TRADE BARRIERS FACING DEVELOPING COUNTRIES

TRADE BARRIERS FACING DEVELOPING COUNTRIES

by Alexander J. Yeats
Institute for International Economic Studies

ST. MARTIN'S PRESS   NEW YORK

All rights reserved. For information, write:
St. Martin's Press, Inc. 175 Fifth Avenue, New York, NY 10010
Printed in Great Britain
First published in the United States of America in 1979
ISBN 0–312–81207–8

Library of Congress Cataloging in Publication Data

Yeats, Alexander J
  Trade barriers facing developing countries.

  Bibliography: p.
  Includes index.
    1. Underdeveloped areas—Commercial policy.
  2. Nontariff trade barriers. 4. International
  economic relations. I. Title.
  HF1413.Y46 1979   382.1′09172′4   78–10537
  ISBN 0–312–81207–8

HF1413
.Y46
1979

To Jeannie

Contents

List of Tables and Figures

TABLES

FIGURES

Foreword

One of the basic problems of the international economy today is how the economies of the less developed countries (LDCs) could be further integrated into the global economic division of labour for manufactured goods and not only, as now, for raw materials. It is well known that severe obstacles and problems connected with such an integration exist both within these countries themselves and on the international markets. In fact, the most important contribution that the developed countries could make towards the less developed countries is precisely to provide access to markets for manufactured goods.

Alexander Yeats presents in this book a penetrating study of the obstacles on the international markets to an integration of this kind. The study covers not only tariff and nontariff barriers erected by the industrial countries, but also institutional arrangements in international shipping. The most distinguished characteristic of this important book is the relentless attempts to estimate the quantitative size and spread of these various obstacles, as a basis for an evaluation of the economic benefits to the LDCs from their removal. This makes Alexander Yeats's work an important contribution to the international discussion of the potential consequences of changes in the world economic order—a discussion that no doubt has demonstrated the need for this type of empirical research.

The book is the first report from an ongoing research project on the New World Economic Order by researchers at the Institute for International Economic Studies of the University of Stockholm, financed by the Bank of Sweden's Tercentenary Foundation. We are proud that the publication of our studies can start with such an excellent piece of work.

Stockholm   *Assar Lindbeck*
May 1978

Acknowledgements

This book, which constitutes the first of a two-part survey of developing country trade problems, was written during my stay as Visiting Scholar at the Institute for International Economic Studies at the University of Stockholm during the academic year 1977/78. Financial support for this endeavour was provided by the Bank of Sweden's Tercentenary Foundation as part of a comprehensive project on the New World Economic Order.

In the course of my work I have been able to draw on the advice of several individuals at the Institute and the United Nations Conference on Trade and Development. Professor Odd Gulbrandsen read earlier versions of most chapters and was an invaluable source of criticism and constructive comments. I have also drawn from several previous studies written with Professor Gary Sampson, as well as Dr Andrzej Olechowski's expertise on empirical analysis of trade barriers. Several individuals at UNCTAD including Ho Dac Tuong, Jack I. Stone, Alfred Maizels, Craig MacPhee and Robert Ramsey, commented on specific aspects, as did Marian Radetzki, Carl Hamilton, Sven Grassman, Arne Jon Isachsen and several other colleagues at the Institute. Special thanks are also due to members of the secretarial staff at the Institute who prepared the manuscript.

The author would like to express appreciation to the editors of the *Journal of Business and Economics, Quarterly Review of Economics and Business, Journal of Development Studies, Journal of Political Economy, American Journal of Agricultural Economics, Oxford Economic Papers* and *Weltwirtschaftliches Archiv* for permission to use parts of the author's previously published studies.

Stockholm   *Alexander J. Yeats*
March 1978

1 Trade Liberalisation and the New International Order

For more than two decades, the United Nations and its agencies have provided a major international forum for the study, debate, and implementation of measures to assist the poorer countries of the world in their development efforts. For example, in 1964 the first session of the United Nations Conference on Trade and Development (UNCTAD) received Raul Prebisch's report on the requirements of a new trade policy for development.[1] A major feature of the report was a call for the establishment of a new international order which would be more responsive to both global needs, and the needs of developing countries. The proposed system contained suggestions which required basic changes in the framework of trade and finance, as well as other aspects of international relations between developed and developing countries.

While the initial session of UNCTAD had little immediate impact, many of Prebisch's recommendations were later incorporated in the International Development Strategy for the Second United Nations Development Decade.[2] The central concept of the Strategy focused on a world order in which economic growth was transmitted to less developed countries (LDCs) through trade, technology, and development aid from industrial countries. This system implied that economic expansion in developed nations would lead to increased demand for developing country exports, thus increasing the LDCs' real income and capacity to purchase equipment required for industrialisation.

This concept of interdependence and of the process by which growth could be transmitted from rich to poor countries required the removal of artificial barriers to trade, technological transfer, investment, and the regulation of restrictive practices which hindered these flows. The key policy prescriptions of the Strategy were, therefore, focused on measures which would improve access to developed countries' markets, promote the transfer of technology on fair and reasonable terms, and

1

achieve a substantial expansion in the flow of financial resources for development. The quantitative targets set by the Strategy included those for growth in the foreign trade of developing countries, and in the flow of financial resources for development.[3]

Several developments in the early 1970s clearly demonstrated that some important assumptions of the Strategy were invalid. First, the growth of industrial countries, which had been sustained at relatively high rates during the previous two decades, fell off sharply in 1974 and has failed to return to previous levels. This retardation in the economic expansion of industrial countries undermined the central concept of growth transmission in the Strategy. Furthermore, the key recommendations on aid targets, improving the transfer of technology, and the reduction of trade barriers facing LDC exports, went largely unimplemented. Trade relations of many developing countries were also increasingly influenced by multinational corporations whose activities have the potential to distort the industrialisation process.

Due to the growing deficiencies in the Strategy, important developments resulted from initiatives taken by the Sixth Special Session of the United Nations General Assembly in the Spring of 1974. On May 1 the Assembly adopted a Declaration and Programme of Action on the Establishment of a New International Economic Order which constituted a formal recognition by the world body of the need for basic institutional changes.[4] The Declaration begins by stating that its aim is 'to correct inequalities and redress existing injustices and ensure steadily accelerating economic development, peace and justice for present and future generations'. The document incorporates a set of 'inherent' principles stressing national sovereignty and equality of states, and ends by asserting that 'the present Declaration shall be one of the most important bases of economic relations between all peoples of all nations'. The Programme of Action, which accompanied the Declaration, proposed urgent measures on raw materials and primary commodities, the international monetary system and development finance, industrialisation, transfer of technology, transnational corporations, and the promotion of cooperation among developing countries. The Charter of Economic Rights and Duties of States, adopted by the General Assembly some months later, lent support to the concept of the need for a changed order.[5]

BACKGROUND DEVELOPMENTS

Criticism of the current state of the world economy centres on a number of inequalities which operate to the detriment of the developing countries. For example, the differential in per capita incomes between the richest and poorest nations is very large. Of the 4 billion people in the world today, (here, and throughout the book, 'billion' means American billion, i.e. one thousand million) 1·2 billion live in countries with per capita incomes of less than $200 a year. If China were included in this total, the number would increase to 2 billion. As such, half the world's population lives on a subsistence income of less than 50 cents a day. As for the other half, about 1·3 billion live in countries with an income of between $200 and $2000. Thus, the abject poverty in many developing countries places people below the minimum level of subsistence with the result that famine, disease, and malnutrition are a constant threat to existence.

Gross differences also exist in other measures of economic well-being. At present, life expectancy in some of the advanced developed countries reaches well over 70 years, yet a number of developing countries have not been able to attain half this level. Educational opportunities also vary widely between developed and developing nations. In North America and Europe, literacy rates are well over 90 per cent, but in many of the developing countries of Asia and Africa more than 90 to 95 per cent of the population can neither read nor write. Gross differences exist in employment opportunities between the developed and developing world. While unemployment rates for many industrial countries typically average between 4 to 6 per cent, Algeria, Bolivia, Jamaica, Surinam, and a number of other developing countries report that over 20 per cent of their population is without gainful employment.

Recent developments have also made it clear that citizens of the industrialised countries are not being well served by the existing economic order. The international monetary system, which was based on fixed parities and the convertibility of currencies into gold, has largely collapsed, with the result that unstable exchange rates and disequilibriating movements of capital are a common occurrence. High rates of inflation persist in many developed nations in spite of continuing conditions of slack economic activity, while unemployment remains high by historical standards. Many industrial countries have still not fully adjusted to the shock of markedly higher energy costs which resulted from the Organization of Petroleum Exporting Countries' (OPEC) price increases. The socialist countries have not been without their share of problems. For example, the debt position of some of the socialist countries in Eastern Europe is unprecedented, and debt service is fast becoming a serious strain on some economies. Also, many of these nations have been showing an increased dependence on Western technology with the result that conditions for improved access and transfer must be established. Due to this increasing *interdependence* of the socialist, market economy, and third world countries, new institutions must evolve, or adapt, to accommodate international relations between countries or country groups. It is precisely to this problem that many of the deliberations on the new world economic order are addressed.

ESSENTIALS OF THE NEW ECONOMIC ORDER

The basic changes in the framework of international relations which were envisioned by the General Assembly are outlined in the Declaration and Programme of Action on the Establishment of a New International Economic Order. The programme clearly places emphasis on structural changes in international institutions as a vehicle for achieving its goals, rather than policies enacted within the framework of existing institutions. While many specific proposals concerning the New International Economic Order have been modified or changed during the debate on these topics, the following are among the major points which appear to have carried consistently through the discussion:

—An improvement in the terms of trade is required for developing countries' exports of commodities and other raw materials, along with a stabilisation programme for commodity prices. These objectives are to be achieved by various measures classified under the general heading of an Integrated Programme for Commodities which includes proposals for commodity cartels, guaranteed minimum prices through industrial country purchase commitments, and large-scale buffer stocks. Plans are also included for indexing raw material prices through links to general price indices, or indices covering manufactures.[6] Measures to increase demand for commodities, by making substitution with artificial products more difficult, have been discussed.

—An increase in developing countries' share of world industrial production to about 25 per cent by the end of the century. This is to be achieved by a permanent reduction of direct and indirect trade barriers, by phasing out certain industries in the industrial countries, by facilitating the transfer of technology, by stimulating the flow of direct investment, and by increasing development aid. The Programme of Action also stresses the need for a vastly increased LDC role in world shipping.

—Increased financial transfers to the developing countries are required with a view toward covering the basic needs of the inhabitants. Related proposals call for a greatly changed International Monetary Fund with both expanded and easier LDC access to credit facilities, and to new liquidity in the form of special drawing rights.

—A major expansion of trade and other contacts is required between the developing countries and socialist countries of Eastern Europe. Also, cooperation among developing countries themselves must be greatly increased. A major element in this effort would be the establishment of a system of preferences for developing country intra-trade.

A new structure for commodity trade

One of the areas slated for major institutional reform centres on the primary commodity trade of developing countries. Even if petroleum is excluded, almost 70 per cent of developing country export earnings originates from the sale of primary commodities. However, on an individual country basis the reliance can be much greater than indicated by this overall average. This is particularly true for some of the poorest developing countries whose export earnings may be almost entirely dependent on one or two major commodities.[7] In these cases, the prosperity of the commodity sector is often a key determinant of the country's economic well-being. It can be a major element influencing the balance of payments, the level of external debt, the domestic budget, and the probability of success for the overall development effort. However, the volatility of most commodity prices on world markets, as well as deteriorating terms of trade relative to manufactures, has been a major problem for development planning and finance.

Previous international action in the area of primary commodities has reflected the view that market intervention should occur only under limited circumstances, and that the primary objective should be the control of excessive price fluctuations rather than any attempt to influence long-term trends. The Havana Charter adopted several measures intended to modify price fluctuations, although this document stressed that international commodity agreements should be confined to short-term protective measures.[8] Furthermore, while the General Agreement on Tariffs and Trade (GATT) is the primary institution concerned with the regulation of international trade, there is no provision for commodity agreements under its charter. While several attempts have been made, the developed country signatories have refused to bring commodity agreements within GATT's framework.

In retrospect, there can be few who are satisfied with the performance of commodity prices or trade over the last decade. During this period, developing countries have been able to make only modest gains in their efforts to shift from unprocessed to processed product exports. Tariffs and other trade restraints in industrial markets have been largely responsible for this lack of progress. Fluctuations in commodity prices also continue to have a serious disequilibriating effect on both developed and developing countries. For example, over the period between 1971 and 1974 the UNCTAD index of agricultural raw materials prices rose more than 100 points from a base of 111 to a peak of 236, and then began a descent which brought the index close to its earlier levels. Mineral prices experienced an even wider fluctuation, rising from a value of 131 to over 400 points, and then dropping almost as sharply. The rapid run-up in commodity prices had a serious inflationary influence on developed economies, while the inflated prices of 1974–5 caused many LDCs to invest in substantial over-capacity which has had a protracted depressant effect on commodity prices.

The integrated programme for commodities

Due to the failure of previous efforts, and the pressing need of developing countries for concrete action in the area of commodities, the UNCTAD Secretariat has advanced a comprehensive strategy in the form of an integrated programme for commodities.[9] Essentially, the integrated programme covers the following five major elements:

(1) Internationally owned stocks covering a wide range of commodities;

(2) A common financial fund that will make resources available for the acquisition of stocks;

(3) The institution, in circumstances which justify it, of a system of medium- to long-term commitments to purchase and sell commodities at agreed prices;

(4) The institution of measures to provide compensatory financing to producers to cover shortfalls in export earnings; and

(5) The initiation of an extensive programme to further the processing of commodities by the producing countries themselves.

Under the programme, UNCTAD proposes the establishment of buffer stocks for key commodities such as copper, bauxite, rubber, tea, coffee, cocoa, sugar, jute, hard fibres, and cotton. Stocks are to be released in times of shortages and held back in periods of surplus, thus stabilising supply and demand. The initial cost for the establishment of the buffer stocks is placed at about \$3 billion.[10]

The structure of access to markets at adequate prices is also a vital issue for commodities. For example, UNCTAD (March 1977) states that the problem of nontariff and tariff barriers restricting the commodity exports of developing countries is no less important than depressed and fluctuating commodity prices and earnings. These trade restrictions are reflected in the systems of agricultural protection in developed countries, and in the complex array of tariffs, quotas, variable levies, subsidies, etc., which severely curtail potential export earnings. While these problems figure in the multilateral trade negotiations, it need hardly be emphasised that liberalising access to markets is an essential element in the arrangements contemplated for individual commodities within the integrated programme.[11]

Industrialisation and developing countries
While commodity trade is of considerable current importance to the majority of developing countries, and for that reason needs to be restructured on more equitable lines, a broadened manufacturing and trade base is required to substantiate the overall development effort. A sound commodity sector may be regarded as a base for the further transformation of the economy, but this transformation itself must be accompanied by industrialisation. For example, the overall importance of the industrialisation objective was stressed at the Second General Conference of the United Nations Industrial Development Organization (UNIDO) held in 1974. While the present share of developing countries in world production is only about 7 per cent, UNIDO established a target of 25 per cent by the turn of the century. Such a goal implies that industrial expansion must accelerate from a rate of 6 or 7 per cent per annum which was achieved during the 1960s, to about 10 per cent over the next quarter of a century.

As was the case with commodities, attainment of these industrialisation objectives have important implications for trade in industrial products. Although the satisfaction of domestic needs will undoubtedly absorb much of the increased output, it is scarcely conceivable that such growth can be directed to the domestic market alone. Based on the past experience of both industrialised and developing countries, trade in manufactured goods will need to expand even more rapidly than industrial production. Preliminary UNCTAD (April 1976b) estimates of the magnitudes involved suggests that developing country exports of manufactures must increase twenty-fold in the next 25 years, at an annual rate of 12 per cent, compared to a rate of about 10 per cent in 1972. As a result, exports as a proportion of gross product should rise from 10 per cent in 1972 to about 18 per cent by the year 2000.

SCOPE OF THE PRESENT STUDY

As indicated in the preceding discussion, efforts to promote significant trade expansion for developing countries are at the core of policy proposals associated with the new world economic order. However, when discussing the factors which work to limit LDC exports, a distinction should be made between two different types of restraints. First, a variety of problems which are, to some extent, endogenous to the developing, countries themselves certainly contribute to the curtailment of exports. Under this general heading may be classified factors which would cause general *supply constraints*. Here we have such diverse elements as lack of trained manpower, capital equipment, managerial skills, inadequate transport services and other infrastructure. Secondly, there are a variety of largely exogenous factors such as tariffs, quotas, export restraints, etc., which work to limit LDC exports. These are due to policies in external markets over which the LDCs have little if any policy control. Hence, if these trade restraints are to be reduced the initiative must come from the developed nations themselves.

While supply constraints are undoubtedly a factor limiting some developing countries' exports, this book focuses on trade barriers which are largely outside the influence of LDC policy-makers. There are several reasons for this approach. First, many of the apparent supply constraints in developing countries are, at least partially, a result of the restrictive policies pursued by industrial countries. If appropriate opportunities were created, through a general reduction in artificial trade barriers, this should produce an external environment in which LDCs have a stronger incentive to initiate internal measures which could alleviate many of the apparent supply problems. It must be admitted that, at present, the incentives that could result from an opening of these external markets are nowhere near their potential.[12]

Artificial trade barriers also play an important role in limiting the size of the market served by producers in developing countries. Since expanded outlets are often required to employ techniques which depend on large-scale operations for efficiency, or for the achievement of economies associated with specialisation and scale of operations, the external barriers may be the cause of some seemingly inefficient production procedures employed by LDCs. Furthermore, what appear to be inefficient production techniques can be a direct result of the technology, manpower and training, capital acquisition, cartelisation, or production and distribution policies of transnational corporations. If further research should show that the international operations of these giant organisations do not normally result in practices which are complementary to the industrialisation objectives of developing countries, this too will have to be corrected by appropriate policy action.

This book, which deals with commercial policy measures and shipping, constitutes the first part of a systematic survey of the nature and magnitude of the external trade barriers that limit LDC penetration of industrial markets. Such an effort appears especially timely in view of the fact that trade liberalisation is assuming an increasingly important role in aspects of international development policy and discussions concerning the new world economic order. As such, a comprehensive analysis of these restraints should provide a useful input for any systematic plan aimed at dismantling these barriers. The persistence of slack demand and high unemployment in some sectors of developed countries' economies has resulted in growing pressure to insulate domestic producers from foreign competition. It is further hoped that the arguments and data advanced in this book will contribute toward offsetting such protectionist sentiments.

To evaluate the effects of a liberalisation of trade barriers, Chapter 2 examines the potential benefits from expanded trade opportunities for developing countries. Aside from an analysis of the theoretical ties between trade and development, recent empirical evidence which bears on the theory is also discussed. The economic consequences of concentration in a narrow range of exports is analysed, as well as the advantages of moving toward a more diversified export base. Chapter 3 reviews the recent export performance of developing countries with special attention devoted to LDC efforts to shift from primary product exports to semi-finished goods and manufactures.

Chapters 4 and 5 are devoted to a thorough evaluation of the protection afforded by tariffs and nontariff barriers in major industrial markets. In addition to an assessment of previous empirical findings, considerable new evidence is developed on the trade effects of these barriers. Detailed statistical appendices to these chapters summarise the tariff and nontariff barriers applied to individual developing country exports. Partial equilibrium models, or other related procedures, are also employed to estimate the volume of trade flows which would occur in the absence of these restrictions. Chapter 6 evaluates procedures which might be employed for the reduction of these restraints including the Generalised System of Preferences, Off-Shore Assembly, effects of alternative tariff cutting formula, and proposals for the elimination of nontariff barriers.

Previous empirical investigations have largely focused on such artificial trade control measures as tariffs or nontariff barriers among the various types of restraints that limit developing country penetration of industrial markets. However, recent studies have shown that ad valorem freight costs (i.e., shipping costs as a percentage of product price) frequently exceed most-favoured-nation tariffs applied to LDC exports, and that freight as a percentage of price has generally been rising over time. Chapter 7 empirically examines the level and structure of transportation costs on LDC exports and also discusses procedures which could lower shipping costs of developing countries.

Before proceeding, however, it should be noted that the results and arguements presented in the forthcoming chapters should not divert attention from an integrated assessment of the barriers to expansion of developing countries' export trade. While commercial policy measures and transport barriers are often of key importance, transfer of technology, finance, operations of multinationals, domestic policies in LDCs, or a number of other factors may also have a serious retardation effect on trade.

2 International Trade and Economic Development

In principle, several different relations can be envisaged between the performance of the foreign trade sector and an economy in the process of development. To the extent that the classical economists offered a judgement, it was held that foreign trade could make an impressive contribution to a country's growth and development. Trade was not only considered a device for achieving production efficiency, but was a powerful 'engine of growth' which incorporated a variety of dynamic effects that could raise living standards. On the other hand, several alternative growth models accent potentially negative aspects of trade and recommend that export promotion be given less weight than production geared to local needs. Finally, some models relegate the export sector to a more or less neutral role, in which export revenues are just sufficient to cover capital equipment costs.[1]

While there is a widespread view that international trade was a major factor in the development of periphery economies in the nineteenth century, there is less optimism in some quarters that trade will necessarily have such a stimulating effect on developing countries today. In cases such as Korea, Taiwan, Hong Kong, Singapore, etc., it is recognised that a dynamic export sector provided a key stimulus to growth and development. However, there are other situations where foreign trade has had few beneficial effects. In these cases, export production resulted in a form of economic dualism in which the foreign trade sector essentially remains an 'enclave', with little practical contribution to the development of the traditional economy. Certain failures of the foreign trade sector to provide a stimulus to growth have lead some developing countries to pursue import-substitution policies rather than export-oriented growth strategies.

Proper assessment of the role of trade in development is of key importance in any attempt to evaluate the influence of barriers to developing countries' exports. While numerous empirical studies have estimated potential trade which would occur if a barrier such as a tariff or quota were eliminated, these analyses are essentially static in that they fail to indicate the longer-term implications of trade liberalisation for growth and development. For this objective, recourse must be made to the theoretical trade models. This chapter attempts to summarise the key points of the theory in order to provide a framework for assessing the benefits which might accrue to the LDCs from any systematic trade liberalisation. The summary begins with the basic postulates of the classical trade model and continues to an evaluation of some contemporary variations. A section also examines the economic implications of developing countries' concentrating in too narrow a range of exports, as opposed to a more diversified trade structure. Where possible, an effort is made to assess empirical evidence which has been advanced in connection with various postulates of the theory.

TRADE AND GROWTH: SOME BASIC PRINCIPLES

The classical model of trade according to comparative advantage is essentially a static analysis based on very limiting assumptions. Given a two-commodity, two-factor, two-country world with full employment, identical production functions, and perfect competition in domestic and international markets it was demonstrated that both countries will be better off with free trade or, at the least, one country will be better off while the other's position would not deteriorate.

The model rests on production and exchange based on the principle of comparative advantage. This states that countries should specialise in the production of commodities which require relatively large inputs of those factors in which they are well endowed.[2] Thus, the doctrine recommends that a nation with an abundant supply of relatively cheap labour specialise in the production of labour-intensive items (such as commodities), while a capital-rich country specialise in items which require relatively large capital inputs, such as sophisticated manufactures.

Extensions of this static model introduced important dynamic considerations. For example, if countries specialise according to comparative advantage and trade, it was held that other important benefits result. Since specialisation is held to be a function of the size of the market, more efficient production techniques could be employed due to the enlarged markets resulting from trade. Thus, international trade allows producers to overcome constraints associated with the size of domestic markets and adopt more efficient production techniques.

Another potential benefit from trade was the opening of new markets which created a 'vent' or outlet for surplus production. Both these elements were clearly acknowledged by Adam Smith (1937) in the following passage from the *Wealth of Nations*,

> Between whatever places foreign trade is carried on, they all derive two distinct benefits from it. It carries out that surplus part of the produce of their land and labour for which there is no demand among them, and brings back in return for it something else for which there is a demand. It gives a value to their superfluities, by exchanging them for something else, which may satisfy a part of their wants, and increase their enjoyments. By means of it, the narrowness of the home market does not hinder the division of labour in any particular branch of art of manufacture being carried to the highest perfection. By opening a more extensive market for whatever part of the produce of their labour may exceed the home consumption, it encourages them to improve its productive powers, and to augment its annual produce to the utmost, and thereby to increase the real revenue and wealth of society.

Thus, there are three distinct elements in classical trade theory. First, static comparative cost states that, when a country specialises in production according to its comparative advantage, and trades at the international exchange rate, it achieves an increase in real income. This point can be illustrated with reference to Figure 2.1. Shown on the horizontal axis are quantities of an exportable (i.e., a good requiring relatively large inputs of abundant factors), while the vertical axis measures goods which require relatively scarce inputs. The production-possibility frontier PP shows various combinations of the goods which can be produced with the economy's factor endowment and the level of available technology.

Initially, the economy is in equilibrium at point P_0, where I_0 and X_0 of the goods are produced and consumed domestically. However, given the opportunity to trade, comparative advantage recommends that the country specialise in the manufacture of goods in which it is relatively efficient, thus moving to a point such as P_1. Some of the additional production of the exportable $(X_0 X_1)$ would then be exchanged for the other good, whose production has been reduced by $I_0 I_1$, with the result that the net position of the economy is better off than before trade occurred.

Trade gains of a considerably different nature are stressed in the

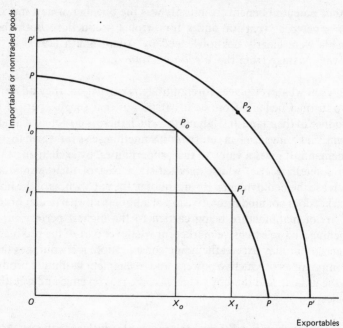

FIGURE 2.1 Illustration of Comparative Advantage and Productivity Gains from International Trade

passage from the *Wealth of Nations*. On the one hand, these relate to potential *productivity effects* in the trading country. Since trade extends the size of the effective market, it permits the adoption of new production technologies, allows increased specialisation, stimulates innovations, raises the productivity of labour, and generally allows the country to experience increasing returns and accelerate economic development.[3] A second result is the *vent for surplus effect*, which involves utilisation of formerly unemployed or underemployed resources and allows a country to expand production without any sacrifice in the manufacture of other goods and services. The productivity effects and vent for surplus differ from static comparative costs in that they involve utilisation of new production technologies. Thus, these elements involve movement to a point such as P_2, on a higher production-possibility frontier, while static comparative costs involve a shift along a given curve. The implications of the movement to a higher production-possibility frontier are important. Given the fixed factor endowments of the economy (labour and capital), new technologies can be adopted which allow increased production even though the supply of basic inputs to the manufacturing process have not changed.

Criticisms of comparative advantage

While the productivity gains are discussed in a later section, it should be noted that the static comparative cost doctrine has come under attack on several points. Essentially, the criticisms stem from the limitations of the basic assumptions of the model as well as the difficulty in generalising to a multi-period time frame. While production according to comparative advantage may yield optimal results in a single (current) time period, there remains the question of whether some alternative pattern of resource allocation might lead to more advantageous results over the long run. In other words, there is no assurance that current allocation of resources based on comparative advantage will be optimal over time, even though it may be optimal in the current period.[4]

Framed in terms of Figure 2.1, current production and investment decisions will influence the position of the production-possibility curves which are achievable in the future. If current production is allocated according to comparative advantage, with the economy operating at a point such as P_1, this may foreclose the possibility of achieving a higher position in the future. Even though point P_0 is not optimal in the short run, there may be long-term advantages in operating here if new skills or investments are generated, or other changes occur that allow movement to a curve such as P_1P_1 in the future. Such considerations may be especially important for developing countries since trade according to comparative advantage could lead these nations to specialise in raw materials, with declining terms of trade, as contrasted with the more favourable prospects of developed countries which produce manufactures.

A related objection to comparative advantage centres on the infant industry agrument. The term 'infant' refers to new, or not yet established industrial activities, that are prevented from developing because production volumes and prices are kept too low by foreign competition. If the industry were allowed to develop, so the argument goes, a comparative advantage could be established, or at least the industry could compete in the home market given the natural protection afforded by international transportation costs. Comparative advantage is based on the *current* structure of relative prices. The infant industry argument suggests that certain policy decisions influence the structure of relative prices, and comparative advantage in the future. This argument has had considerable appeal in numerous developing countries just beginning to industrialise, and has been used to justify subsidies or high levels of protection for domestic industry.

Other objections to trade based on comparative advantage rest on the short-term instability of prices in various export markets. Several studies have demonstrated that commodity prices may be considerably more volatile than those of semifinished goods or manufactures. Since widely fluctuating export prices and revenues can make development planning difficult, a country may be advised to plan some export ventures with a view toward achieving stable revenues, even if these new ventures are not consistent with comparative advantage. Furthermore, comparative advantage may not be a useful guide for planning new export ventures. If demand is not perfectly elastic, estimation of revenues from any new venture must account for the return on that investment as well as the impact on profits from inframarginal sales. It may happen that a country will be well advised to leave resources currently engaged in exports where they are, but to invest additional resources elsewhere.

PRODUCTIVITY EFFECTS OF INTERNATIONAL TRADE

While the static doctrine of comparative advantage has been criticised on several important points, there is a wider consensus that opening up an economy to international trade can bestow benefits which have important long-term consequences. In general, these productivity gains may have the following favourable influences on the domestic economy; (1) increasing returns connected with economies of scale and market size, (2) learning effects and the improvement of human capital, (3) beneficial effects from competition and close communication with advanced countries, including the familiarisation with advanced technologies from abroad, and (4) potentially favourable demonstration effects which accompany the opening up of the domestic economy.[5]

Scale effects and market size
Given the relatively small size of many developing countries' domestic markets, inefficiencies and high costs associated with production, marketing, and distribution operations geared solely to local needs may constitute a serious obstacle to industrialisation. Various statistical studies have confirmed that such basic industries as chemicals, metals, food processing, beverages, furniture, publishing, etc., are sometimes characterised by declining costs as production volumes increase.[6] Thus,

some industries have natural characteristics which could saddle a developing country with inefficiencies if production had to be geared solely to the domestic market. Similarly, the manufacturing *techniques* which can be employed are frequently determined by the size of the market. If production volumes were constrained by domestic require- ments, this might not allow small developing countries to achieve efficiencies and lower costs associated with specialisation or scale effects in manufacturing.[7]

International trade offers a means whereby LDCs can circumvent these natural limitations of domestic markets. Through joint pro- duction for both domestic and export demand, it may be possible to achieve practical cost saving benefits which might be diffused through the economy in a variety of ways. For example, increased production of exports will have direct effects on domestic income, but there may also be important 'backward linkage' effects. An expansion in the export sector may induce production increases elsewhere in industries which provide inputs. A chain of cost-savings may result if the larger production volumes produce efficiencies or lower prices in these service industries. In so far as the output of the export industry is also employed as an input by other domestic firms, there may be important *forward linkage* effects. Since this would lower production costs in user industries, efficiencies and expanded production might also occur in these sectors.[8]

Learning effects and competition

To the extent that international trade brings individuals in developing countries into contact with new technologies, products, and skills, it can have important beneficial effects for the domestic economy. By promoting the development of human capital and new skills, the learning effects produce an outward shift of the production-possibility frontier since more efficient technologies and production methods can be adopted. The lack of technological or managerial skills may be a key constraint hampering the overall development. By providing an oppor- tunity for nationals to establish contacts, study and evaluate foreign ideas and technologies, international trade can do much to rectify this deficiency.

One potentially important aspect of this educational effort is connected with the training activities of foreign subsidiaries within the developing countries. If processing or manufacturing plants are located in the LDCs, a need for local skilled and semi-skilled labour— accountants, construction personnel, machinists, transport and distribution services, etc.—could result which may be filled by on-the-job training of the developing country's nationals.[9] Similar developments may occur as local entrepreneurs become acquainted with trading opportunities in foreign markets. To the extent that these opportunities stimulate investment in production ventures, new jobs and skill requirements will be created. The linkage effects also provide a means whereby the educational and employment opportunities can spread to other sectors of the economy.

Aside from the expansion of employment opportunities and new skills, there are also potential benefits on the import side. International trade can create educational opportunities if it allows nationals to familiarise themselves with products and technologies of advanced countries. Often this will introduce individuals to new ideas, goods, production techniques, etc., which can be successfully adapted for the domestic market.[10] The advanced economies are likely to be suppliers of modern and efficient capital equipment, so trade provides an opportunity to learn about these techniques and products. The potential benefits of foreign competition should not be overlooked since many developing countries' industries are dominated by a small number of concerns. Competition from outside sources can weaken the monopoly position of these firms and result in lower prices and better service for consumers. There can also be important long-term benefits if foreign competition forces local producers to modernise and keep abreast of recent developments and technologies.

While there are positive educational benefits associated with both export and imports, adverse consequences may result from attempts to retard the flow of trade by erecting artificial barriers to this exchange. In discussing these *negative* educational effects, Keesing (1967, p. 309) suggests 'consider the human-resource impact of excessive protection. Government officials, from the customs service to the exchange-control authorities, to people who give licenses and dole out subsidies, acquire experience in the finer arts of corruption and graft. Managers learn to worry about their political connections and spend much of their energy trying to manipulate officials to improve their supplies. Cutting costs of production, raising the quality of the product or marketing it more effectively become difficult and secondary ways of making profits are stressed—if they are profitable at all in view of the captive markets, uncertain supplies, and the fact that lowered costs may bring about reduced protection. Skilled professionals such as engineers pick up the listless and careless ways of their fellows in a stifling bureaucracy, and learn to avoid technical suggestions and decisions. There is little call for their expertise, and it would frequently prove more dangerous to their careers to point out what is being done wrong than to go along and say nothing. Workers learn lackadaisical ways, not being pressed to raise their productivity. Thus, the *wrong skills are learned.*'

Technology, competition and innovation

While there are exceptions, most important innovations in technology, science, medicine, and communications have originated in the developed countries of the world. Even so, the adoption of many of these advances have provided immeasurable benefits for citizens of developing countries. For example, the innovations in agricultural production techniques often referred to as the 'green revolution' have done much to combat famine in the developing world, although serious problems undeniably remain. Similarly, improved medical and health facilities have increased life-spans, and have done much to eradicate the threat of disease. Improved communications have broadened the perspectives of developing country nationals, and brought increased awareness of ideas, products, and commercial opportunities in foreign markets.

Since trade establishes a network for the physical exchange of goods, it also creates systems which facilitate the international exchange of ideas. Lines of communication established for commercial transactions can also contribute to the spread of cultural, scientific, and technological knowledge which can have a profound impact on developing countries. Often these nations are locked in rigid sociological patterns that are a serious handicap in the development effort. Foreign trade, and the resulting exposure to new opportunities and ideas, can have a profound impact on these conditions. While every nation gains from exposure to new ways of thinking, these benefits can be particularly impressive given the isolated situation of many LDCs. Through the exchange of goods, and resulting contacts, trade can do much to weaken sociological and cultural barriers to development.

Aside from these considerations, the material content of trade can be of vital importance. Most developing countries do not have the internal capacity to produce much of the machinery and other capital equipment required for industrialisation and growth. Through exchange for traditional products, trade provides a means whereby this equipment can be acquired. Since these imports broaden the developing country's capital base, they permit more efficient and higher levels of production than would occur without trade. In other words, imports of capital equipment produce an outward shift of the production-possibility frontier which raises incomes and living standards in the developing country.

Due to the small size of many LDCs' home markets, domestic demand may be only sufficient to sustain a relatively small number of firms in industries where there are scale economies, while in other cases supply may be limited by scarcity of certain factor inputs. As such, monopolistic structures may be a natural feature of some developing country markets with potentially adverse consequences for prices and operating efficiency. However, competition from foreign firms through trade can be an important incentive to reduce prices and costs while improving quality and service. Also, competition with foreign suppliers, and the necessity of keeping abreast of industry developments, can be an important source of information on new products and technologies. When secure behind a high wall of protective tariff and nontariff barriers, firms in developing countries may lose many of these incentives, while the flow of new ideas and communication will also be restricted.

The fact that local conditions and markets may not provide an appropriate stimulus to innovational activity is often a constraint to the development process. Since innovation in new products or production techniques normally involves the adoption of some risks, the potential rewards from local markets may not be sufficent to justify certain undertakings. However, international trade can provide more lucrative opportunities, so the incentive and rewards from innovational activity become stronger. The example of entrepreneurs who are successful may create an atmosphere which is conducive to experiment and change, while new employment and production opportunities should also be associated with innovational efforts.[11]

The demonstration effect

The creation of a new set of work incentives is another potential result of international trade. In many developing countries, domestic production of consumer goods may be limited to a few varieties, while certain luxury goods may not be available. Due to inferior quality, lack of variety, or absence of nonessentials, the incentive to work for the acquisition of material goods may be low.

As a result of international trade, the local populace may become acquainted with consumption standards or products available in advanced countries. Thus, a 'demonstration effect' occurs in which citizens of the developing country try to emulate consumption patterns in the advanced nations. While this can have harmful repercussions if the propensity to consume is increased, with corresponding reductions in saving and investment, the net result may be more than sufficient to offset this negative aspect. To the extent that the demonstration effect results in the increased consumption of imported goods, it raises the incentive to work. Mill (1848) clearly describes the way in which the international demonstration effect increases incentives and raises productivity in developing countries: 'A people may be in a quiescent, indolent, uncultivated state, with all their tastes either fully satisfied or entirely undeveloped, and they may fail to put forth the whole of their productive energies for want of any sufficient object of desire. The opening of a foreign trade, by making them acquainted with new objects, or tempting them with easier acquisition of things which they had not previously thought attainable, sometimes works a sort of industrial revolution in a country whose resources were previously undeveloped for want of energy and ambition in the people: inducing those who were satisfied with scanty comforts and little work, to work harder for the gratification of their new tastes, and even to save, and accumulate capital, for the still more complete satisfaction of those tastes at a future time.'

While generally discussed in terms of consumer behaviour, there may be parallel results in the field of industrial techniques and production. If trade heightens the LDC producers' awareness of procedures employed by their business counterparts in advanced nations, it may stimulate the desire to copy these techniques. This phenomenon seems at least partially responsible for the proliferation of iron mills and other capital goods industries in some developing countries. While the possibility exists that this aspect of the demonstration effect may result in the adoption of technologies which are not appropriate for domestic conditions, such as the implementation of labour-saving innovations, emulation of developed country business procedures may raise the efficiency and output of local producers.

Import substitution
While the preceding discussion outlines the potential advantages of an export-oriented development strategy, import-substitution has been advocated as an alternative approach. Many LDCs have adopted import-substitution policies in response to balance-of-payment pressures resulting from the rising import demand which normally accompanies industrialisation and growth. Import substitution has also been employed as a strategy for industrialisation itself, for employment creation, long-term income maximisation, foreign exchange con-

servation, or all of these objectives simultaneously.[12]

Under an import-substitution policy, a country erects high protective tariff and nontariff trade barriers around domestic industry to replace foreign supply. The process has normally been introduced in nondurable consumer goods sectors where relatively simple labour-intensive production techniques are employed. This is often followed by the developing country moving into the final processing stage of some assembly-operations (i.e., transportation equipment, electronics, some tools and machinery, etc.), thereby producing a shift in the composition of imports away from these fabricated products toward their components and intermediate inputs. To accommodate the new import-substitution industries, the structure of domestic protection is increased or escalated by degree of processing with final assembly-stage items normally more heavily protected than primary goods or semi-manufactures.[13]

One of the advantages of an import-substitution policy is that it avoids the uncertainties of scheduling production and investment for new markets in which the LDC has little or no policy control. By ejecting barriers to imports, it secures the established domestic market for local industry. However, there are a number of other factors often associated with import-substitution which have had serious adverse consequences. A major drawback is that it normally confines the import-substituting industry to a long-term growth rate equal to that of domestic markets.

While an industry can grow faster than domestic demand when import substitution is first implemented, and thus appear to be a leading sector, this process can only continue for a limited period. Eventually, import-substitution opportunities will be exhausted and further growth is tied to internal demand for manufactures. While exports could permit achievement of higher growth rates, a prolonged policy of import-substitution can lead to an industrial structure unsuited for export production. Moreover, domestic demand may be restricted by high internal prices, while inefficient import-substitution may actually inhibit the development process by increasing input costs for potentially forward-linked industries.

A primary objective of import-substitution policies often is the development of domestic industries whose operations will conserve foreign exchange. To the extent that imports of fabricated goods are displaced by domestic manufactures, the policy may appear to be successful. However, it may create import demand for a variety of new materials, parts, and components used in the assembly stage or for the equipment used in these manufacturing operations.[14] Demand for imported consumer goods may also increase if the new manufacturing activities succeed in raising real income.

Certain other aspects of import-substitution may result in indirect foreign exchange losses. Local producers often operate under less efficient conditions and with higher costs than foreign firms. If the output of the import-substitution industry is an input for the export sector, the competitive position of firms producing for foreign markets can be eroded. Furthermore, by restricting import demand through high tariffs and other restraints, the domestic currency's exchange rate is artificially inflated, making it more difficult to export traditional products. Thus, the policy discriminates in favour of import-competing industries and against export-production in a variety of different ways.

While import-substitution policies once were viewed favourably as a vehicle for stimulating industrialisation or conserving foreign exchange, current thinking is generally critical. Numerous attempts to apply import-substitution in practice have been thwarted by a variety of adverse consequences ranging from diminished agricultural productivity to overvalued exchange rates. In addition, the important learning and productivity effects, as well as other competitive benefits from trade are sacrificed. As such, it is generally conceded that import-substitution is not an alternative to a progressive outward-looking export-oriented growth strategy, but a policy that must be applied with considerable caution in special circumstances.[15]

TRADE CONCENTRATION AND DEVELOPING COUNTRIES

As indicated in the preceding discussion, the principle of trade determined by comparative advantage has been opposed on the basis that it can lead to LDC export concentration in a narrow range of commodities which are subject to volatile short-term price movements. These fluctuations in prices and export revenues may constitute a serious impediment to industrialisation and growth. If export earnings are a sizeable percentage of national product, and these revenues vary markedly, serious multiplier effects on income and investment may result.[16] Specifically, there may be important consequences for the level and stability of income, the development potential of the economy, and on trading possibilities. Since exports of many developing countries are concentrated in a narrow range of items, the potential causes and consequences of instability and concentration should be examined.

Analysis of price instability

Price instability for commodity exports can be attributed to changes in quantities demanded on world markets or those supplied. One source of variation are the cyclical fluctuations in industrial countries' economic activity which has a strong influence on demand for many commodities. The fact that developed countries are the major markets for commodity exports, coupled with generally inelastic supply, can produce sizeable price changes if demand shifts. Thus, one potential cure for commodity price instability is the reduction of cyclical fluctuations in developed nations' business activity. The prolonged inflation of the 1970s also seems to have injected a new factor, as many commodities were viewed as a hedge against inflation, which further increased demand and prices.

Agricultural commodities are obviously susceptible to a variety of different factors which influence quantities offered on world markets. Droughts, temperature variations, excess rainfall, plant disease, etc., have had a major influence on supply. For example, in the early 1970s production shortfalls due to unfavourable climatic conditions in the Soviet Union were a factor leading to the price run-up for wheat and other grains. Drought in the Sahel and other regions influenced prices for various foodstuffs, while unseasonal frosts in Brazil and other South American countries in the mid-1970s resulted in a significant reduction in coffee production and marked price increases.

Analysis of price fluctuations is facilitated by dividing commodities into three groups based on market characteristics; those where world supply fluctuates while demand holds fairly steady; those for which both supply and demand fluctuate; and those where demand tends to be more unstable than supply.[17] The first category includes agricultural foodstuffs such as grains, coffee, cocoa, oil seeds, and tea. Demand for these items is normally slow growing and predictable while supply can be influenced by exogenous factors such as weather. Agricultural raw materials like rubber, flax, jute, and some vegetable oils are classified in the second group since both supply and demand may be unstable.[18] The remaining commodity group, with stable supply and fluctuating demand, includes metals, minerals and fuels. Here demand is largely determined by the pace of economic activity in major markets so prices reflect the industrial countries' business cycle.

The realisation that price instability has its roots in such broad forces has important policy implications for developing countries. However, in cases where a LDC is heavily dependent upon a single export commodity it matters little whether price variations are demand induced, or are associated with exogenous supply changes. Foreign exchange earnings will be more directly in line with the price of the export item. The normal situation, however, is where a developing country specialises in a narrow range of related commodities whose prices are likely to be influenced by similar (supply or demand) factors. In other words, the range of exports of many LDCs is likely to fall largely within one of the three commodity classifications with the result that prices for individual items are highly correlated, and fluctuations in aggregate export earnings are amplified.[19]

Consequences of export concentration
Economists have argued that countries dependent on a single export commodity, or on a narrow range of commodities, are liable to experience a greater instability in export earnings than one whose trade structure is more diversified. This line of reasoning holds that the more unrelated are the products exported, the more stable will export revenues be in the face of fluctuations within particular product groups.[20] Thus, countries which are trying to dampen fluctuations in export earnings should consider diversification into products with different supply and demand characteristics.

This proposition can be demonstrated through recourse to a simple algebraic formulation. If a country exports two commodities, whose standard deviation of export revenues are σ_1 and σ_2 for good 1 and 2 respectively, the standard deviation of the country's total export earnings is,

$$\sigma_t = \sqrt{\sigma_1^2 + \sigma_2^2 + 2r\sigma_1\sigma_2} \qquad (2\text{--}1)$$

where r is the correlation coefficient for the two products' export revenues.[21]

For illustration, suppose a country exports \$10 million per year in both goods 1 and 2. Exports of both items have a standard deviation of \$3 million, or 30 per cent of the mean. Taken together, the relationship of total export variability to total export revenues depends on the correlation between earnings from the two products. In the extreme case of a perfect negative correlation ($r = -1$), the standard deviation of total earnings is zero, each decline in one product is exactly offset by an increase in the other. However, if exports of the two goods are closely correlated ($r = 1$), so declines in one match those in the other, the standard deviation of total revenues is \$6 million, or 30 per cent of total exports.

A plausible goal for a country trying to stabilise export earnings might be to diversify into items that have an approximately independent

TABLE 2.1 Commodity Shares in Exports and Gross National Product of Selected Developing Countries

Exporting country	Major commodity exports[1]	1973 Exports Value ($m)	1973 Exports Percentage of GNP	Commodity share in exports Largest commodity	Commodity share in exports Second largest	Commodity share in exports Three main commodities
Zambia	Copper, Zinc, Tobacco	1136	47	94	2	97
Gambia	Oil seeds, Vegetable oils, Feeds	41	66	53	32	96
Cuba	Sugar, Nonferrous metals, Fish	859	18	76	16	94
Chad	Cotton, Meat, Live animals	26	7	65	21	90
Uganda	Coffee, Cotton, Copper	299	17	68	16	89
Somalia	Live animals, Fruit, Meat	43	18	54	26	87
Sri Lanka	Tea, Rubber, Vegetable oils	324	12	59	16	83
Togo	Crude fertilisers, Cocoa, Coffee	61	15	45	25	83
Bolivia	Nonferrous metals, Silver, Coffee	198	20	76	5	82
Uruguay	Meat, Wool, Hides and skins	214	8	46	25	81
Sudan	Cotton, Oil seeds, Crude materials	414	18	56	18	80
Ghana	Cocoa, Wood rough, Wood shaped	565	79	60	13	79
Upper Volta	Live animals, Cotton, Oil seeds	20	4	41	20	77
Ethiopia	Coffee, Oil seeds, Hides and skins	165	7	48	14	75
Niger	Oil seeds, Live animals, Nonferrous ore	38	7	32	19	70
Cambodia	Rubber, Rice, Live cattle	65	10	40	17	65
Burma	Rice, Wood, Animal feeds	121	5	34	17	61
Congo	Wood, Sugar, Precious stones	39	9	41	10	57
Tanzania	Cotton, Coffee, Spices	318	17	24	22	57
Peru	Animal feeds, Nonferrous metals, Sugar	893	10	31	12	51

[1] Defined at the three-digit SITC level. Commodities listed in order of export importance.

relation between changes in export revenues ($r = 0.0$). In such a case, the cross-product term in equation 2–1 vanishes, and the standard deviation of total exports is the square root of the sum of individual variances. However, Table 2.1 shows that developing countries' exports are often highly concentrated in a few commodities which should have highly correlated price movements, so fluctuations in total earnings are amplified. In part, this concentration reflects a lack of financial and technical capacity to support a wide range of export industries. Exports of many LDCs have developed around plantations established to produce tropical products for shipment to metropolitan states, or from the exploitation of mineral resources. Due to the narrow range, and high correlations between the prices of the goods exported, the trade structures of many LDCs are such as to make these countries susceptible to cyclical fluctuations in export earnings.[22]

While the preceding discussion deals with the causes and consequences of export instability it must be noted that stability, by itself, cannot be a policy objective. Stability can be achieved by diversifying into products with stagnant growth, but this would be accomplished at the expense of long-term income increases. For many combinations of products a trade-off exists between stability of earnings and growth. In formulating a diversification strategy, the trade-off between these alternative objectives must be assessed. However, there is evidence that the export structures of many LDCs balance the worst of these two factors. Products are often exported which combine unstable export earnings with low annual growth rates.[23]

These points can be illustrated with reference to Table 2.2. Shown here are compound annual growth rates and price instability indices for 20 major commodities exported by LDCs over 1954–73. Separate information on price changes is also given for 1950–60, 1960–70, and 1970–73. For comparison, the growth rate and price instability index for manufactures is shown. Total exports of each commodity are also given to assist in evaluating the importance of each item in LDC trade.

As Table 2.2 shows, several of these commodities are characterised by low growth even though their instability indices are considerably above the group mean. For example, linseed oil actually experienced declining exports in spite of having an instability index second only to sugar. Lead, rice, and cocoa had relatively low growth rates ranging from 0.4 to 1.2 per cent with price instability indices that averaged more than 40 per cent. Countries which specialised in such items experienced a two-fold detrimental effect on trade and development prospects: price instability, which can have a serious destabilising influence on export

TABLE 2.2 Export Growth and Price Instability in Primary Commodity Trade, 1954–73

Commodity	1973 LDC exports ($m)	Percentage price change			1954–73 LDC exports[1]	
		1950–60	1960–70	1970–73	Growth rate	Price instability
Sugar	2147·5	-27	19	99	4·6	129
Linseed oil	28·2	—	—	—	-2·7	80
Sisal	151·4	23	-41	345	3·9	76
Palm oil	299·6	-17	15	45	5·6	60
Rice	571·5	-10	12	170	0·7	57
Groundnut oil	155·7	-2	25	24	4·5	54
Cocoa	931·7	1	19	102	1·2	47
Maize	571·0	-21	20	92	6·7	46
Beef	1120·2	126	42	131	16·2	43
Lead	155·3	—	—	—	0·4	41
Tin	729·6	6	68	-49	4·6	41
Copper	3748·9	36	107	38	9·5	40
Cotton	2114·0	-37	2	130	2·5	36
Coffee	4089·8	-24	46	30	2·7	31
Rubber	1846·5	1	-49	92	3·6	30
Jute	190·0	32	-7	-2	0·6	23
Manganese	78·1	-10	35	66	1·3	23
Iron	1252·5	75	-6	23	10·4	22
Tea	572·6	0	-20	-6	-0·5	15
Bauxite	274·8	7	90	14	8·1	15
Manufactures[2]	15490·0	—	—	—	10·8	18

[1] Annual compound rate of growth. Price instability measured by the coefficient of variation expressed as a percentage.
[2] Annual compound rate of growth is for world exports of manufactures.

Source: Adapted from Kathryn Morton and Peter Tulloch, *Trade and Developing Countries* (London: Croom Helm, 1977), p. 101 and Walter C. Labys, 'Optimal Portfolio Analysis of Multicommodity Stocking Arrangements', *Oxford Bulletin of Economics and Statistics* (August 1977), p. 221.

revenues, and low growth rates, which can produce income stagnation.

Another factor emerging from the table is that the performance of these commodities, measured in terms of growth and instability, has been poor relative to manufactures.[24] The latter averaged a 10·8 per cent growth rate over the 19 year period, which was 6·6 percentage points above the commodity average. Manufactures also experienced considerably less price instability than the commodities (18 per cent versus an average 45 per cent), with only bauxite and tea having lower instability indices. However, the figure for tea was accomplished in the face of declining LDC exports, as trade fell by 0·5 per cent per year.

Thus, Table 2.2 shows that countries specialised in the export of commodities have generally experienced two adverse consequences relative to nations trading in manufactures. Lower growth rates have a retardation effect on incomes and financial reserves available for purchase of capital equipment required for industrialisation. The *development potential* of a country is therefore reduced. The volatile nature of some commodity prices can also have a destabilising influence on export earnings. This latter factor can have adverse consequences for investment incentives, due to risk aversion, as well as on development planning efforts. Some economists also suggest an association exists between commodity and geographic concentration of exports. If LDCs specialise in a narrow range of commodities, this forecloses some trading possibilities and makes them dependent upon given export markets. The resulting inequalities in bargaining and economic power can have serious adverse consequences on LDC import and export trade.

Advantages of trade diversification

Due to the potentially serious adverse economic consequences of specialisation in a narrow range of commodities, an incentive exists for these LDCs to broaden their export base. In fact, a comprehensive trade diversification programme can form an integral part of an overall development strategy since development and diversification are interdependent. When economic development has reached an advanced stage, however, diversification becomes more a consequence than a cause of development, whereas in the earlier stages the reverse seems to be true.

Diversification may take one of two forms: horizontal or vertical. Horizontal diversification refers to widening the *range* of exports, as when a country dependent on (say) cotton begins to produce related products like tobacco, oil seeds, wheat, and cattle. Vertical diversification involves movement into exports at different stages of fabrication such as the processing of primary commodities. Thus, a cotton-exporting country may diversify vertically into yarn, fabric or clothing, while a country which exports rough or simply worked wood may expand into plywood, veneers, paper, or wood manufactures. Since processing activities normally require inputs from other service industries, vertical diversification may often involve important linkage effects whereby benefits are transmitted to other sectors of the economy.

It is difficult to generalise about problems encountered by LDCs in efforts to diversify horizontally since situations vary from country to country. However, UNCTAD (1975b, p. 6) has identified several factors which are often a common constraint:

(a) *Lack of knowledge* about alternative products which can be as profitable, or even more profitable than traditional exports.

(b) *Lack of labour skills and know-how* necessary for a shift from traditional to new products. In cases, agricultural extension services, if available at all, are concerned with problems of the staple export commodities and fail to take the initiative for new export ventures.

(c) *Lack of infrastructure* in the form of roads, port and transport facilities, marketing and distribution, etc., needed by alternative products.

(d) *Capital and input requirements.* A shift (say) from field to tree crops may be hampered by capital requirements which are beyond the reach of producers. Some new crops may involve a gestation period of from three to seven years before marketable quantities are produced. Many producers cannot afford such a delay.

(e) *Crop rotation.* The staple export commodity may form part of a crop rotation which has to be followed over a fixed cycle. A shift from one crop to another therefore involves a transition from a certain crop rotation to a different one. The diversification problem is compounded by the fact that this may involve entirely new production cycles or systems.

(f) *Institutional constraints.* Various regulations can work against diversification. For example, cropping patterns may not permit deviations by individual producers, while regulations may prescribe minimum acreages for principle exports to maintain foreign exchange earnings. Similarly, credit facilities and other financial or institutional support may be devoted primarily to traditional exports with managers unwilling to take risks associated with new ventures.

(g) *External economies.* Due to the size of operations, traditional exports often benefit from external economies in marketing, distribution, credit, and insurance, as well as from specialised skills not available to other producers. Such economies enhance the profitability, or reduce the cost, of traditional as opposed to new crops.

(h) *External protection and support* are often a key factor working against diversification. Complex systems of protection limit trading opportunities even though LDCs have a comparative advantage in many commodities. High support prices and subsidised production in developed nations often lead to surpluses which, when exported, displace developing country products in third markets. This produces uncertainties which work against new ventures.

These factors cause production rigidities which cannot be ignored in any effective diversification programme. Their existence indicates that the introduction of new exports cannot normally be left to the free play of market forces. Interventions in the form of subsidies, tax incentives, training, research on alternative products and production techniques, development of infrastructure, international finance and technical assistance may be needed. Horizontal diversification also raises the problem of harmonisation of different programmes since there is a danger that countries might move into products in actual or potential surplus, or which face problems such as competition from synthetics. A key effort is also needed to liberalise tariffs and nontariff restraints since these artificial protectionist measures are often the primary constraint for LDC diversification efforts.

Programmes aimed at vertical diversification often face similar problems except that technological factors and protectionist policies in industrial markets may assume increased importance. Some processing functions, such as the fabrication of metals, involve capital requirements and technologies which are beyond the capacity of many developing countries. Natural forces preclude vertical integration in these products since the items require a high degree of technical competence, on large capital expenditure. The structure of protection in industrial markets is often a major factor limiting vertical integration efforts. Typically, trade barriers escalate with the degree of processing involved in a product. Since fabricated items face more restrictive tariffs and nontariff barriers, these artificial protectionist measures may be the primary limiting factor working against LDC diversification efforts.[25] If developing countries are to break out of the narrow range of exports

which constrain industrialisation efforts, a major liberalisation of trade
barriers in industrial markets is required.

CURRENT PERSPECTIVES ON TRADE AND DEVELOPMENT

Although economists have extensively explored the links between trade
and growth in theoretical models, there have been relatively few
empirical studies aimed at quantifying this relation. In part, the
difficulty stems from statistical problems in isolating the influence of
trade from a host of other economic and cultural factors which also
affect growth. However, the available evidence suggests that trade has
played an important role in the industrialisation and development of
some economies, while in others it has had a neutral effect. The
differences seem largely related to variations in external and internal
conditions in individual countries. Where trade provides a successful
stimulus to growth, other elements such as factor mobility, appropriate
monetary and fiscal policies, attitudes toward risk, work, and reward,
etc., were required to provide an environment in which the expansion
became cumulative.

A study by Irving Kravis (1970) empirically examined the influence of
trade on the growth of current industrialised societies in a historical
perspective, and also assessed the trade-growth prospects of developing
countries today.[26] A primary objective of this investigation was to test
the hypothesis that the tremendous expansion of Western Europe's
demand for foodstuffs and raw materials in the nineteenth century
provided the basic inducement for the development of the periphery
countries (i.e., Canada, United States, Australia, Argentina, etc.), and
that trade in this period was an 'engine of growth'. The issue has
important implications for current development policy. If demand
conditions were basically different, the nineteenth-century model of
growth through trade may be of little practical consequence to
developing countries today.

The major conclusions of the study may be summarised as follows: (a)
trade expansion should be seen as a 'handmaiden' of successful growth
rather than an autonomous engine of growth, (b) where growth
occurred in the nineteenth century it was mainly the result of favourable
internal factors, and the differentials in export expansion did not
distinguish between successful and unsuccessful countries,[27] (c) export
growth and increases in national product are correlated for LDCs
today, and (d) external markets for developing countries are now more

favourable than nineteenth-century markets were for the periphery countries. This latter finding is important since it implies that the *size* of current export markets is sufficient to support LDC development objectives. Specifically, Kravis (1970, p. 860) concludes that 'it is clear that the markets of today's centre countries loom much larger relative to the output of the LDCs than was the case in the nineteenth century. Also, post-Second World War markets have expanded about twice as fast per annum as in the nineteenth century, with the increase between 1950 and 1965 being more than four times the 1950 aggregate GNP of the LDCs.'[28]

Several observations are made concerning the export performance of developing countries since the end of the Second World War. While this trade expansion has been quite high by historical standards, a failure to capitalise on existing opportunities has resulted in declining market shares for the LDCs as a group. In part, this was due to these countries' pursuance of import substitution policies, with their unfavourable economic effects, a failure to shift into new lines of production, and the neglect of traditional exports in favour of manufactures. However, a significant positive correlation between growth in exports and growth in real product for the non-petroleum exporting LDCs shows that increased exports are tied to real growth and development. Given the existence of this relation, an attempt is made to identify factors leading to the higher export growth in the successful developing countries.

Three indices of export performance are employed for this purpose. A 'world market factor' shows what the export performance of each LDC would have been had variations in world demand for traditional products been the only source of change. A second 'competitive factor' index shows the variation in export earnings associated with actual changes in the country's market shares, while a 'diversification factor' is computed as the residual change in a country's actual export earnings after account is taken of the first two factors.[29] The world market factor is employed as a measure of external demand changes on export earnings, while the competitive and diversification indices measure the influence of increased competitiveness and product diversification; elements which reflect the 'own competitiveness' position of individual countries.

Comparison of the overall export performance of individual LDCs with each of these indices suggests that export success did not depend primarily on world demand, although this was an important factor. The largest differences among the developing countries occur for the competitiveness factor; the LDCs with the fastest growing exports were distinguished from the less successful primarily by improvements in market shares for traditional exports rather than by demand increases.[30] The successful exporters were also found to have done better at diversification, although the margins of superiority were smaller.

The implications of these findings for development policy should be carefully noted. First, Kravis' correlations between LDC trade expansion and growth rates in GNP are positive and significant. Trade and growth are thus shown to be complementary factors. However, a key question centres on what causes trade to expand fastest; external demand, which is exogenous from the viewpoint of developing countries, or endogenous internal factors which make the country more competitive in world markets. According to Kravis' findings, the latter is generally more important, so the potential for trade expansion and growth is capable of being influenced by LDC policy measures.[31]

More recent empirical evidence provides additional support for the proposition that trade provides an important stimulus to growth and development, although it is difficult to establish clear lines of causation in these studies. For example, Michael Michaely (March 1977) has correlated the rate of change in exports as a percentage of national product against the change in per capita product for 41 developing countries over the period 1950 to 1973 and found a highly significant positive relation between the variables. The association between economic growth and increases in the export share appears to be particularly strong for the more advanced developing countries (Taiwan, Israel, Yugoslavia, Korea, etc.) and not to exist at all among the least developed nations. These tests show that a dynamic export sector is associated with more rapid rates of economic growth and development.

In a related investigation, Cohen (May 1968) employs a multiple regression model to assess the relative impact of additional export earnings and additional foreign aid on LDCs' gross national products. In each of the two-time periods tested, the export variable's regression coefficient was significant and considerably larger than that for the foreign aid term. This is interpreted to mean that the growth effects of additional export earnings are larger than those from foreign aid. As an explanation, Cohen cites the contribution of the dynamic productivity and learning effects of trade on growth, while foreign aid conveys relatively static benefits in these areas.

Emery (1967) has also employed regression analysis to test the relation between export expansion and economic growth for a selection of 50 developed and developing countries. As in the other studies, a high positive correlation between growth in exports and gross national product is observed. Emery also concludes that, on average, a 2·5 per cent increase in exports leads to a 1 per cent increase in gross national product although there is considerable variation among individual countries.

The role of internal factors

Empirical studies have confirmed that a general positive association exists between export expansion and economic growth rates. However, for some individual developing countries exposure to foreign trade has not resulted in the favourable cumulative growth process that is observed in other cases. A key question, therefore, centres on the nature of the factors which retard the growth-stimulating effects of international trade. In an assessment of this problem Meier concludes that the failure of trade to result in sustained growth is often the result of the character of the export base, the production techniques adopted to satisfy export demand, policies concerning the internal distribution of gains from trade, unfavourable effects of export instability, domestic rigidities or market impediments, and the absence of certain preconditions necessary for a take-off into sustained growth.[32]

While an analysis of the role of these internal constraints is beyond the scope of this book, it must be noted that cumulative growth through trade requires a removal of these obstacles and the establishment of an environment which is conducive to industrialisation and development.[33] However, the potential magnitude of this task should not be underestimated. Many of these inhibiting factors are the result of long established economic, political, and social customs, existing distributions of income and wealth, or lack of infrastructure. Thus, the necessary changes often require an extensive restructuring of basic institutions in many developing countries.

3 Recent Trends in Developing Country Exports

As indicated in the preceding discussion, theoretical models of the development process often assign a key role to various aspects of commercial trade policy. Aside from maintenance of a steady growth in exports, with accompanying increases in foreign exchange earnings, recent thinking has also emphasised the need for developing countries to reduce their dependence on traditional primary product exports. Factors cited for this proposed shift are a deterioration in the terms of trade for commodities relative to manufactures, as well as the instability of primary product prices and resulting uncertainty for development planning and finance.[1] In addition, a transfer of the processing function to the LDCs should provide an efficient method for absorbing some of the surplus labour existing in these countries.

While there has been general agreement that considerable benefits would accrue to the developing countries from a shift in the composition of exports toward manufactures, it is acknowledged that there are obstacles working against such a change. For example, analyses of industrial country tariffs suggest that the structure of these charges discourages the importation of processed goods. Other studies have also concluded that the structure of ocean freight rates may often favour the exportation of primary or unprocessed products from developing countries rather than manufactures. Finally, it is acknowledged that developing countries are frequently deficient in the technical knowledge and capital equipment required for the production of some manufactured goods.

Aside from individual efforts by developing countries to increase the proportion of manufactures in total exports, there have been several recent occurrences which may have influenced the level and structure of LDC exports. In 1968, most industrial countries initiated the first in a series of broad cuts in import duties agreed upon during the Kennedy

Round trade negotiations. Under the provisions of this agreement, tariffs on manufactured goods were reduced considerably over a period of five consecutive years. Many industrial nations also initiated 'generalised system of preference' (GSP) programmes which have the stated objective of stimulating exports of processed goods from the LDCs. Under the provisions of these plans, some developing country manufactures can be imported at zero tariffs, or at duties below most-favoured-nation rates. Finally, various programmes conducted under the auspices of the United Nations Industrial Development Organization and other international organisations have attempted to assist developing countries in acquiring the technical knowledge and capital equipment required for production of manufactures.

This chapter examines recent changes in the level and composition of developing country exports to determine if these programmes have resulted in any marked improvement in LDC trade performance. Specifically, the analysis investigates growth in developing country trade over the 1960s and early 1970s, as well as changes in market shares, terms of trade, and export concentration. Changes in the composition of exports over various processing chains (i.e., a manufacturing process in which a primary input progresses through successive stages of increased fabrication) are analysed to determine the extent to which LDCs succeeded in shifting from primary products to semi-finished and manufactured goods. Developing country trade with the Union of Soviet Socialist Republics is also analysed to determine if the level and structure of imports by this centrally planned economy differs from that of the developed market economy countries.

THE EXPORT PERFORMANCE OF DEVELOPING COUNTRIES

As an indication of the recent trade experience of developing nations Table 3.1 compares these countries' exports, both in total and on a geographic basis, with those of other selected countries or country groups. Aside from total values, the table also shows the LDC share of exports as well as that of other nations in 1950, 1960, and 1973. While these initial comparisons are confined to the period prior to the Organization for Petroleum Exporting Countries' price increases, a later section evaluates the impact of the OPEC price policy on developing country and world trade.

Over the thirteen-year period extending from 1960–1973, total

TABLE 3.1 Comparison of Values, Shares and Growth Rates of Total Exports from Major Country Groups in Selected Years

Region or country	Value of exports ($m)			Share in total exports (%)			Average annual growth rate	
	1950	1960	1973	1950	1960	1973	1960–70	1950–70
World	60700	128300	570100	100·0	100·0	100·0	9·2	7·4
Developed market economy	37200	85700	408300	61·3	66·8	71·6	10·0	8·0
European Economic Community	16250	41900	211170	26·8	32·7	37·0	10·1	8·9
European Free Trade Association	3340	7840	37700	5·5	6·1	6·6	9·9	8·2
Japan	820	4055	36930	1·4	3·2	6·5	17·5	15·7
United States	10149	20412	70223	16·7	15·9	12·3	7·7	5·8
Socialist countries in Europe	4140	13000	52900	6·8	10·1	9·3	8·7	9·8
Socialist countries in Asia	790	2040	4920	1·3	1·6	0·9	3·1	4·6
Developing countries	18500	27400	99400	30·5	21·4	17·4	6·9	4·6
Latin America	6600	8570	28980	10·9	6·7	4·4	5·3	3·4
Other America	950	1410	4010	1·6	1·1	0·7	4·6	3·8
Africa	3110	5330	20160	5·1	4·2	3·5	9·1	6·2
Asia	7740	11870	49230	12·8	9·3	8·6	7·0	4·9
Oceania	60	170	920	—	0·1	0·2	10·3	8·5

Source: Adapted from UNCTAD, *Handbook of International Trade and Development Statistics* (New York: United Nations, 1976).

exports of developing countries rose approximately 250 per cent from a level of $27·4 to $99·4 billion. On a geographic basis, exports of LDCs in Asia were among the fastest growing (up to 314 per cent), while those of Latin American and Caribbean countries rose at below average rates of 240 and 180 per cent respectively. Overall, the developing nations managed a 6·9 per cent average annual growth rate for the period 1960–70, which was more than 2 percentage points higher than the corresponding rate for 1950–70.[2] In the recent decade, the 9 per cent African export growth rate is largely accounted for by petroleum shipments, while the 7 per cent rate for Asian countries is explained by petroleum and rapidly growing exports of manufactures from semi-industrialised countries like Korea, Hong Kong, India, Taiwan and Singapore.

In spite of the developing countries' registering what appear to be impressive increases in the overall level of exports, the LDC *share* in world trade shows a persistent decline. In 1950, these exports accounted for over 30 per cent of total trade, but dropped to 21 per cent in 1960 and 17 per cent in 1973. In retrospect, the 1973 share may have been somewhat inflated due to abnormally high primary commodity prices. In any event, the 13 percentage point decline in developing countries' export share is primarily accounted for by a 10 percentage point increase in that for the European Economic Community, a 5 point rise for Japan, and a 2·6 percentage point increase for the socialist countries in Europe. The United States runs counter to the generally favourable performance of developed countries with a 4 percentage point decline, from 16·7 to 12·3 per cent, over the 1950–73 interval.

On a geographic basis, the export shares of the developing countries in Latin America and the Caribbean record the largest relative declines, with each falling by more than 50 per cent. In absolute terms, the 6·5 percentage point drop for Latin American nations is the largest in the table. With the exception of developing countries in Oceania (largely New Guinea, New Caledonia, Fiji and Guam), export shares of each other geographic group also registered persistent declines. To some extent, the overall reduction for the Asian and African LDCs, down 4·2 and 1·6 percentage points respectively, is inflated by the performance of petroleum exporters in both regions, and the fast growing exporters of manufactures in Asia.[3] Aside from these countries, the market performance of other Asian and African LDCs was generally more unfavourable than suggested by the overall averages.

Table 3.2 attempts to identify product groups primarily responsible for the erosion of the developing countries' market position. Shown in

TABLE 3.2 The Level and Share of Developing-Country Exports of Major Commodity Groups; 1960 to 1973 with Estimated 1980

	1960	1965	1970	1973	Est. 1980
Commodity group		(values in $ billion)			
Total merchandise exports	27·4	36·0	52·9	99·4	330·3
Total excluding fuels	19·7	24·7	37·5	67·0	151·6
Primary commodities excluding fuels	17·1	20·5	26·7	44·0	77·4
Foodstuffs (SITC 0 +1)	8·1	10·4	13·2	20·3	40·0
Industrial raw materials (SITC 2 +4)	7·6	8·2	10·0	19·3	31·4
Nonferrous metals (SITC 68)	1·4	1·9	3·5	4·4	6·0
Fuels (SITC 3)	7·5	10·9	17·6	43·5	178·7
Manufactures (SITC 5 through 9–68)	2·6	4·6	10·6	22·8	74·3
	(share of world exports)				
Primary commodities excluding fuels	36·1	33·2	30·5	29·0	25·6
Foodstuffs (SITC 0 +1)	35·5	34·6	31·7	27·1	24·4
Industrial raw materials (SITC 2 +4)	38·2	32·8	29·8	32·3	28·5
Nonferrous metals (SITC 68)	29·6	28·4	28·3	25·4	21·5
Fuels (SITC 3)	59·9	62·5	62·2	61·1	61·1
Manufactures (SITC 5 through 9–68)	3·9	4·4	5·4	6·3	6·3

Source: Adapted from UNCTAD, *Trade Prospects and Capital Needs of Developing Countries, 1976–1980*, (TD/B/C.3/134) (Geneva: United Nations, 15 April 1976).

the top half of the table are actual values of exports, both in total and for broad product groups, which occurred over the period 1960–73. The table also gives a 1980 projection for LDC exports which was made by the LINK econometric model.[4] The lower half of the table indicates the developing countries' actual share of exports for each product group, as well as their projected shares for 1980.

Several points emerge from the data presented in Table 3.2. First, the figures show that developing countries maintained their market position for both fuels and manufactures, with their share of exports rising by 1·2 and 2·4 percentage points respectively during 1960–73. However, the LDCs remain a relatively unimportant source of supply for manufactured goods, producing only about 6 per cent of the total trade. Erosion of the developing countries' market position for primary commodities is the major factor accounting for their overall declining percentage of world exports, as the LDC share for this product group fell more then 7 percentage points (from 36·1 to 29 per cent) over 1960–73. An analysis of the components shows foodstuffs recorded the largest absolute decline (8·4 percentage points), while industrial raw materials and nonferrous metals fell 5·9 and 4·2 points respectively.[5] According to the LINK estimates, further erosion of the developing country market position can be expected for these items over 1973–80, with LDC shares falling an average of 3 to 4 percentage points.

Table 3.2 also indicates that there have been major shifts in the composition of developing country exports. For example, fuels rose from 27 per cent of the total in 1960 to 44 per cent in 1973. The LINK projections suggest these exports should grow further in importance and account for over 50 per cent of LDC exports by 1980. The share of manufactures has also doubled over 1960–73, rising from 9 to 23 per cent. These increases were mainly at the expense of primary commodities whose share dropped from 63 per cent of total exports in 1960 to 44 per cent in 1973.

The trend toward declining shares for foodstuffs and other primary commodities in developing country and world trade can be attributed to several factors. First, industrial country governments have made extensive use of export subsidies for agricultural products with the result that the competitive position of developing countries has been undercut in foreign markets. Indeed, one of the features of the European Economic Community's Common Agricultural Policy provides for export subsidisation of items produced in surplus. High levels of domestic protection in industrial nations raises returns and stimulates investment in agriculture, with the result that surpluses may be generated which need to be disposed of internationally. Furthermore, as real incomes rise, the pattern of demand for various types of goods shifts. The most obvious example is that food consumption grows more slowly than real income. Indeed, the income elasticity of demand for some basic foodstuffs such as grains may be near zero. Shifts in the pattern of food consumption are also important since items which have a relatively high income elasticity of demand, such as meats, are to a large extent produced in developed countries. On the other hand, primary commodities such as sugar and tropical beverages, which are produced by the developing countries, have lower elasticities with the result that a given increase in real income tends to produce a relatively lower export growth rate.[6]

Concentration of developing country exports
Aside from a general reduction in market shares, there are other

unfavourable aspects of the developing countries' export position. Specifically, many LDCs are highly specialised in the exportation of closely related primary goods whose prices may fluctuate widely from year to year. Due to the uncertainties caused by these fluctuations, the prospects for rational development planning become dubious. For this reason, economists have generally agreed that many developing countries should attempt to broaden their export base. A shift from primary commodities to semi-finished goods and manufactures has a number of positive aspects, among which is relatively stable demand and prices for processed goods.

Several statistical indices are available for measuring export concentration of individual countries. One such measure employs the absolute deviations of a country's commodity export shares from the share of those commodities in world trade. This index (S_j) is defined by,

$$S_j = \frac{\sum_i |h_{ij} - h_i|}{2} \qquad (3\text{--}1)$$

where h_{ij} is the share of each (three-digit) commodity i in total exports of country j, while h_i is the share of commodity i in total world exports. The index measures the extent that each country has diversified against the total world demand structure for exports. It ranges between zero and one with the former indicating complete diversification.[7]

Table 3.3 summarises results when the concentration index was computed for over 100 countries using information on their 1962 and 1972 export structures. In addition to showing averages for the developed and developing country groups, values for selected countries are presented. The net change in the index has been computed to serve as a measure of increased or decreased export concentration. To assist in evaluating the economic implications of export concentration, an index of annual fluctuations in export earnings is also shown for each nation.[8]

One point emerging from these results concerns the different degree of export concentration in developed and developing countries. For the industrial nations, an average 1972 index value of about 50 per cent is approximately 36 points below the corresponding average for LDCs. Furthermore, the data also reveal a strong inverse correlation between export concentration and the level of per capita GNP between developing country income groups. For example, the average concentration index value for the over $1000 GNP group is 0·809, while the index takes progressively higher values with each move to a lower

TABLE 3.3 Developed and Developing Country Indices of Export Concentration and Fluctuations Ranked by Income Group; Totals and Selected Countries

Country or country group	Diversification index[1]			Index of export fluctuations[2]
	1962	1972	Net change	
DEVELOPED MARKET ECONOMY[3]	·582	·496	−·086	3·0
France	·295	·236	−·059	3·3
United Kingdom	·377	·301	−·076	2·5
Germany, Federal Republic	·439	·315	−·124	1·6
United States	·349	·335	−·014	2·3
Belgium	·439	·341	−·098	3·8
Italy	·420	·343	−·077	2·0
Sweden	·506	·402	−·104	2·6
Japan	·548	·423	−·125	4·3
Austria	·512	·425	−·087	2·8
Denmark	·578	·473	−·105	2·5
Canada	·558	·489	−·069	2·6
Spain	·664	·503	−·161	4·6
Switzerland	·600	·547	−·053	1·4
Norway	·615	·587	−·028	2·5
Australia	·694	·666	−·028	3·9
Greece	·811	·695	−·116	3·5
Turkey	·813	·760	−·053	2·7
DEVELOPING COUNTRIES[4] by income category:	·884	·856	−·028	6·4
Over $1000 per capita GNP	·849	·809	−·020	4·2
Singapore	·531	·557	+·026	4·0
Israel	·760	·668	−·092	2·2
Argentina	·805	·762	−·043	5·4
Hong Kong	·773	·772	−·001	2·8
Trinidad and Tobago	·853	·811	−·042	2·5
Martinique	·962	·892	−·070	7·3
Cyprus	·914	·893	−·021	3·8
Gabon	·921	·895	−·026	5·0
Reunion	·976	·956	−·020	4·4
$401 to $1000	·884	·883	−·001	5·5
Mexico	·690	·537	−·153	2·0
Korea, Republic of	·835	·672	−·163	3·2
Brazil	806	·682	−·124	5·5
Colombia	·831	·715	−·116	5·7

TABLE 3.3 *continued*

Country or country group	Diversification Index[1] 1962	1972	Net change	Index of export fluctuations
Guatemala	·893	·723	−·170	5·5
Nicaragua	·879	·745	−·134	3·1
Costa Rica	·931	·769	−·162	3·2
Angola	·840	·783	−·057	4·3
Tunisia	·857	·784	−·073	3·0
Malaysia	·845	·828	−·017	5·3
Chile	·868	·864	−·004	3·6
Ivory Coast	·918	·867	−·051	5·2
Panama	·915	·882	−·033	5·2
Paraguay	·903	·885	−·018	6·2
Congo, People's Republic	·824	·886	+·062	11·7
Dominican Republic	·912	·910	−·002	6·4
Peru	·831	·933	+·102	3·7
Ecuador	·913	·951	+·038	4·7
Zambia	·959	·971	+·012	8·7
Cuba	·945	·971	+·026	11·0
$201 to $400	·896	·851	−·045	6·8
El Salvador	·866	·738	−·128	9·0
Egypt	·821	·757	−·064	7·2
Senegal	·919	·762	−·157	6·1
Thailand	·870	·789	−·081	3·8
Mozambique	·840	·796	−·044	4·7
Morocco	·842	·802	−·040	2·9
Cameroon	·837	·816	−·021	4·9
Honduras	·873	·846	−·027	9·0
Philippines	·885	·847	−·038	4·2
Jordan	·915	·858	−·057	6·5
Bolivia	·926	·923	−·003	5·2
Liberia	·943	·934	−·009	9·5
Ghana	·943	·934	−·009	6·2
Mauritius	·977	·950	−·027	9·6
$200 and below	·892	·896	+·004	7·9
India	·739	51·3	−22·6	3·7
Madagascar	·849	·802	+·047	4·3
Pakistan	·782	·820	+·038	3·0
Indonesia	·821	·828	+·007	6·9
Kenya	·867	·828	−·039	3·0
Togo	·931	·833	−·098	8·8
Upper Volta	·875	·873	−·004	13·6

Country or country group	Diversification index[1] 1962	1972	Net change	Index of export fluctuations[2]
Tanzania	·898	·873	− ·025	6·6
Mali	·945	·877	− ·068	21·4
Ethiopia	·912	·892	− ·020	4·3
Niger	·938	·898	− ·040	9·5
Malawi	·918	·907	− ·011	5·0
Zaire	·860	·913	+ ·053	7·6
Burma	·893	·914	+ ·021	10·2
Sri Lanka	·912	·914	+ ·002	3·3
Bangladesh	·733	·915	+ ·182	3·6
Central African Republic	·890	·923	+ ·033	9·7
Chad	·907	·927	+ ·020	8·0
Sierra Leone	·947	·927	+ ·020	9·2
Sudan	·936	·934	− ·002	5·7
Uganda	·913	·934	+ ·021	6·0
Afghanistan	·919	·943	+ ·024	4·2
Somalia	·956	·951	− ·005	5·2
Rwanda	·949	·951	+ ·002	16·5
Gambia	·981	·972	− ·009	11·8

[1] Average absolute deviation of country commodity shares from world trade structure.
[2] Average annual percentage deviation from trend.
[3] Excludes Iceland.
[4] Excludes OPEC countries.

income category. The data also suggest an association exists between income level and the *change* in export concentration over 1962–72. Developed market economy countries evidence the highest degree of deconcentration, with an average decline of 8·5 percentage points, while the indices for the low income group ($200 per capita GNP and below) suggest increased concentration has occurred.

Examination of individual developing country concentration indices reveals that the drop of almost 23 percentage points in India's index is by far the most impressive example of export diversification. This movement is primarily the result of industrialisation projects which allowed India to move into such diverse export markets as steel, metal products, machinery, and chemicals, as well as its traditional textile and crude material exports. Another factor was that real wages in some other developing countries which are important exporters of manufactures drifted upwards, giving India a competitive cost advantage. Other important examples of export deconcentration occurred for developing countries with the index dropping more than 10 points for Korea, Brazil, El Salvador, Guatemala, Nicaragua, Costa Rica and Mexico. Aside from their own industrialisation programmes, diversification in the Latin American countries was encouraged by off-shore assembly provisions in the United States tariff code. These provisions permit primary and semifinished goods produced in the United States to be assembled into manufactures in other countries and re-exported to the USA under reduced tariffs. One estimate suggests that these provisions were worth more than $6 billion to Mexico alone over the period 1968–74.[9] However, aside from these exceptions, Table 3.3 suggests that few developing countries experienced important export deconcentration over 1962–72, while some evidence indicates trade structures of the poorest LDCs may have become more concentrated.

The data in Table 3.3 also underscores the positive correlation between export concentration and instability in foreign exchange earnings. For example, the most diversified group of exporters, the developed market economy countries, experienced average year-to-year fluctuations in export revenues of about 3 per cent, which was less than half that for the developing nations (6·4 per cent). Within the LDC groups, a rather wide range of experience is evidenced, but the tendency is clearly for increased instability with higher levels of export concentration. For example, developing countries with a GNP of over $1000 per capita had an average annual 4·2 per cent fluctuation in export earnings, but this figure increases with each move to a lower income group. The average for $200 GNP countries is close to 8 per cent, or more than two-and-one-half times the instability level for the developed nations.

Developing country terms of trade
Aside from instability in export earnings, changes in the terms of trade are of primary importance to developing countries. The net barter terms of trade measure the price ratio of exports to imports, while changes in the terms of trade reflect movements in these price relatives over some time period. If the change in terms of trade exceeds unity, the implications are favourable since this indicates the prices of a nation's exports have risen relative to import prices.[10]

While the theoretical concept appears relatively simple, there are several factors which make practical measurement difficult. First, it has been demonstrated that measures of the terms of trade may be very sensitive to any change in the time period chosen for these comparisons. Shifting the base period by even a few years may reverse the indicated directional movement in the terms of trade. Another difficulty is that, due to a lack of alternatives, these calculations employ unit values as proxies for transaction prices. However, unit values are notorious for their inability to distinguish true price movements from quality or product mix changes. There are also the familiar index number problems common to any intertemporal comparison of prices. One aspect is that the composition of a country's imports and exports changes over time with the result that the index may be quite sensitive to the system of weights used. Finally, there is the problem of distinguishing cyclical movements in the terms of trade from the more important secular changes.

In spite of these difficulties, economists tend to agree that long-run changes in the terms of trade have generally been unfavourable to developing countries.[11] A number of factors have been suggested as contributing to this trend. For example, it is recognised that raw material production is characterised by diminishing returns on the supply side, and low elasticities of demand with respect to price. Working in tandem, these forces would tend to lower primary producers' margins over time. Estimates of the income elasticities for primary materials are also low, so the long-term demand prospects for commodities relative to manufactures are not favourable.[12] Prebisch expanded on these observations and demonstrated that raw materials entering international trade have been subject to highly unstable prices, and that over the long run the terms of trade for raw material exporting countries had worsened.[13] Therefore, LDCs could not count on a given sum of foreign exchange earnings from the sale of their raw materials. Furthermore, Prebisch suggested that an increasing amount of raw material exports would be required over time to obtain the same import volume of manufactured goods.[14]

Overall, the data shown in Table 3.4 are in agreement with the proposition that terms of trade have been declining for developing countries. From the mid-1950s to 1973, the ratio of developed country export to import unit values rose 10 per cent, while a similar ratio for all developing countries registered no change. However, the overall LDC index was inflated by the performance of petroleum exporting countries whose terms of trade actually rose by 30 per cent.

A separate analysis for non-petroleum exporting countries shows that their terms of trade actually declined by 13·3 per cent. When arranged by income group, the data suggest that the deterioration was

TABLE 3·4 Changes in the Terms of Trade for Developed Market Economy and Developing Countries from the Levels which Prevailed during 1954 to 1956

Country or country group	Change in the terms of trade (%)[1]			
	1960	1965	1970	1973
Developed market economy countries	+6·6	+8·9	+11·1	+10·0
America	+6·6	+8·9	+11·1	+6·7
Europe	+6·6	+8·9	+11·1	+10·0
European Economic Community	+9·1	+11·4	+13·6	+12·5
European Free Trade Association	+3·3	+7·7	+9·9	+7·7
Other Europe	+1·1	+8·8	+9·9	+12·1
Japan	+12·2	+2·2	+11·1	+12·2
Oceania	−14·8	−12·5	−21·9	+3·1
Developing countries	−10·2	−8·3	−7·4	0·0
Petroleum exporters	+1·0	+3·1	+3·1	+30·9
Other developing countries *of which:*	−13·4	−11·6	−10·7	−13·3
Fast growing exporters of manufactures	−15·1	−14·2	−5·7	−11·3
All other developing countries *of which*:	−13·3	−11·5	−11·5	−12·4
Countries with a per capita GNP over $40	−18·1	−13·8	−13·8	−12·9
With a per capita GNP of $200 under $200	−1·9	−4·8	−3·8	−5·8
	−8·9	−9·8	−10·7	−17·9

[1] Unit value of exports over import unit values for each year divided by the average 1954–6 ratio of export to import unit values.

Source: Computed from information published in UNCTAD, *Handbook of International Trade and Development Statistics* (New York: United Nations, 1976).

most severe for the lowest income group, where the rise in import prices was approximately 18 per cent above that for exports.

THE COMMODITY COMPOSITION OF EXPORTS

Any investigation of structural changes in developing country exports is complicated by a classification problem for goods involving different stages of fabrication (i.e., primary products, semifinished goods, manufactures, etc.). However, this difficulty can be surmounted by drawing on a scheme employed by UNCTAD for analysis of tariff escalation in the major industrial countries. Essentially, the UNCTAD classification scheme covers almost all important commodities exported by developing countries in primary and processed form with the exception of petroleum. Altogether, twenty-one processing chains are identified: meat, fish, fruits, vegetables, cocoa, leather, groundnuts, copra, palm kernel, rubber, wood, paper, wool, cotton, jute, sisal and henequen, iron, copper, aluminium, lead and zinc. On average, three different stages of processing were distinguished for these commodities: two in seven cases, three in eleven others, and four or more for the remaining products.[15]

Trade data on the industrial market economy country imports of these items was taken from official United Nations publications, while an UNCTAD document provided information on the Soviet Union's imports from developing countries.[16] These sources presented detailed trade statistics through the four-digit SITC level, so components of the processing chains were easily identified. Since imports are tabulated separately for developed and developing countries, data was available for calculation and analysis of change in LDC market shares.

To illustrate the changes which have occurred in the structure of LDC exports of these commodities to the major industrial countries, Table 3.5 gives total values of each stage of the 21 processing chains.[17] Shown here are imports from both developing countries and all sources in 1964 and 1974, as well as LDC market share in each year. The table gives the percentage of imports in each processing stage, and also provides summary information on imports and market shares by stage of processing.

Table 3.5 shows that while total exports of the components of these processing chains were experiencing a threefold increase over the decade, from $7.2 to 22 billion, this expansion was generally accomplished in the face of declining LDC market shares. Analysis of individual product data shows that the metals experienced the largest declines with copper, lead, and zinc falling by at least 8 percentage points, and iron and aluminium falling by about 4 points. However, the sharpest decline was the 28 percentage point drop for rubber where developing countries almost totally failed to participate in the rapidly expanding trade in manufactured goods.

On an overall basis, the LDC market shares generally registered declines for the ten year period, falling for total exports of 16 of the 21 processing chains. An examination of trade figures by processing stages shows that most of these declines were due to erosion of developing country market positions for the primary stage items, with reductions

TABLE 3.5 Analysis of Changes in the Structure of Industrial Countries' Imports from Developing and Developed Nations during the Interval 1964-74: Selected Commodity Groups[1]

Product	1964 Imports					1974 Imports				
	From LDCs		Total imports		LDC share (%)	From LDCs		Total imports		LDC share (%)
	Value ($m)	%	Value ($m)	%		Value ($m)	%	Value ($m)	%	
Meat products										
1. Fresh or frozen meat	248·6	74·3	1310·1	76·6	19·0	471·6	64·0	3916·1	76·4	12·0
2. Meat preparations	86·2	25·7	399·6	23·4	21·6	264·7	36·0	1209·4	23·6	21·9
Total	334·8	100·0	1709·7	100·0	19·6	736·3	100·0	5125·5	100·0	14·4
Fish and seafood										
1. Fresh or frozen fish	162·9	78·1	625·8	68·5	26·0	1285·8	85·9	3039·5	81·4	42·3
2. Fish preparations	45·7	21·9	287·3	31·5	15·9	211·7	14·1	693·6	18·6	30·5
Total	208·6	100·0	913·1	100·0	22·8	1497·5	100·0	3733·1	100·0	40·1
Fruits and nuts										
1. Fresh fruit or nuts	711·6	85·5	1522·7	79·9	46·7	1309·1	81·6	3157·5	73·9	41·5
2. Preserved fruit	120·8	14·5	384·2	20·1	31·4	295·6	18·4	1114·1	26·1	26·5
Total	832·4	100·0	1906·9	100·0	43·7	1604·7	100·0	4271·6	100·0	37·6
Vegetables										
1. Fresh vegetables	179·7	75·4	734·1	79·6	24·5	504·2	65·7	2015·5	66·2	25·0
2. Preserved vegetables	58·5	24·6	188·1	20·4	31·1	263·0	34·3	1029·9	33·8	25·5
Total	238·2	100·0	922·2	100·0	25·8	767·2	100·0	3045·4	100·0	25·2
Cocoa and chocolate										
1. Cocoa beans	300·5	90·9	304·2	67·0	98·8	753·4	73·4	787·6	55·0	95·7
2. Cocoa powder	29·5	8·9	73·7	16·2	40·0	262·2	25·6	391·5	27·3	67·0
3. Chocolate	0·5	0·2	75·8	16·7	0·7	10·2	1·0	253·8	17·7	4·0
Total	330·5	100·0	453·7	100·0	72·8	1025·8	100·0	1432·9	100·0	71·6
Leather and products										
1. Hides and skins	113·3	48·1	406·9	36·8	27·8	101·4	8·5	604·5	14·3	16·8

2. Leather	72.5	30.8	235.3	21.3	225.7	30.8	665.6	19.0	33.9	15.8
3. Leather goods	49.9	21.2	462.4	41.9	862.5	10.8	2945.4	72.5	29.3	69.9
Total	235.7	100.0	1104.6	100.0	1189.6	21.3	4215.5	100.0	28.2	100.0
Groundnut oil										
1. Groundnuts	123.8	77.9	135.2	64.0	154.1	91.6	247.2	43.4	62.3	51.1
2. Groundnut oil	35.1	22.1	76.2	36.0	200.8	46.1	236.2	56.6	85.0	48.9
Total	158.9	100.0	211.4	100.0	354.9	75.2	483.4	100.0	73.4	100.0
Coconut oil										
1. Copra	157.2	69.4	159.1	67.6	185.6	98.8	190.0	35.8	97.7	33.2
2. Coconut oil	69.4	30.6	76.1	32.4	332.6	91.2	382.8	64.2	86.9	66.8
Total	226.6	100.0	235.2	100.0	518.2	96.3	572.8	100.0	90.5	100.0
Palm kernel oil										
1. Palm kernels	69.2	89.5	69.5	81.8	67.7	99.6	68.4	36.9	99.0	30.9
2. Palm kernel oil	8.1	10.5	15.5	18.2	115.8	52.3	153.2	63.1	75.6	69.1
Total	77.3	100.0	85.0	100.0	183.5	90.9	221.6	100.0	82.8	100.0
Rubber and products										
1. Natural rubber	592.2	99.4	593.9	72.5	1224.2	99.7	1240.9	95.8	98.7	43.0
2. Rubber products	3.8	0.6	225.7	27.5	53.9	1.7	1646.7	4.2	3.3	57.0
Total	596.0	100.0	819.6	100.0	1278.1	72.7	2887.6	100.0	44.3	100.0
Wood and products										
1. Wood in the rough	4.5	2.0	184.3	9.4	39.6	2.4	1537.2	3.5	2.6	22.2
2. Plywood	214.5	94.0	1615.7	82.6	891.4	13.3	4697.9	79.1	19.0	67.7
3. Wood manufactures	9.2	4.0	156.1	8.0	195.5	5.9	702.9	17.4	27.8	10.1
Total	228.2	100.0	1956.1	100.0	1126.5	11.7	6938.0	100.0	16.2	100.0
Paper and products										
1. Pulpwood	4.8	26.7	72.0	2.4	13.9	6.7	146.3	9.7	9.5	1.4
2. Wood pulp	6.7	37.2	1185.8	39.0	29.9	0.6	3744.9	20.9	0.8	34.7
3. Paper and articles	6.5	36.1	1780.5	58.6	99.3	0.4	6901.9	69.4	1.4	63.9
Total	18.0	100.0	3038.3	100.0	143.1	0.6	10793.1	100.0	1.3	100.0
Wool and products										
1. Raw wool	139.9	96.7	1123.3	68.5	65.3	12.5	1005.9	79.2	6.5	61.6
2. Wool yarn	1.7	1.2	199.6	12.2	6.0	0.9	187.5	7.3	3.2	11.5

TABLE 3.5 *continued*

Product	1964 Imports					1974 Imports				
	From LDCs Value ($m)	%	Total imports Value ($m)	%	LDC share (%)	From LDCs Value ($m)	%	Total imports Value ($m)	%	LDC share (%)
3. Wool fabrics	3·0	2·1	316·2	19·3	0·9	11·1	13·5	438·7	26·9	2·5
Total	144·6	100·0	1639·1	100·0	8·8	82·4	100·0	1632·1	100·0	5·0
Cotton and products[2]										
1. Raw cotton	634·8	64·9	1001·2	48·8	63·4	1129·8	31·2	1825·8	23·8	61·9
2. Cotton yarn	21·9	2·2	60·5	2·9	36·2	181·0	5·0	407·4	5·3	44·4
3. Cotton fabrics	136·8	14·0	436·8	21·3	31·3	564·5	15·6	1602·7	20·9	35·2
4. Clothing	184·5	18·9	553·5	27·0	33·3	1749·9	48·3	3822·7	49·9	45·8
Total	977·8	100·0	2052·0	100·0	47·7	3625·2	100·0	7658·6	100·0	47·3
Jute and products										
1. Raw jute	86·7	32·0	92·2	30·2	94·0	73·8	20·1	77·9	19·3	94·7
2. Jute fabrics	173·3	64·0	197·3	64·6	87·8	239·5	65·1	256·6	63·5	93·3
3. Sacks and bags	10·9	4·0	15·9	5·2	68·6	54·4	14·8	69·9	17·3	77·8
Total	270·9	100·0	305·4	100·0	88·7	367·7	100·0	404·4	100·0	90·9
Sisal and products										
1. Raw sisal	94·2	78·0	94·7	57·4	99·5	124·6	45·7	125·6	28·2	99·2
2. Cordage	26·6	22·0	70·3	42·6	37·8	147·9	54·3	320·4	71·8	46·2
Total	120·8	100·0	165·0	100·0	73·2	272·5	100·0	446·0	100·0	61·1
Iron and products										
1. Iron ore	811·2	92·9	1454·7	47·5	55·8	2088·0	80·6	4359·1	41·2	47·9
2. Pig iron	55·9	6·4	432·1	14·1	12·9	364·0	14·0	1646·4	15·6	22·1
3. Steel ingots	2·0	0·2	325·0	10·6	0·6	6·5	0·3	1067·7	10·1	0·6
4. Mill products	4·3	0·5	742·1	24·3	0·6	125·2	4·8	2937·9	27·8	4·3
5. Special steel items	0·0	0·0	105·5	3·4	0·0	7·7	0·3	565·3	5·3	1·4
Total	873·4	100·0	3059·4	100·0	28·5	2591·4	100·0	10576·4	100·0	24·5

Copper and products										
1. Copper ores	108·6	11·9	166·6	9·9	65·2	1209·7	34·1	2039·2	25·7	59·3
2. Unwrought copper	792·3	87·0	1336·7	79·0	59·3	2331·6	65·6	4782·0	60·4	48·8
3. Copper wrought	10·2	1·1	188·0	11·1	5·4	10·7	0·3	1101·5	13·9	1·0
Total	911·1	100·0	1691·3	100·0	53·9	3552·0	100·0	7922·7	100·0	44·8
Aluminium										
1. Bauxite	158·9	75·5	178·9	19·3	88·8	262·9	43·2	373·3	11·6	70·4
2. Alumina	28·0	13·3	126·6	13·6	22·1	143·9	23·6	603·2	18·8	23·9
3. Unwrought aluminium	22·2	10·5	485·5	52·3	4·6	190·9	31·4	1406·6	43·7	13·6
4. Wrought aluminium	1·5	0·7	136·9	14·8	1·1	11·1	1·8	833·4	25·9	1·3
Total	210·6	100·0	927·9	100·0	22·7	608·8	100·0	3216·5	100·0	18·9
Lead and products										
1. Lead ores	35·0	44·5	79·0	30·7	44·3	89·2	71·0	232·3	37·4	38·4
2. Unwrought lead	43·5	55·3	175·6	68·2	24·8	36·3	28·9	381·1	61·3	9·5
3. Wrought lead	0·2	0·3	2·8	1·1	7·1	0·1	0·1	8·1	1·3	1·2
Total	78·7	100·0	257·0	100·0	30·6	125·6	100·0	621·5	100·0	20·2
Zinc and products										
1. Zinc ores	71·6	72·9	143·3	41·6	50·0	235·6	73·1	621·7	40·3	37·9
2. Unwrought zinc	26·6	27·1	190·2	55·2	14·0	81·0	25·1	877·7	56·8	9·2
3. Wrought zinc	0·0	0·0	11·2	3·2	0·0	5·9	1·8	45·0	2·9	13·1
Total	98·2	100·0	344·7	100·0	28·5	322·5	100·0	1544·4	100·0	20·9
Aggregate imports										
Stage 1	4809·2	67·0	10451·7	43·9	46·0	11389·5	51·8	27611·5	35·5	41·2
Stage 2	1920·6	26·8	7552·1	31·7	25·4	6678·5	30·4	25428·1	32·7	26·3
Stage 3	251·2	3·5	4256·2	17·9	5·9	2011·6	9·2	16544·2	21·3	12·2
Stage 4	190·3	2·7	1538·0	6·5	12·4	1893·9	8·6	8159·3	10·5	23·2
Total	7171·3	100·0	23798·0	100·0	30·1	21973·5	100·0	77743·1	100·0	28·2

[1] Imports of Denmark, France, Germany, Japan, Sweden, United Kingdom and the United States. 1974 imports of the USSR have been excluded from this summary table.

[2] Includes cotton blends and other types of clothing in the final stage of processing.

for metal ores being of special importance.[18] Moving counter to this general trend, however, were developing country shares for the final stage of each processing chain where *increases* occurred in 16 of 21 cases, as opposed to the same number of reductions in the primary round. However, the intermediate and final stage share increases were generally not of sufficient magnitude to offset the declines which occurred in the primary product stages. The significance of these falling market shares can be appreciated by noting that, had the developing countries merely *maintained* their overall 1964 market position (30·1 per cent of total exports) this would have increased their 1974 foreign exchange earnings by about $1·4 billion.[19]

While there are exceptions to the general pattern, Table 3.5 shows that developing country exports continue to be heavily concentrated in primary or semi-processed goods. In 1974 for example, 52 per cent of LDC exports consisted of primary product (stage 1) items, while 82 per cent fell in the first two processing stages. In contrast, the developed countries are considerably more diversified with only 29 per cent of total exports composed of primary goods.

In spite of the continuing concentration of LDC exports in primary products, Table 3.5 provides evidence that progress has been made in efforts to move up the processing chains. Specifically, 67 per cent of total LDC exports were composed of stage 1 items in 1964, while this share fell to 52 per cent in 1974.[20] Analysis of the individual product figures shows that major shifts occurred in aluminium, sisal, cotton, leather, palm kernel, coconut and groundnut oil where the percentage of primary product exports fell by 20 points or more, while this share for meat, vegetables, cocoa, paper and wool products declined by at least 10 points. However, in spite of these changes, the impression emerging from Table 3.5 is that the exports of LDCs remain heavily concentrated in primary goods in spite of a recent shift toward semi-finished goods and manufactures.

A comparative analysis of importing markets

As an illustration of the overall importance of the individual industrial markets for developing country products, Table 3.6 shows the total value of imports of items comprising these major processing chains. The table shows both 1964 and 1974 import values, and also gives the percentage change over the decade. To assist in comparing these figures, the total value of each country's imports has been deflated by two measures of market size; population and gross national product. Of the eight industrial markets, the United States is the largest single

TABLE 3.6 Comparative Analysis of Industrial Country Imports of Products of Special Export Interest to Developing Nations

| Importing country | Value of imports adjusted for market size[1] | | | | Value of imports from developing countries ($m)[2] | | Percentage change |
| | Gross national product | | Population | | | | |
	1964	1974	1964	1974	1964	1974	
Denmark	·0060	·0072	11·5	39·0	54·5	195·9	259·4
France	·0105	·0100	19·5	49·0	981·6	2541·6	158·9
Germany	·0108	·0104	19·0	58·5	1145·2	3615·1	215·7
Japan	·0146	·0139	11·5	53·0	1170·9	5741·9	390·4
Sweden	·0072	·0070	17·0	43·0	133·9	348·4	160·2
USSR	n.a.	·0033	n.a.	7·0	n.a.	1692·3	n.a.
United Kingdom	·0163	·0155	27·5	48·5	1515·5	2711·8	78·9
United States	·0034	·0052	11·0	32·5	2169·7	6818·8	214·3
Total					7171·3	23665·8	230·0

[1] Population and Gross National Product figures taken from UNCTAD, *Handbook of International Trade and Development Statistics* (Geneva, various issues).

[2] Imports of primary and processed forms of meat, fish, fruits and nuts, vegetables, cocoa, leather, groundnut oil, coconut oil, palm kernel oil, rubber, wood, paper, wool, cotton, jute, sisal, iron, copper, aluminium, lead and zinc.

buyer of these developing country products with close to $7 billion of imports in 1974 (28·8 per cent of the total), while Japan was second with 5·7 billion. Japan was the most rapidly growing LDC market, however, as imports increased by 390 per cent over the 1964 base. Overall, developing country exports to these industrial markets averaged about a 200 per cent increase over the decade, with the United Kingdom and France on the low end of the scale.

When the aggregate import values are deflated by the size variables, considerable change is evidenced in the relative positions of the individual countries. For example, in 1974 Germany registered close to $60 of LDC imports per capita, followed by Japan, France and the United Kingdom. The fact that the UK has a relatively high LDC penetration ratio in 1964 ($27.5 per capita) accounts in part for its low growth rate. Another factor emerging from the size adjusted import figures is that the Soviet Union's performance as a developing country market falls well below that of the industrial market economy countries. If the USSR raised its per capita imports to the average for the seven other developed nations (about $46), this would produce *additional* LDC exports of approximately $9 billion.[21]

Table 3.7 presents supplementary information on the structure of imports from developing countries. Shown here are 1964 and 1974 import values, by stage of processing, for the seven market economy countries along with information on the Soviet Union's 1974 imports. The table gives developing country market shares and also shows the percentage of imports falling in each processing stage. Table 3.8 presents two summary concentration measures for LDC exports to the industrial markets, and also shows the change in these indices over the decade. The first of these measures, the primary product ratio, indicates the percentage of developing country exports falling in the initial production stage, while the second measure is based on each stage's share in total exports (see equation 3–2 in Note 7).

Analysis of the individual industrial country import figures (Table 3.7) along with the summary indices, shows that wide differences exist in the concentration of LDC exports to each market. For example, whether measured by the primary product ratio or the concentration coefficient, the Soviet Union's trade is far more heavily centred on primary goods than any of the Western market economy countries. About 79 per cent of the USSR's imports were composed of stage 1 items, while almost 90 per cent fell in the first two stages. Thus, while the tariff structures of the developed market economy countries have been blamed for the concentration of LDC exports in primary goods (see

TABLE 3.7 Analysis of the Structure of Industrial Country Imports from Developing Nations in 1964 and 1974

Importer-processing stage	1964			1974		
	Imports from LDCs Value ($m)	%	LDC market share	Imports from LDCs Values ($m)	%	LDC market share
Denmark						
Stage 1	34·2	62·8	40·1	60·9	31·1	30·0
Stage 2	14·7	27·0	8·1	77·5	39·6	13·6
Stage 3	2·3	4·2	1·3	21·2	10·8	3·4
Stage 4	3·3	6·0	4·2	36·3	18·5	10·4
Total	54·5	100·0	10·6	195·9	100·0	11·2
France						
Stage 1	759·7	77·4	48·7	1417·1	55·8	39·2
Stage 2	191·3	19·5	28·6	951·8	37·5	28·5
Stage 3	30·5	3·1	7·5	117·7	4·6	4·3
Stage 4	0·1	0·0	0·0	55·0	2·1	4·4
Total	981·6	100·0	34·4	2541·6	100·0	23·2
Germany						
Stage 1	819·8	71·6	37·9	1991·1	55·1	34·1
Stage 2	289·1	25·2	19·3	993·5	27·5	19·0
Stage 3	9·8	0·9	1·1	171·0	4·7	4·3
Stage 4	26·5	2·3	7·3	459·5	12·7	25·0
Total	1145·2	100·0	23·2	3615·1	100·0	21·4
Japan						
Stage 1	1035·9	88·5	52·2	3948·0	68·7	41·1
Stage 2	129·4	11·1	27·0	1118·0	19·5	40·8
Stage 3	5·2	0·4	6·9	400·0	7·0	29·9
Stage 4	0·4	0·0	4·1	275·9	4·8	62·1
Total	1170·9	100·0	45·9	5741·9	100·0	40·7

TABLE 3.7 *continued*

Importer-processing stage	1964 Imports from LDCs Value ($m)	%	LDC market share	1974 Imports from LDCs Values ($m)	%	LDC market share
Sweden						
Stage 1	68·1	50·9	30·8	103·2	29·6	20·9
Stage 2	47·1	35·2	19·5	152·5	43·8	17·4
Stage 3	3·5	2·6	2·2	47·5	13·6	7·9
Stage 4	15·2	11·3	9·8	45·2	13·0	8·8
Total	133·9	100·0	17·3	348·4	100·0	14·0
USSR						
Stage 1	n.a.	—	—	1327·7	78·5	n.a.
Stage 2	n.a.	—	—	175·6	10·4	n.a.
Stage 3	n.a.	—	—	162·1	9·6	n.a.
Stage 4	n.a.	—	—	26·9	1·5	n.a.
Total	n.a.	—	—	1692·3	100·0	n.a.
United Kingdom						
Stage 1	835·2	55·1	37·7	1053·3	38·8	34·0
Stage 2	506·4	33·4	21·6	1217·1	44·9	21·5
Stage 3	120·2	7·9	12·4	195·6	7·2	7·2
Stage 4	53·7	3·6	33·9	245·7	9·1	25·3
Total	1515·5	100·0	26·7	2711·8	100·0	21·8

United States						
Stage 1	1256·3	57·9	56·6	2815·8	41·3	59·0
Stage 2	742·6	34·2	34·7	2168·1	31·8	30·9
Stage 3	79·7	3·7	5·1	1058·6	15·5	23·3
Stage 4	91·1	4·2	16·3	776·3	11·4	27·8
Total	2169·7	100·0	33·5	6818·8	100·0	35·7
Total[1]						
Stage 1	4809·2	67·1	46·0	12717·2	53·7	41·2
Stage 2	1920·6	26·8	25·4	6854·1	29·0	26·2
Stage 3	251·2	3·5	5·9	2173·7	9·2	12·1
Stage 4	190·3	2·6	12·3	1920·8	8·1	23·2
Total	7171·3	100·0	30·1	23665·8	100·0	28·3

[1] Developing country market share figures and the 1964 totals exclude imports of the Soviet Union.

TABLE 3.8 Summary Concentration Measures for Industrial Countries' Imports from Developing Nations; 1964 and 1974

Importing country	Primary product ratio (%)[1]			Concentration coefficient[2]		
	1964	1974	Change	1964	1974	Change
Denmark	62·8	31·1	−31·7	68·7	54·7	−14·0
France	77·4	55·8	−21·6	79·9	67·4	−12·5
Germany	71·6	55·1	−16·5	75·9	63·0	−12·9
Japan	88·5	68·7	−19·8	89·2	71·9	−17·3
Sweden	50·9	29·6	−21·3	63·0	56·1	−6·9
USSR	n.a.	78·5	n.a.	n.a.	79·8	n.a.
United Kingdom	55·1	38·8	−16·3	65·0	60·4	−4·6
United States	57·9	41·3	−16·6	67·5	55·6	−11·9
Total[3]	67·0	51·8	−15·1	72·4	61·4	−11·0

[1] Defined as the ratio of stage 1 product imports to total imports.

[2] Defined as $100 \cdot [\Sigma(x_i/X)^2]^{\frac{1}{2}}$ where x_i is the value of stage i imports ($i = 1$ to 4) and X is the total value of imports. The index ranges between 0 and 1 with the latter value indicating imports totally concentrated in a single processing stage.

[3] The 1974 totals exclude imports of the Soviet Union.

Chapter 4), state trading by this centrally planned economy results in an even more detrimental structure. Aside from the Soviet Union, Japan emerges as the most heavily concentrated market with about 70 per cent of total 1974 imports composed of primary goods. At the opposite end of the scale, the Scandinavian countries, Sweden and Denmark, have the most favourable structure with close to 70 per cent of LDC imports composed of semi-finished goods or manufactures.

Another factor emerging from these data is that the shift in composition of LDC exports toward semi-finished goods and manufactures, evidenced in Table 3.5, extends to all industrial market economy countries.[22] As measured by the primary product ratio, Denmark experienced the largest decline in concentration, with stage 1 products falling from 63 to 32 per cent of total imports. Analysis of the Danish trade data shows that this shift was largely due to sizeable increases in imports of leather manufactures, clothing, and fish. Increases in Japan's leather manufactures and clothing imports, the latter rising from almost a zero base in 1964 to over $265 million a decade later, largely accounts for the 17 point decline in this country's concentration coefficient.

While the data presented in Tables 3.7 and 3.8 pertain to aggregate trade flows, they suggest the desirability of a further analysis aimed at identifying the LDC products primarily responsible for the overall deconcentration of exports. To examine this question, the statistics shown in Table 3.5 were used to compute 1964 and 1974 primary product ratios and concentration coefficients for each of the 21 individual processing chains. These indices were then differenced with the result serving as an indicator of the change in export concentration. While these figures suggest that deconcentration occurred in most product groups, leather, vegetable oils, clothing, sisal, and aluminium experienced *at least* a 30 percentage point decline in the primary product ratio. Aside from aluminium, these indices show that the nonferrous metals (copper, lead and zinc) were moving counter to the general trend with increased LDC trade concentration in the primary product.

IMPLICATIONS OF OPEC FOR DEVELOPING COUNTRIES

A major adverse change in the economic position of most developing countries took place with the quadrupling of petroleum prices at the end of 1973. Over the first three years of the 1970s the developing countries, as a group, achieved an average annual growth rate of 6 per cent for real gross product, which was the target envisaged in the International Development Strategy. The growth rate of 3·5 per cent per annum in real product per capita was also in conformity with the Strategy's goal. However, from 1974 on, the economic position of the developing countries deteriorated rapidly. In part, this was due to the reduction in effective demand for LDC exports associated with the induced recession in the Western economies, as well as the very unfavourable effects of the petroleum price increase on developing country balance of payments.[23] As a result, the growth rate in real product per head for non-petroleum exporting LDCs dropped to less than 1·5 per cent per year, a rate only two-fifths of the Strategy's target for the decade. However, the rate of increase in per capita real product for the poorest (under $200 per capita GNP) developing countries appears to have declined or been static.

While it is difficult, at this point, to quantitatively assess the long-term economic implications of OPEC policy on the foreign trade position of developing countries, it is still possible to identify some of the major adverse consequences. In general, these consequences work to limit developing country access to the industrial markets, or to reduce the LDCs' ability to finance projects which would expand, or diversify, their export base.

Several different factors contribute to a reduction in LDC access to the industrial markets. First, the recession in Western economies resulted in a sizeable drop in export demand for developing country products. One recent estimate by UNCTAD (March 1977a, p. 9) suggested that the decline in demand caused a deterioration in the LDC trade balance amounting to $12 billion a year, while a further $8 billion loss was attributed to increased oil prices. The impact of increased petroleum product prices seems to have had a serious adverse effect on LDC transportation costs, which limits foreign exchange earnings and the competitive position of these goods in export markets. A recent study by Finger and Yeats (1976) examined the behaviour of liner and tramp freight rate indices and suggested that the OPEC price rise increased developing country *ad valorem* frieght rates from an average of 9 to 13 per cent. An increase of this magnitude would be sufficient to offset the 4 percentage point reduction in tariffs negotiated during the Kennedy Round. If such an increase in transportation costs has occurred, the trade gains through reduced tariffs facing developing country products have been offset by increased penetration costs.

While the recession-induced reduction in demand, and higher freight costs, are serious *immediate* effects of the OPEC action, the longer term implications for developing country trade expansion may be even more foreboding. The results of the four-fold increase in oil prices demonstrated the susceptibility of industrial economies when strategic materials become concentrated in the hands of foreign suppliers. As such, the developed nations now seem clearly reluctant to liberalise trade barriers on other key products, such as foods, in which the developing countries might be expected to realise substantial trade gains. The fact that sluggish economic conditions persist in industrial economies also reduces prospects for a significant liberalisation of trade barriers from the Tokyo Round negotiations.

The OPEC action, combined with the growing protectionist tendencies in the industrialised countries, may have had a serious detrimental effect on the ability of the developing countries to attract international investment for new production ventures, or to generate such funds from normal export earnings. Much of the increased borrowing that has occurred on the part of the LDCs has gone largely for higher energy import costs, and will not result in an expanded output of exports or domestic consumption goods. Thus, it appears that available funds for new capital investment have declined in many developing countries.[24] The industrial country search for stable sources of supply may also have damaged the long-term trade prospects of some developing countries. As noted, recent shifts in Japan's imports of metal ores may have cost some LDCs as much as $800 million in foreign exchange earnings, while the inducement to develop synthetic substitutes or alternative supply sources for commodities which have the potential for cartelisation may further erode the competitive position of developing countries.

In short, the future trade prospects of developing countries may be heavily influenced by political considerations. It is clear that the foreign trade position of most non-petroleum exporting LDCs has been essentially static or deteriorated over the last few decades, while recent international developments hold further unfavourable prospects. As such, we now appear to be in a period which is of key importance for future international relations. Failure to grant freer access to industrial markets, through removal of artificial protectionist devices, will undoubtedly contribute to a worsening of the legitimate trade and development aspirations of developing countries. This would undoubtedly be accompanied by increased polarisation and discord between the developed and developing world. However, solutions are needed which also convey guarantees to the industrial countries. Specifically, liberalisation of international trade barriers must be accompanied by assurance of continuing supplies under terms which are considered equitable by both exporting and importing nations.

4 Tariff Protection in Industrial Markets

While developing country exports frequently face a variety of trade barriers in industrial markets, the type of restraint most often encountered is the import tariff. Stated simply, a tariff is little more than a tax or duty levied on a commodity when it crosses a national frontier. However, when discussing the effects of tariffs a distinction should be made between three different types: the *ad valorem*, specific, or compound tariff. An *ad valorem* duty is stated as a fixed percentage of the import's value, as when foreign shirts are taxed at a rate of 20 per cent of product price, while a specific tariff is quoted as a fixed sum of money per unit of the commodity, i.e., a $2 charge for each shirt. While most industrial countries rely on a mixture of both specific and *ad valorem* tariffs some, like Switzerland, exclusively apply the former.[1] Finally, some countries also use compound tariffs which apply joint specific and *ad valorem* duties (say 10 per cent of product value plus a fixed charge of $1) to imports.

In previous times, tariffs were employed jointly as a source of government revenue and to offer protection to domestic industry. However, industrial country governments have come to rely more on other revenue-generating measures so the primary function of industrial tariffs today is that of protection. Quite obviously, tariffs exert their protective effect by raising the landed costs of foreign goods which enter into competition with domestic produce. In general, it has been assumed that the higher are national tariffs, *ceteris paribus*, the more heavily protected are domestic producers from foreign competitors, although recent studies have demonstrated that the structure of a nation's tariffs may have important repercussions.

The analysis in this chapter examines the general level of tariff protection applied by industrial countries to developing country products, and attempts to evaluate the overall importance of these trade restrictive measures. After discussion of some of the technical problems involved in making inter-country comparisons of tariffs, the levels and types of import duties facing developing country shipments to the major industrial markets are examined. Attention is also directed toward the problem of tariff escalation, i.e., the tendency of national tariffs to increase with the degree of product fabrication, and the economic consequences for LDCs. A section is also devoted to the development of empirical techniques, such as the effective protection model, which will be used throughout the book for analysis of trade barriers.

PROBLEMS IN TARIFF COMPARISONS

While it would appear to be a relatively simple matter to compare levels of tariff protection in various industrial countries, such comparisons are in fact hampered by a number of practical problems. First, most developed nations employ a cost-insurance-freight (c.i.f.) basis for valuation of imports so *ad valorem* duties are levied on the foreign price of the commodity plus all transportation and insurance charges involved in shipment to the importing country. However, a relatively few countries such as the United States, Canada and Australia exclude freight costs from the valuation base and impose their tariffs on a free-on-board (f.o.b.) basis. This difference in valuation practices results in the tariffs of a country using f.o.b. valuations being overstated relative to those which employ a c.i.f. base. Since the forthcoming analysis will show that transportation and insurance costs for developing country exports may come to 50 per cent or more of product price, the degree to which United States tariffs are overstated relative to those of the European countries may be considerable.[2]

American selling price system
Certain industrial countries make departures from these valuation practices which cause further difficulties for comparative analyses of industrial tariffs. For example, the United States employs two practices which result in protection for domestic producers being higher than that indicated by national tariff schedules. The first procedure values certain products such as footwear, knit gloves and benzenoid chemicals at their equivalent American selling price (ASP) rather than the foreign invoice price. Since the equivalent (wholesale) American price may often be considerably higher, this means that the actual tariff rate is above that published in the official United States tariff schedules.[3] The second practice is to impose tariffs on whisky imports as if the alcohol content were 100 per cent proof even though the actual percentage may be well

below this level. While the ASP system has been the subject of considerable controversy among chemical exporting industrial countries, these valuation practices have also had an important detrimental effect on expanding developing country exports of shoes and knitted textiles.

Preferential trade arrangements
Aside from valuation problems, international comparisons of tariff levels are often complicated by the fact that more than one tariff rate may be applied to items included in a tariff line depending on the country of origin. While most trade between industrial countries is conducted under most-favoured-nation (MFN) tariffs, some trade with socialist countries takes place under duties above MFN rates. Also, in recent years most industrial countries have initiated Generalised System of Preference (GSP) schemes which permit selected imports from developing countries to be admitted under zero tariffs or rates below those applied to other trading partners' goods. The stated objective of these GSP schemes is to provide the LDCs with a competitive advantage which could act as a stimulus to the development of their export sectors. Similarly, the European Economic Community has a number of important preferential trade arrangements with former colonial associates which permits goods from these nations to enter duty free, or at tariffs below MFN rates. Customs unions, such as the European Economic Community or the European Free Trade Association have also been established to permit the duty free trade of goods between member states. Thus, in comparative analyses of tariff rates it must be determined what type of duty is being discussed, the normal MFN rate, reduced or zero tariffs due to a preference system, or trade within the confines of a customs union.[4]

Specific tariffs
Specific tariffs also pose special problems for any comparative analysis of national tariffs. When analysing the influence of these charges, the normal practice has been to compute *ad valorem* equivalents by taking the ratio of the tariff to the average unit value for the imported good. However, this procedure can obscure important differential effects if there are various grades of the imported good since *ad valorem* equivalents will vary inversely with product price. If LDC exports generally have lower unit values than similar items from industrial nations, due to quality differentials or the execution of monopoly power by importers, specific tariffs will result in higher *ad valorem* equivalents

and a more regressive effect on developing countries.

Switzerland's tariff schedules and import statistics were employed in a test of this differential incidence hypothesis. This industrial country was selected for analysis since the Swiss exclusively employ specific tariffs for levying import duties. Information on the incidence of these charges was generated via a two-stage procedure. At the first pass, *ad valorem* equivalents were computed for over 1200 tariff lines which recorded dutiable imports from both developed and developing countries.[5] Next, differences in the *ad valorem* equivalents for the two country groups were recorded so the incidence of the import duty on each tariff line item could be assessed. Table 4.1 shows the differences in *ad valorem* equivalents for industrial and developing country products to which a common specific import tariff was applied.

Examination of the data in Table 4.1 reveals the regressive effect of the specific tariffs on imports from developing countries. While 25 per cent of the tariffs have an approximately equal *ad valorem* rate on developed and developing countries, over 50 per cent of these charges fall more heavily on the LDCs. Indeed, almost 10 per cent (119) of these fixed import charges resulted in *ad valorem* equivalents for the LDCs which were at least 10 percentage points higher than on competing shipments from industrial countries, while the difference in favour of the industrial countries was at least 5 percentage points in about 22 per cent of the tariff lines sampled. Conversion to an *ad valorem* duty based on the total tariff average for these items would lower the actual tariff liability of LDCs, resulting in an increase in their exports, while the liability of the developed nations would increase.[6]

For several reasons it may be argued that the distribution of tariff rates shown in Table 4.1 understates the true incidence of specific tariffs on LDC exports. First, some of the Swiss duties appear to be set at levels which prohibit imports from developing countries. Thus, comparisons of the *ad valorem* incidence of these fixed import charges was not possible for some tariff lines in which the LDCs had an export capability. In addition, the regressive impact of the Swiss duties may have restricted exports of certain developing country products that could have been imported at even lower values (prices) than those recorded for the LDC group. In other words, the trade restrictive effect of the specific tariffs probably resulted in the average developing country unit value being upward biased with the result that estimates of the duties, *ad valorem* incidence are biased downward. Thus, those LDC products which were actually imported probably represent the upper value-quality range of *potential* developing country products. Finally,

TABLE 4.1 Analysis of the Differential Incidence of Switzerland's Specific Tariffs on Imports from Developed and Developing Nations; Computations Based on Tariff Line Information

Differential of the ad valorem incidence	Ad valorem incidence falling heaviest on[1]			
	Developed countries		Developing countries	
	No. of tariff line items	Percentage of total	No. of tariff line items	Percentage of total
10·5 percentage points or more	26	2·1	119	9·6
8·5 to 10·5 percentage points	10	0·8	41	3·3
6·5 to 8·5 percentage points	10	0·8	49	3·9
4·5 to 6·5 percentage points	27	2·2	63	5·1
2·5 to 4·5 percentage points	65	5·2	118	9·5
0·5 to 2·5 percentage points	178	14·3	235	18·9
Total	316	25·4	625	50·3

[1] Of the 1244 tariff lines with imports from both developed and developing countries, 303, or 24·3 per cent, had an equal *ad valorem* incidence on both country groups.

the data in Table 4.1 understate the true importance of specific tariffs on LDC products because they do not show separately the rates on those semi-finished and processed goods which are of direct interest to developing countries in their attempts to expand exports of domestic processing industries. Analysis of tariff line data suggests that the *ad valorem* incidence of specific tariffs falls more heavily on these manufactured products than on crude or unprocessed goods.[7]

Since specific duties have been demonstrated to have an adverse differential impact on developing country products, the question arises as to how frequently are these tariffs employed, and on what types of products do they generally fall. For answers, special GATT-UNCTAD tariff tapes for the major industrial countries were employed. Since these computerised files contain binding codes which indicate the type(s) of duty levied on each tariff line item, it was possible to tabulate the number of products and the value of imports covered by specific tariffs. For purposes of this analysis, variable levies were included in the Swedish and EEC tabulations as specific tariffs. These charges are expressed in fixed-rate-per-unit terms and have the same differential effect as specific duties. Their only real difference is that they are changed more frequently, often several times a year. Table 4.2 shows the per cent of products and import values covered by specific tariffs in the European Economic Community, Japan, Norway and the United States. Also given are country coverage totals using weights based on OECD imports, and on imports from developing nations.

In terms of all items, coverage by the specific duties ranges from about 3 per cent of the tariff line products in Japan to approximately 35 per cent in the United States. In general, the percentages for value of imports entered under specific duties are usually lower, although application of these tariffs on fuels reverses the normal picture for Japan.

While there is considerable variation from country to country, the highest overall incidence of these specific duties appears to fall on the foods, beverages, and animal-vegetable oil groups. Japan and the United States rely heavily on specific duties for fuel imports, but in most cases these charges are concentrated on crude and semifinished goods, as well as some manufactured products, which form the bulk of developing country exports. The overall averages show this clearly as the percentage of developing country products imported under specific tariffs is higher than that for the developed countries in all cases but the European Economic Community. Thus, specific tariffs constitute a serious problem for developing countries since they cover a sizeable

TABLE 4.2 Percentage of Tariff Line Items and Value of Imports Covered by Specific Tariffs in Major Standard International Trade Classification Product Groups: Selected Industrial Countries

SITC	Description	EEC		Japan		Norway		Sweden		USA	
		Items	Value	Items	Value	Items	Value	Items	Value	Items	Value
0	Food and live animals	38·8	46·8	4·6	14·1	56·9	46·0	60·3	65·0	45·0	42·6
1	Beverages and tobacco	74·6	81·4	43·8	16·9	41·4	32·6	82·7	70·8	93·7	99·9
2	Crude materials, inedible	2·3	1·7	5·6	9·7	14·7	3·5	7·5	7·1	33·7	23·5
3	Mineral fuels	3·6	9·4	18·2	71·0	17·1	4·3	8·1	0·5	39·7	89·1
4	Animal and vegetable oils	16·0	13·4	15·4	4·8	56·2	51·4	55·2	65·0	59·8	74·2
5	Chemicals	1·9	2·4	1·1	0·8	11·9	4·6	4·0	1·7	38·5	37·9
6	Manufactured goods	2·7	5·5	1·6	8·2	34·4	30·5	6·5	5·9	32·3	30·2
7	Machinery and transport equipment	0·6	0·1	0·2	0·1	9·1	3·8	1·4	1·1	7·3	1·3
8	Miscellaneous manufactures	4·4	2·0	5·8	2·7	28·3	28·9	4·2	3·3	30·9	21·7
	Imports from:										
	Developing countries	—	7·5	—	42·7	—	a	—	24·4	—	42·6
	Developed countries	—	10·8	—	6·7	—	a	—	8·1	—	22·9
	All sources	10·2	10·1	3·4	21·1	27·9	28·9	13·9	9·7	34·7	28·3

a Due to special format changes on the Norwegian tariff tape this information could not be tabulated.

portion of LDC exports, and have been shown to have a differential regressive incidence on these products.[8]

Tariff averaging

A further problem connected with international comparisons of nominal tariffs is that different importing countries employ various classification schemes for imported goods. For example the European Economic Community distinguishes between about 3300 tariff line items, while some of the Scandinavian countries have about 6000 classifications. If international comparisons are to be made, some procedure must be used to aggregate data to a common level in all countries. Ideally, this aggregation system should be based on weights of hypothetical imports which would occur under free-trade. These data being unobtainable, a variety of averaging procedures, admittedly biased, are employed as approximations to this true average. These techniques include:

(a) a simple average of tariff rates over the relevant group of products,
(b) an average of tariff rates weighted by the values of imports for each product in the group,
(c) an average of tariff rates weighted by domestic production values for each product,
(d) an average of tariff rates weighted by the values of domestic demand for each product,
(e) the average of tariff rates weighted by world trade values for each product in the group.

Various combinations of (a), (b) and (e) have been derived for use in the recent Kennedy Round negotiations, while averages (c) and (d) have proven more difficult to calculate due to a lack of comparable data.[9]

As a practical matter, most of the advantages and disadvantages of the tariff averaging formula are apparent. Averages based on a country's own trade weights (b) are known to be downward biased since import values will be inversely related to tariff levels. If a commodity's tariff is set at a prohibitive level, the value weight would be zero and this duty would fail to enter into the calculation of an overall tariff average. Other products facing high tariffs would be imported below free trade levels, so averages based on a country's own trade weights understate the importance of items facing high trade barriers.

The simple average procedure (a) has the advantage of being easy to compute, but it rests on the assumption that all items in the group are of equal importance. When one considers the variety of (say) four-digit BTN products entering international trade, from passenger cars to hair combs, the assumption of equal importance is clearly unacceptable. While weights based on domestic production or consumption patterns have considerable conceptual appeal, these data, when available, are generally compiled on a different classification scheme from that of foreign trade statistics, and establishment of a correspondence between the two systems frequently is difficult. As a compromise, world trade-weighted averages, or those derived from a major country group such as the OECD nations, are generally considered superior to either averages (a) or (e) since the aggregate weighting procedure can moderate the influence of high protection rates in an individual country's tariff structure. However, these figures must be regarded with caution since economists have noted similarities between the tariff structures of industrial nations. In general, low or zero duties are applied to raw materials and semi-processed goods while *ad valorem* rates rise with the degree of fabrication. Thus, a world or composite country trade-weighted average will be downward biased to the extent that common high tariffs on manufactures retard imports of these items relative to crude materials or semi-processed goods.

While the present analysis does not deal in depth with technical problems of tariff averaging, it is meant to caution the reader that summary statistics on protection levels in individual countries may be sensitive to the aggregation techniques employed in the derivation of such data. For example, in an analysis involving tariff averages for over 100 categories of goods imported by ten industrial countries, Tumlir and Till (1971) noted that the differences in overall averages computed with four different weighting schemes were large enough to cause extreme changes in the rankings of countries by protection levels when one type of weighted average was substituted for another. While sections of the forthcoming analysis will conduct comparative analyses of import duties at low levels of aggregation, where problems connected with weighting techniques may not be so serious, the qualification concerning potential sensitivity of averages to different weighting systems should be kept in mind when evaluating aggregate statistics on tariff levels.

Developing country differences
Another qualification which must be made concerns the tendency to discuss trade and tariff barriers facing developing countries as a group. In actual practice, the developing countries are a very heterogeneous mixture involving different natural resource and factor endowments, different levels of development, different trade structures, etc. As such,

the artificial trade barriers erected by industrial countries to protect domestic producers from foreign competition are not of equal importance to all developing nations. In general, trade restraints most heavily protect domestic manufacturing, so industrial country tariffs are more of a concern to Hong Kong, Brazil or Korea, where exports are composed of a larger percentage of manufactures, than they would be to a country which was primarily a supplier of basic raw materials. Appendix Tables 1 to 3 present summary information on the protection profiles facing individual developing countries in the major industrial markets.

SOURCES OF TARIFF STATISTICS

For information concerning tariffs facing developing country exports, extensive use was made of documents published by the United Nations Conference on Trade and Development and the General Agreement on Tariffs and Trade, as well as other national and international agencies. The UNCTAD (1968) study *The Kennedy Round Estimated Effect on Tariff Barriers* is a basic source of information on pre- and post-Kennedy Round tariffs, and the general structure of tariff protection in industrial markets. This document also includes useful information concerning tariffs facing a sample of about 450 tariff line items which are of special export interest to developing countries. A section of this document also estimates effective protection facing LDC exports to the European Community, United States, Japan, United Kingdom and Sweden.

When required data could not be obtained from this source, documents published by other departments or agencies were used. A GATT study, *Basic Documentation for Tariff Study*, provides extensive information on tariffs compiled by Brussels Tariff Nomenclature headings. Since this document also calculates tariff averages for composite product groups using a variety of weighting systems, it provides useful information for analysing the sensitivity of summary tariff statistics to alternative aggregation procedures. The Belgian International Customs Tariff Bureau's publication *International Customs Journal* translates national tariff schedules into five major languages. Tariff information for foreign countries is also given in various issues of *Overseas Business Reports*, a publication of the US Department of Commerce. The document *Atlantic Tariffs and Trade* published by the United Kingdom Political and Economic Planning

Commission (1962) gives tariff statistics for the late 1950s and early 1960s period. Finally, the United States International Trade Commission (1975) study *Protection in Major Trading Countries* provides tariff statistics for the EEC, Japan, and the United States, and is also a comprehensive source of effective protection estimates for these countries.

With the exception of the UNCTAD study, a deficiency with much of the published statistical material is that tariff information is often compiled in a manner best suited for analysis of barriers facing developed country trade. Since special computerised GATT-UNCTAD trade and tariff tapes had translated national tariff schedules and related import statistics into machine-readable form, these internal data sources were used for several empirical tariff-trade analyses which required special information concerning LDCs such as the derivation of tariff averages using preferential tariff trade weights. These trade-tariff tapes were also used for derivation of the tariff profiles facing individual developing countries which are shown in the Appendix to this study.

TARIFF PROFILES OF INDUSTRIAL COUNTRIES

For an overview of current tariff levels in industrial countries, Figure 4.1 shows combined average *ad valorem* tariff rates for broad product groups in the United States, European Economic Community and Japan. The vertical axis indicates the OECD trade-weighted import duty, while the horizontal axis designates various one-digit SITC or lower-level product groups. The width of the bar for each group average is drawn proportional to its value weight in total OECD imports. For example, the bar for manufactures is roughly 20 times that for animal and vegetable oils (SITC 4) due to far greater trade in the former. The chart also provides a basis for assessing the depth of Kennedy Round tariff cuts for each group since average pre-Kennedy rates are also indicated.

While the Kennedy Round tariff agreements resulted in an overall reduction of 36 per cent in industrial country tariffs, the chart shows that these reductions were not evenly distributed across product groups. Chemicals, machinery, transport equipment and instruments, items of primary importance to industrial countries, experienced the deepest tariff reductions, while products in which LDCs are generally held to have a comparative advantage, i.e., clothing, textiles, animal and vegetable oils, foodstuffs, etc., experienced lower cuts. The differential

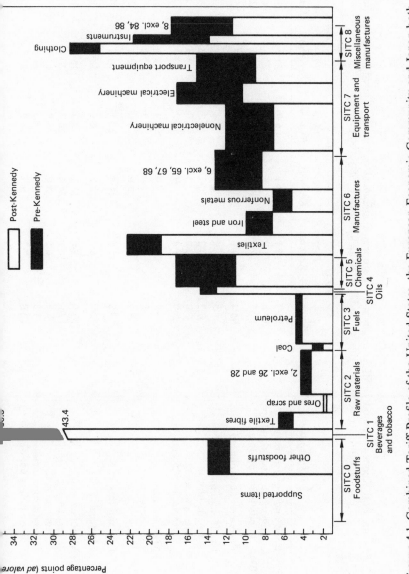

FIGURE 4.1 Combined Tariff Profile of the United States, the European Economic Community and Japan both before and after the Kennedy Round

TABLE 4.3 Pre- and Post-Kennedy Round Tariff Averages in the European Economic Community, United States and Japan for Products of Export Interest to Developing Countries[1] (percentages)

SITC	Description	EEC		USA[2]		Japan	
		Pre-Kennedy	Post-Kennedy	Pre-Kennedy	Post-Kennedy	Pre-Kennedy	Post-Kennedy
0	Food and Foodstuffs	18·7	15·1	8·1	6·9	25·9	22·0
07	Coffee, tea, cocoa and spices	19·8	11·9	1·8	1·6	22·5	15·0
0 excl. 07	Foodstuffs excluding 07	17·9	17·2	12·3	10·4	28·1	26·6
1	Beverages and tobacco	66·4	49·9	32·4	30·8	223·8	222·1
2	Crude materials	1·7	0·8	4·7	3·6	2·1	1·6
26	Textile fibres	0·2	0·2	10·7	8·2	0·0	0·0
28	Ores and scrap	0·0	0·0	2·3	1·6	0·0	0·0
Other 2	2, excluding 26 and 28	3·0	1·4	2·9	2·2	4·0	3·1
3	Mineral fuels	3·8	1·9	3·9	3·9	13·2	13·0
33	Petroleum	3·8	1·9	3·9	3·9	13·1	12·9
Other 3	Gas	3·5	1·5	0·0	0·0	20·0	20·0
4	Oils and fats	11·8	11·8	21·4	17·1	16·6	14·7
5	Chemicals	12·0	6·6	12·0	6·1	18·4	12·4
6	Manufactures	10·6	8·0	12·1	8·3	15·6	10·1
65	Textiles	17·3	14·9	24·4	18·7	20·7	12·7
67	Iron and steel	8·7	6·5	5·0	3·9	13·1	7·8
68	Nonferrous metals	3·3	2·7	7·2	4·1	11·5	8·7
Other 6	6, excluding 65, 67 and 68	12·0	7·7	9·9	6·0	15·7	10·1

7	Machinery	12·9	7·5	10·3	6·1	16·8	8·4
71	Nonelectrical machinery	13·0	7·1	9·9	4·8	16·7	8·3
72	Electrical machinery	14·5	9·1	12·2	8·5	17·5	8·6
73	Transportation equipment	8·0	4·0	6·2	3·1	15·0	7·5
8	Misc. manufactures	18·1	11·7	26·0	20·8	22·3	14·6
84	Clothing	20·8	15·2	32·1	30·0	25·6	17·8
Other 8	8, excluding 84	16·2	9·0	21·5	14·0	19·9	12·2
5 to 8	Industrial manufactures	12·4	8·5	14·4	10·1	17·2	10·9
	Total	10·9	7·7	10·2	7·9	20·5	17·1

[1] Based on a sample of approximately 300 individual tariff line items. Group averages are based on weights derived from total OECD country imports from developing nations.

[2] United States tariff averages have been re-stated on a cost-insurance-freight valuation base.

Source: Data have been adapted from UNCTAD, *The Kennedy Round Estimated Effects on Tariff Barriers* (New York, 1968).

trade benefits from the Kennedy Round were noted by the UNCTAD Secretariat which estimated that the average tariff reduction for products of interest to developing countries was only about 20 per cent as opposed to a reduction of 35 to 40 per cent for industrial nations. Even if one excludes primary products and looks only at semifinished goods and manufactures the disparity is still substantial: an average Kennedy Round cut of 28 per cent for developing countries as against 38 per cent for developed.[10]

Figure 4.1 also shows that current tariffs of industrial countries are unevenly distributed across product groups. Beverages and tobacco are characterised by import duties averaging more than 40 per cent of product value; which probably is a factor accounting for the group's relatively low trade weight. Of the items of special interest to LDCs, tariffs on clothing average over 20 per cent, while those on textiles and foodstuffs are set at about 17 and 11 per cent. While these levels appear imposing, subsequent chapters will show that these products are also covered by extensive nontariff restraints such as quotas, prohibitions, export restraints, variable levies, etc., which may have even more serious trade retardation effects. In contrast, crude materials and fuels, important *inputs* for manufacturing processes in industrial countries, face average tariffs of only 3 to 4 per cent and relatively few nontariff barriers. Thus, Figure 4.1 indicates why it has been argued that the tariff *structures* of industrial countries retard LDC exports of manufactured goods. While crude and raw materials typically face zero or low import duties, tariffs and other trade barriers applied to processed goods increase with the degree of fabrication. The net effect of such a system is to bias LDC exports in the direction of primary materials.

For a closer examination of trade barriers facing developing countries, UNCTAD frequently utilises a special sample of approximately 450 narrowly defined products. The items from this sample were selected from lists submitted by LDCs to the GATT concerning products in which developing countries had a special interest.[11] The advantage of the sampling approach is that some form of selection is required to deal with the vast number of items in the tariff schedules when an in-depth analysis is intended. This procedure also allows one to focus on trade barriers facing products of special importance to developing countries and exclude extraneous information on items in which they have little interest. A sample also gives more control over the data so it is easier to ensure that results are not biased by aggregation (averaging) problems, or other large-scale data handling difficulties.

Table 4.3 provides information concerning the pre- and post-

Kennedy Round tariff profiles facing these products in the European Economic Community, United States and Japan. Comparison of these data with the information shown in Figure 4.1 generally supports the proposition that existing tariffs on products of export interest to developing countries are higher than duties on industrial goods, and that the LDC items benefited less from the Kennedy Round reductions. For example, the average reduction on these developing country products in the EEC, USA, and Japan was 29, 23, and 17 per cent respectively, well below the average 36 per cent reduction achieved in the negotiations. Also, some of the industrial country tariff averages for the LDC products are considerably higher than the OECD trade-weighted figures shown in Figure 4.1. For example, LDC beverages and tobacco products (SITC 1) face virtually prohibitive Japanese tariffs of over 220 per cent, while the United States applies average tariffs of 30 per cent to clothing, and duties of about 20 per cent on textiles and fats and oils. Post-Kennedy tariffs of 15 and 22 per cent for foodstuffs exported by developing countries to the EEC and Japan are well above the OECD weighted average indicated in Figure 4.1, while the EEC tariff of 15 per cent on clothing and textiles must have an important retardation effect on LDC exports.[12]

Tariff structure

While the industrial country tariffs certainly influence the value of some LDC exports, available evidence indicates the structure of these charges is also important. For example, the tendency of tariffs to escalate or increase with the level of processing may seriously hamper developing country efforts to shift from traditional exports into manufactures. According to those who expound such views, application of zero or low tariffs to raw materials, with the level of duty increasing as the items goes through successively higher stages of processing, is a reason why the trade of many LDCs is heavily concentrated in raw materials and semi-manufactures.

Table 4.4 provides some empirical support for this suggestion. The leftmost columns of the table reproduce the processing stage schema used in Chapter 3, while the figures in the body indicate the *ad valorem* tariffs applied to each item in the USA, EEC, Sweden and Japan. To assist in making comparisons, the table shows the magnitude of the tariff change (in points) as one moves from a lower to a higher processing stage. Summary information by stage of processing is also given to assist in evaluating the general relation between processing activity and tariffs.

TABLE 4.4 Analysis of the Structure of Post-Kennedy Round Tariffs in Industrial Countries on Primary and Processed Goods Exported by Developing Countries

Commodity	United States		EEC		Sweden		Japan		Average	
	Nominal tariff	Net change	Nominal tariff	Net change	Nominal tariff	Net change	Nominal tariff	Net change	Nominal tariff	Net change
Meat products										
1. Fresh and frozen meat	4·6	—	17·8	—	0·0	—	6·2	—	7·2	—
2. Meat preparations	5·9	1·3	19·5	1·7	0·0	0·0	17·9	11·7	10·6	3·6
Fish and seafood										
1. Fresh and frozen fish	1·3	—	14·9	—	0·0	—	5·3	—	5·4	—
2. Fish preparations	6·0	4·7	21·5	6·6	3·7	3·7	13·6	8·3	11·2	5·8
Fruit										
1. Fresh fruit or nuts	5·6	—	13·9	—	2·5	—	14·0	—	9·0	—
2. Preserved fruit	14·8	9·2	20·5	6·6	10·3	7·8	18·5	4·5	16·0	5·0
Vegetables										
1. Fresh vegetables	8·9	—	9·9	—	7·8	—	8·1	—	8·7	—
2. Preserved vegetables	8·0	-0·9	14·8	4·9	6·8	-1·0	20·0	11·9	12·4	3·7
Cocoa										
1. Cocoa beans	0·0	—	3·2	—	3·6	—	3·0	—	2·5	—
2. Cocoa powder	1·6	1·6	18·2	15·0	3·9	0·3	12·2	9·2	9·0	6·5
3. Chocolate	4·8	3·2	18·0	-0·2	11·3	7·4	35·0	22·8	17·3	8·3
Leather										
1. Hides and skins	1·1	—	0·0	—	0·0	—	0·0	—	0·3	—
2. Leather	4·7	3·6	4·8	4·8	1·7	11·6	1·7	11·6	5·7	5·4
3. Leather goods[1]	11·3	6·6	9·6	4·8	11·2	9·5	17·4	5·8	12·4	6·7
Groundnut oil										
1. Groundnuts	25·7	—	0·0	—	0·0	—	20·0	—	11·4	—
2. Groundnut oil[2]	27·1	1·4	11·2	11·2	0·0	0·0	23·6	3·6	15·5	4·1

Coconut oil										
1. Copra	0·0	—	0·0	—	0·0	—	0·0	—	0·0	—
2. Coconut oil²	17·7	17·7	12·5	12·5	0·0	0·0	10·0	10·0	10·1	10·1
Palm kernel oil										
1. Palm kernels	0·0	—	0·0	—	0·0	—	0·0	—	0·0	—
2. Palm kernel oil²	2·8	2·8	11·5	11·5	0·0	0·0	7·3	7·3	5·4	5·4
Rubber and products										
1. Natural rubber	0·0	—	0·0	—	0·0	—	0·0	—	0·0	—
2. Rubber products	4·6	4·6	7·9	7·9	6·6	6·6	6·4	6·4	6·4	6·4
Wood and products										
1. Wood in the rough	0·0	—	1·0	—	0·0	—	0·0	—	0·3	—
2. Plywood	8·5	8·5	11·3	10·3	3·5	3·5	14·0	14·0	9·3	9·0
3. Wood manufactures	6·7	-1·8	8·7	-2·6	6·9	3·4	11·5	-2·5	8·5	-0·8
Paper and products										
1. Pulpwood	0·0	—	0·0	—	0·0	—	0·0	—	0·0	—
2. Wood pulp	0·0	0·0	3·3	3·3	0·0	0·0	5·0	5·0	2·1	2·1
3. Paper and articles	2·5	2·5	6·1	2·8	1·0	1·0	7·7	2·7	4·3	2·2
Wool and products										
1. Raw wool	9·7	—	0·0	—	0·0	—	0·0	—	2·4	—
2. Wool yarn	20·7	11·0	5·7	5·7	2·9	2·9	5·0	5·0	8·6	6·2
3. Wool fabrics	20·7	0·0	16·0	10·3	11·1	8·2	10·0	5·0	14·5	5·9
Cotton and products										
1. Raw cotton	6·2	—	0·0	—	0·0	—	0·0	—	1·6	—
2. Cotton yarn	10·5	4·3	10·0	10·0	8·7	8·7	2·8	2·8	8·0	6·4
3. Cotton fabrics	13·8	3·3	12·0	2·0	10·5	1·8	7·9	5·1	11·1	3·1
4. Clothing³	18·3	4·5	14·7	2·7	12·2	1·7	15·0	7·1	15·1	4·0

TABLE 4.4 continued

Commodity	United States		EEC		Sweden		Japan		Average	
	Nominal tariff	Net change	Nominal tariff	Net change	Nominal tariff	Net change	Nominal tariff	Net change	Nominal tariff	Net change
Jute and products										
1. Raw jute	0·0	—	0·0	—	0·0	—	0·0	—	0·0	—
2. Jute fabrics	0·0	0·0	19·6	19·6	19·6	7·9	20·0	20·0	11·9	11·9
3. Sacks and bags	3·6	3·6	15·5	-4·1	8·8	0·9	12·5	-7·5	10·1	-1·8
Sisal and products										
1. Raw sisal	0·0	—	0·0	—	0·0	—	0·0	—	0·0	—
2. Cordage	3·6	3·6	10·3	10·3	10·4	10·4	9·6	9·6	8·5	8·5
Iron and products										
1. Iron ore	0·0	—	0·0	—	0·0	—	0·0	—	0·0	—
2. Pig iron	0·7	0·7	4·0	4·0	0·0	0·0	1·9	1·9	1·7	1·7
3. Steel ingots	6·3	5·6	4·0	0·0	3·8	3·8	6·4	4·5	5·1	3·4
4. Mill products	3·5	-2·8	5·5	1·5	5·1	1·3	8·9	2·5	5·8	0·7
5. Special steel items	4·0	0·5	7·5	2·0	5·0	-0·1	7·8	-1·1	6·1	0·3
Copper and products										
1. Copper ores	0·1	—	0·0	—	0·0	—	0·0	—	0·0	—
2. Unwrought copper	2·3	2·2	0·0	0·0	0·0	0·0	7·0	7·0	2·3	2·3
3. Copper wrought	4·2	1·9	8·0	8·0	2·0	2·0	17·8	10·8	8·0	5·7
Aluminium										
1. Bauxite	0·0	—	0·0	—	0·0	—	0·0	—	0·0	—
2. Alumina	0·0	0·0	5·6	5·6	0·0	0·0	0·0	0·0	1·4	1·4
3. Unwrought aluminium	4·0	4·0	5·8	0·2	0·0	0·0	10·4	10·4	5·1	3·7
4. Wrought aluminium	5·9	1·9	12·8	7·0	2·0	2·0	13·6	3·2	8·6	3·5
Lead and products										
1. Lead ores	6·0	—	0·0	—	0·0	—	0·0	—	1·5	—

2. Unwrought lead	8·3	2·3	7·2	7·2	0·0	0·0	6·5	6·5	5·5	4·0
3. Wrought lead	10·3	2·0	6·6	−0·6	0·0	0·0	14·9	8·4	8·0	2·5
Zinc and products										
1. Zinc ores	12·0	—	0·0	—	0·0	—	0·0	—	3·0	—
2. Unwrought zinc	6·6	−5·4	5·8	5·8	0·0	0·0	6·5	6·5	4·7	1·7
All items										
Stage 1	3·9	—	2·9	—	0·7	—	2·7	—	2·6	—
Stage 2	7·3	3·4	10·7	7·8	3·2	2·5	10·4	7·7	7·9	5·3
Stage 3	7·6	0·3	9·9	−0·8	5·6	2·4	13·9	3·5	9·3	1·4
Stage 4	7·9	0·3	10·1	0·2	6·1	0·5	11·3	−2·6	8·9	−0·4

[1] Leather products including shoes.
[2] Includes crude and refined oils.
[3] Includes cotton blends and other types of clothing.

Source: Data adapted from Alexander J. Yeats, 'Effective Tariff Protection in the United States, The European Economic Community, and Japan', *Quarterly Review of Economics and Business* (Summer 1974), p. 45 and UNCTAD, *The Kennedy Round Estimated Effects on Tariff Barriers* (New York: United Nations, 1968), pp. 209–13.

On an overall basis, an average *ad valorem* tariff of 2·6 per cent is applied to stage 1 products while this rate rises to about 9 per cent for processing stage 3 or 4 items. The same pattern of escalation is observed for each of the individual country averages with the stage 3 Japanese products reaching a level of almost 14 per cent, some 11 percentage points above that for the primary stage. While some levelling or declines are evident in the stage 4 items, these are probably of little practical consequence for most developing countries. Specifically, the hypothesis has been advanced that at higher levels of fabrication developing countries substitute technological protection for tariffs. Since many developing countries do not have the required technology to produce sophisticated goods, industrial nations need not continually escalate tariffs to protect domestic producers.

On an individual product basis, the degree of tariff escalation seems highest for cocoa and chocolate, leather, wool, cotton and jute. In each of these processing chains, the raw material is imported at zero or low tariffs while the average duty for the final stage has climbed to 10 percentage points or more. However, the picture in the USA is altered since domestic wool and cotton producers are covered by tariffs which range from 6 to 9 per cent. However, since they start from a higher base, tariffs on the final stage items (wool fabrics or clothing) have risen to 18 or 20 per cent. While most of the declines which occur are relatively minor, or are in areas where the importing industrial country has little or no domestic processing, the evidence from Table 4.4 is that the tariffs of industrial nations escalate with the result that processed goods from developing countries typically face considerably higher tariffs than do primary product exports.

Finally, the behaviour of transportation costs over these processing chains has the potential to be of importance. Since the processing function typically raises product value, while lowering bulk or stowage factors, there is some basis for believing that shipping costs should decline as one moves to higher stages of fabrication. If so, transport charges have the potential to offset escalated tariffs. However, analysis of data on international shipping costs suggests that these charges may also increase with fabrication, or have a neutral effect on many processing chains. While this relation will be examined in Chapter 7, the basic problem is that liner conferences frequently follow the practice of 'charging what the traffic will bear' or subsidising primary good exports through higher rates on manufactures. As such, the revenue objectives of the liner conferences run counter to the interests of developing countries in shifting from traditional to processed goods exports.

THE EFFECTIVE TARIFF CONCEPT

While the preceding analysis shows that tariffs facing many LDC manufactured exports are set at imposing levels, there is an additional empirical approach which is often useful for analysing the structure of trade restraints. Specifically, this is the effective protection concept which argues that the protection of value added in a production process is of prime importance to domestic producers. The higher is the effective protection afforded by the structure of a nation's tariffs and other trade restraints, the more foreign producers must lower returns to labour and capital if they are to sell in the protected market.

The effective rate of protection of industry j (E_j) is normally defined as the percentage difference between the industry's value added per dollar of output under tariff protection (V'_j), and its value added per dollar of output in the absence of protection (V_j),

$$E_j = (V'_j - V_j)/V_j \qquad (4\text{--}1)$$

Underlying this definition are the basic assumptions of the effective protection model: (1) all production functions are of a fixed coefficient form with zero elasticity of substitution between intermediate inputs and primary factors (labour and capital), (2) primary factors are internationally immobile, and (3) import supply is perfectly elastic whereas the demand for exports is infinite.[13]

The model can be developed as follows. If a_{ij} is defined as the value of the input of factor i per dollar value of output j, in the absence of all tariffs, then value added can be expressed in terms of the m inputs.

$$V_j = 1 - \sum_{i=1}^{m} a_{ij}. \qquad (4\text{--}2)$$

If imports which are perfect substitutes for the final product j are now subject to a tariff (t_j), the price of j can rise by the amount of the duty in the domestic market. Since material inputs in the production of j are assumed to be in perfectly elastic supply, none of the price increases will be observed in the values for the a_{ij}, but will be allocated to an increase in value added,[14]

$$V'_j = 1 + t_j - \sum_{i=1}^{m} a_{ij}. \qquad (4\text{--}3)$$

This formulation can easily be expanded to account for duties on the material inputs,

$$V'_j = 1 + t_j - \sum_{i=1}^{m} a_{ij}(1 + t_i), \qquad (4\text{-}4)$$

which can also be expressed as,

$$V'_j = V_j + t_j - \sum_{i=1}^{m} a_{ij}t_i. \qquad (4\text{-}5)$$

Finally, through substitution in equation 4–1 it is possible to express the effective rate of protection in terms of the input coefficients and duties on the intermediate and final products,[15]

$$E_j = \left(t_j - \sum_{i=1}^{m} a_{ij}t_i \right) \Big/ \left(1 - \sum_{i=1}^{m} a_{ij} \right). \qquad (4\text{-}6)$$

One modification is required before the foregoing can be employed in the calculation of effective rates of production. Equation 4–6 calls for the use of free trade input coefficients (a_{ij}), but what is typically observed are these coefficients distorted by tariffs on the intermediate inputs and final product. However, by deflating these observed shares (a_{ij}) by tariffs on inputs and the final product,

$$a_{ij} = a'_{ij}[(1 + t_j)/(1 + t_i)], \qquad (4\text{-}7)$$

it is possible to approximate these free trade input coefficients.[16]

Before proceeding, the implications of the effective rate concept for LDC producers and the differences between effective rates and nominal protection should be carefully noted. While the effective rate of protection (ERP) shows the percentage increase in value added domestic firms experience as a result of the structure of protective tariffs, it also indicates the extent to which value added of foreign producers must be reduced if they are to sell in the protected market.[17] Since capital is, to some extent, internationally mobile, the depressed value added in the foreign export sector will result in lower returns to productive factors. While some of the required reduction in value added will be accomplished by forcing foreign wages down, the protection in industrial nations will also result in reduced returns to capital invested in the LDCs. As a result of the reduced returns, international capital flows to developing countries will be lower than that which would occur in the absence of protection. This may be very important since capital shortfalls in developing countries are often a key factor constraining development planning. It should be noted that effective protection in industrial countries also influences the domestic allocation of resources within the developing countries. Since it artificially depresses returns in the export sector, a lower proportion of domestic capital and labour will be allocated to export-oriented industries with consequent reductions in potential production volumes. The full extent of this reduction in factor returns, and in the output of the export sector, is a function of the height of effective protection in the industrial markets.

Thus, the insight provided by the theory of effective protection concerns the restrictive effect some seemingly low tariffs in industrialised countries have on the development of industries in LDCs. For example, many of the developing countries are located in tropical climates, and provide the industrial nations with such products as cocoa beans, coffee, copra, and various tropical fruits. An apparently logical step in the development process would be the establishment of factories in the LDCs for the processing of these raw materials, such as making oil from copra, roasting coffee, or making cocoa butter and paste.

Analyses of industrial country protection have noted that the barrier preventing the full development of these industries in the LDCs are the apparently low tariffs levied on the importation of processed oil, roasted and powdered coffee, and cocoa products. With value added for these production processes being quite low, seemingly low nominal tariffs represent very high effective protection of the processing function. Consider, for example, a tariff of only 5 per cent on the importation of cocoa paste or butter. If value added for these products is 5 per cent, the process is protected by an effective rate of 100 per cent. This means that producers in the developing country can spend less than half the amount on labour and capital as producers in the developed country if they are to be competitive. While wage rates in the LDCs are low, the lower efficiency of labour may absorb this differential. Although LDC producers may still be competitive even with the lower labour productivity, they can be rendered non-competitive by the high effective rates of protection in the developed countries.

A diagrammatic analysis
While the effective rate of protection indicates the extent to which value added increases, or decreases, as a result of the joint influence of tariffs on inputs and the final product, the formulation given in equation 4–6 is deceptively simple since it can conceal complex interrelations between various parameters of the model. The nature of these interrelations can be examined with the aid of Figure 4.2. Here the ratio of effective to

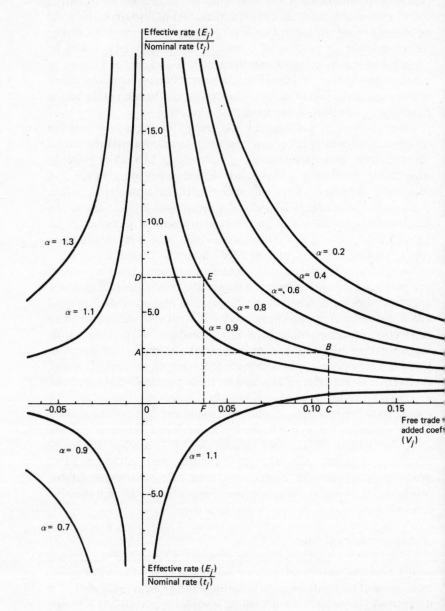

FIGURE 4.2 Analysis of the Relation between the Effective Rate of Protection, the Value Added Coefficient, and Nominal Rates of Protection

nominal protection (E_j/t_j) is shown on the vertical scale, while the free trade value added coefficient is on the horizontal. The curves in the four quadrants trace out the relation between these variables at different ratios (α) of nominal tariffs for inputs over that for the final product.[18]

Starting with the upper right quadrant, the curves show that the effective rate of protection is inversely related to the size of the free trade value added coefficient. For example, with an alpha of 0·8 and a free trade value added of 15 per cent, the ratio of effective to nominal tariff protection would be about two. However, if value added for a production process were about 5 per cent, effective protection would be more than five times the nominal rate, even though neither tariffs on inputs nor those on the final product have changed. Since some of the production processes discussed in the forthcoming analysis have very low value added, the high effective rates are a function of this coefficient's relatively small size.

The curves in Figure 4.2 suggest that the effective protection estimate may be sensitive to measurement errors for tariffs and value added, or any cyclical fluctuations in the latter. Since relative prices for inputs and the final product may change with the level of economic activity, the diagram indicates that some caution must be taken to ensure that any point estimate of value added, like that derived from an input-output table, is representative of longer-term levels. Also, it is frequently necessary to average lower-level tariff statistics in order to develop a correspondence for an input-output classification. Given the bias inherent in all systems of tariff averaging, the alpha value, and resultant effective protection estimates, may be quite dependent on the aggregation procedures employed.[19] In short, it should be realised that any point estimate for effective protection may be quite sensitive to parameter changes or measurement errors. This point should be kept in mind when evaluating some of the estimates presented in the following analyses or in the appendix.[20]

Analysis of Figure 4.2 or equation 4–9 illustrates several other basic characteristics of the effective protection model. For example, if t_i and t_j are equal, the ratio (E_j/t_j) equals alpha which implies that,

$$E_j = t_j = t_i, \qquad \text{if } t_j = t_i \qquad (4\text{–}10.1)$$

it also follows that,

$$E_j > t_j > t_i, \qquad \text{if } t_j > t_i \qquad (4\text{–}10.2)$$

$$E_j < t_j < t_i, \qquad \text{if } t_j < t_i \qquad (4\text{–}10.3)$$

$$E_j < 0, \qquad \text{if } t_j < a_{ij}t_i \qquad (4\text{–}10.4)$$

and that,

$$E_j = t_j/(1 - a_{ij}), \qquad \text{if } t_i = 0 \qquad (4\text{-}10.5)$$

Finally, there is one additional point which should be made concerning the leftmost portions of the diagram where the free trade value added coefficient is negative. Negative value added means that the production technique employed would be unprofitable if world prices were to prevail in the domestic economy. The production of a commodity by such an inefficient technology is only possible because of the distortions in domestic price structure caused by protection and transportation costs. While negative free trade coefficients have been observed in effective rate studies for developed countries, these portions of the diagram are much more relevant for analysis of LDC protectionist profiles where negative V_j is observed with a much higher frequency.

Effective protection in industrial markets
As an indication of the levels of effective protection in industrial markets, Table 4.5 presents summary estimates for the major developed countries. While these figures are based on pre-Kennedy Round tariff rates and, as such, are somewhat dated, they still provide a useful indication of comparative levels of effective protection. To contrast nominal and effective protection these rates are shown separately, while the ERP has also been expressed as a percentage of nominal tariffs. A further breakdown is provided which shows effective protection facing all manufactured goods imported from developed and developing countries, as well as separate ERP estimates for the LDC products.

Two points emerge from the data shown in Table 4.5. First, the effective tariff rates are considerably higher than corresponding *ad valorem* rates, averaging almost twice the latter for developing country products. The fact that this ratio is higher for the LDCs is partly due to the value added coefficients for the types of manufactures they export being generally lower than that for industrial nations. As previously indicated, with given nominal tariffs the levels of effective protection will be inversely related to the size of the value added coefficient. The second point emerging from the table is that both effective and nominal protection facing developing country products is higher than that against manufactures from developed countries. While some of the effective rate differential is undoubtedly due to variations in value added, the fact that nominal duties on LDC products are also 5 percentage points higher suggests that discriminatory tariff policy is a

TABLE 4.5 Averages of Nominal and Effective Tariffs on Manufactures Imported by the Industrial Countries

Importing country[1]	Tariff averages on the total imports of manufactures			Tariff averages on the imports of manufactures from developing nations		
	Nominal	*Effective*	*Effective as a percentage of nominal*	*Nominal*	*Effective*	*Effective as a percentage of nominal*
United States	11·5	20·0	174	17·9	35·4	198
EEC	11·0	18·6	169	14·3	27·7	194
Sweden	6·6	12·5	189	9·8	21·2	216
Japan	16·1	29·5	183	18·0	36·7	207
Industrial countries	12·3	21·7	176	17·1	33·4	195

[1] In averaging tariffs, data on individual countries' non-preferential imports from all sources of supply, and from developing countries respectively have been used as weights. As indicated in a previous section, this may cause some serious downward bias in the developing country averages due to the own trade weight problem.

Source: UNCTAD, *The Kennedy Round Estimated Effects on Tariff Barriers* (New York: United Nations, 1968), p. 205.

TABLE 4.6 Estimated Nominal and Effective Rates of Protection in the EEC, Japan and the USA

Commodity group	EEC tariff rate		Japan tariff rate		United States tariff rate		Free Trade share of value added
	Nominal	Effective	Nominal	Effective	Nominal	Effective	
Food and feeds							
Meat and meat products	19·5	36·6	17·9	69·1	5·9	10·3	0·250
Preserved seafoods	21·5	52·6	13·6	34·7	6·0	15·6	0·300
Preserved fruits and vegetables	20·5	44·9	18·5	49·3	14·8	36·8	0·270
Milk, cheese and butter	22·0	59·9	37·3	248·8	10·8	36·9	0·143
Manufactured and processed foods[1]	14·6	17·7	24·0	59·3	5·0	1·0	0·228
Flour, cereal, and bakery products	16·1	24·9	22·4	46·4	6·9	15·6	0·320
Cocoa products and chocolate	12·8	34·6	22·8	80·7	4·2	16·2	0·210
Soft drinks	14·9	−19·8	35·0	41·0	1·0	−9·5	0·400
Mill products and prepared feeds	11·4	31·6	13·8	32·3	23·4	111·0	0·270
Wood, paper and rubber products							
Wood products	8·2	9·5	12·4	22·0	10·4	18·3	0·445
Paper products and wood pulp	7·4	20·1	6·6	12·1	2·7	5·5	0·415
Rubber products	8·3	19·0	9·3	20·2	6·1	12·5	0·360
Yarns, fabrics and clothing							
Yarns and threads	6·2	19·4	9·9	24·2	19·5	37·1	0·280
Fabrics and clothing	14·3	29·1	13·0	22·0	27·3	40·4	0·340
Jute sacks, bags, and woven fabrics	18·2	42·9	27·1	65·0	1·4	3·2	0·333
Vegetable and animal oils							
Plant and vegetable oils[2]	11·1	138·0	10·1	64·9	9·4	17·7	0·055
Cottonseed oil	11·0	79·0	25·8	200·3	59·6	465·9	0·120
Rapeseed oil	9·0	57·2	15·1	22·3	20·8	60·9	0·150
Soybean oil	11·0	148·1	25·4	286·3	22·5	252·9	0·070
Animal and marine fats and oils	5·2	−26·8	5·1	−1·9	4·2	10·7	0·200

Leather, tobacco and soap						
Leather and leather products	7·8	14·6	14·8	22·6	7·0	12·8	0·397
Cigars and cigarettes	87·1	147·3	339·5	405·6	69·0	113·2	0·530
Soaps and detergents	7·5	14·4	16·6	44·4	7·9	19·3	0·230
Median tariff rate[3]	12·2	33·1	16·5	45·4	8·6	18·0	

[1] Includes roasted coffee.

[2] Consists of both crude and refined palm kernel oil, groundnut oil, and coconut oil.

[3] Median rates for 123 individual products or product groupings.

Source: Alexander J. Yeats, 'Effective Tariff Protection in the United States, the European Economic Community, and Japan', *Quarterly Review of Economics and Business* (Summer 1974), p. 45.

factor. In any event, the average effective rate of over 30 per cent indicates that tariffs have a more restrictive effect on the development of LDC manufacturing capacity than would be suggested by an analysis of *ad valorem* import tariffs.

Turning to the more recent data, the estimates still show that effective rates of protection facing products of interest to developing countries are quite high. For example, Table 4.6 summarises estimates which were derived for over 100 different products exported by LDCs to the European Economic Community, Japan and the United States. This table also presents information on nominal tariff rates so the two figures can be compared. In the interests of brevity, and to illustrate better the underlying pattern of results, data on commodity groups are presented where possible. The estimated free trade value added coefficient is also shown so the reader can assess the influence of this coefficient on the ERP, or on the sensitivity of the effective rate estimate to any changes in this parameter. Finally, the median nominal and effective rates have been computed to serve as a rough indicator of the relative magnitude of the tariff barriers in each of the three markets.

Examination of the data shown in Table 4.6 reveals, with few exceptions, a consistent pattern in the results. In general, the rate of effective protection is several times the nominal tariff with the divergence being particularly high for vegetable oils, where the ERP is about eight times higher. However, the table shows that this is primarily due to the very low value added coefficients for these products which average about 10 per cent. Aside from the oils, there are other cases where effective rates of over 100 per cent occur; cigarettes in all three markets, diary products in Japan, mill products in the United States, etc., while ERPs of 50 per cent or more are observed with a high frequency. The conclusion that emerges is that some seemingly low nominal tariffs conceal very high rates of effective protection, and that ERPs on the order of magnitude shown in Table 4.6 provide a substantial disincentive to the establishment or growth of processing industries in the developing countries.

In several places throughout the table, negative effective rates of protection are observed, even though positive nominal tariffs are applied to these items. Since free trade value added coefficients are positive in these cases, equation (4–10.4) indicates that tariffs on inputs are raising production costs more than the duty on the processed good increases its price. However, it should be noted that products which have negative effective protection rates are generally very bulky low value items that have high shipping costs. While the analysis of transport charges is left to a subsequent chapter, it should be noted that the natural protection provided by these costs may more than offset the influence of tariffs. The net result can be positive *total* effective protection even though the effective tariff rate is negative.[21]

Escalation of effective rates

A question of importance concerns the behaviour of effective tariffs over processing chains. While it was demonstrated that *ad valorem* tariffs increase or escalate with the level of fabrication, ERPs need not follow this pattern if weighted average tariffs on inputs increase faster than those for manufactured goods. Table 4.7 presents estimates of the effective rate of protection for the components of the 21 processing chains used to examine the behaviour of *ad valorem* tariffs.[22] To assist in comparing effective tariffs with *ad valorem* rates, a separate column gives the ratio between the two in each of the four industrial country markets. Averages have also been computed for each processing chain and by stage of processing to illustrate better the general relation between effective protection and level of fabrication.

As was the case with the previous comparisons, the figures in Table 4.7 also indicate that the levels of effective protection for these products are considerably higher than corresponding nominal tariffs. For the second stage items, the average effective tariff of 23 per cent in about 3 times the *ad valorem* rate. While the spread between nominal and effective rates declines, due to higher value added coefficients, with increased product processing the ERPs for stage 4 items still average more than 70 per cent above *ad valorem* tariff rates.

While no strong evidence of effective rate escalation clearly emerges, there are individual processing chains where such a pattern is evident. Effective rates for aluminium never decline with fabrication in any of the four markets, while the processing chains for fish, fruits, vegetables and leather are clearly characterised by rising effective tariffs. However, in the cases where declines in the ERPs are observed it could be argued that some other form of protection is substituted for tariffs. For example, effective rates for steel products are fairly uniform over each processing stage, but capital requirements and technological factors exclude most LDCs from trade in mill products or specialty steels. Similar considerations are also an important limiting factor for LDC trade in wrought lead, zinc, and aluminium as well as some of the higher grades of paper products. For cotton and wool, the stable or declining ERPs are due to a substitution of other forms of protection (quotas, voluntary restraints, etc.,) for tariffs in the higher processing stages.

TABLE 4.7 Analysis of the Structure of Post-Kennedy Round Effective Tariffs in Industrial Countries on Primary and Processed Goods Exported by Developing Countries

Commodity	United States		EEC		Sweden		Japan		Average	
	Effective rate	Ratio to nominal tariff	Effective rate	Ratio to nominal tariff	Effective rate	Ratio to nominal tariff	Effective rate	Ratio to nominal tariff	Effective rate	Ratio to nominal tariff
Meat products										
1. Fresh and frozen meat	4·6	—	17·8	—	0·0	—	6·2	—	7·2	—
2. Meat preparations	10·3	1·8	36·6	1·9	-5·7	—	69·1	3·9	27·6	2·6
Fish and seafood										
1. Fresh and frozen fish	1·3	—	14·9	—	0·0	—	5·3	—	5·4	—
2. Fish preparations	15·6	2·6	52·6	2·4	8·6	2·3	34·7	2·6	27·9	2·5
Fruit										
1. Fresh fruit or nuts	5·6	—	13·9	—	2·5	—	14·0	—	9·0	—
2. Preserved fruit	36·8	2·5	44·9	2·2	21·8	2·1	49·3	2·7	38·2	2·4
Vegetables										
1. Fresh vegetables	8·9	—	9·9	—	7·8	—	8·1	—	8·7	—
2. Preserved vegetables	9·5	1·2	22·7	1·5	9·2	1·4	40·2	2·0	20·4	1·7
Cocoa										
1. Cocoa beans	0·0	—	5·4	—	3·6	—	3·0	—	3·0	—
2. Cocoa powder	11·6	7·3	126·6	7·0	31·6	8·1	98·3	8·1	67·0	7·4
3. Chocolate	1·3	0·3	19·3	1·1	27·0	2·4	68·6	2·0	29·1	1·7
Leather										
1. Hides and skins	1·1	—	0·0	—	0·0	—	0·0	—	0·3	—
2. Leather	12·0	2·6	12·3	2·6	4·3	2·6	34·7	3·0	15·8	2·8
3. Leather goods[1]	18·8	1·7	14·8	1·5	22·5	2·0	25·7	1·5	20·5	1·7
Groundnut oil										
1. Groundnuts	25·7	—	0·0	—	0·0	—	20·0	—	11·4	—
2. Groundnut oil[2]	8·1	0·3	11·2	1·0	0·0	0·0	27·2	1·2	11·6	0·7

Coconut oil										
1. Copra	0·0	—	0·0	—	0·0	—	0·0	—	0·0	—
2. Coconut oil²	23·6	1·3	135·8	10·9	0·0	0·0	47·7	4·8	51·8	5·1
Palm kernel oil										
1. Palm kernels	0·0	—	0·0	—	0·0	—	0·0	—	0·0	—
2. Palm kernel oil²	20·5	7·3	141·9	12·3	0·0	0·0	7·3	1·0	42·4	7·9
Rubber and products										
1. Natural rubber	0·0	—	0·0	—	0·0	—	0·0	—	0·0	—
2. Rubber products	6·6	1·4	16·3	2·1	16·1	2·4	10·3	1·6	18·1	2·8
Wood and products										
1. Wood in the rough	0·0	—	1·0	—	0·0	—	0·0	—	0·3	—
2. Plywood	13·8	1·6	19·6	1·7	2·9	0·8	25·4	1·8	15·4	1·7
3. Wood manufactures	13·6	2·0	16·3	1·9	15·0	2·2	23·2	2·0	17·0	2·0
Paper and products										
1. Pulpwood	0·0	—	0·0	—	0·0	—	0·0	—	0·0	—
2. Wood pulp	-1·1	—	5·0	1·5	-0·5	—	7·5	1·5	2·7	1·3
3. Paper and articles	5·0	2·0	13·0	2·1	2·0	2·0	17·2	2·2	9·3	2·2
Wool and products										
1. Raw wool	9·7	—	0·0	—	0·0	—	0·0	—	2·4	—
2. Wool yarn	49·5	2·4	17·5	3·1	9·6	3·3	14·7	2·9	22·8	2·7
3. Wool fabrics	60·9	2·9	38·1	2·4	28·4	2·6	21·3	2·1	37·1	2·6
Cotton and products										
1. Raw cotton	6·2	—	0·0	—	0·0	—	0·0	—	0·0	—
2. Cotton yarn	25·0	2·4	32·9	3·3	30·4	3·5	6·8	2·4	23·8	3·0
3. Cotton fabrics	24·6	1·8	19·1	1·6	18·1	1·7	17·8	2·3	19·9	1·8
4. Clothing³	18·9	1·0	20·0	1·4	18·6	1·5	27·1	1·8	21·1	1·4
Jute and products										
1. Raw jute	0·0	—	0·0	—	0·0	—	0·0	—	0·0	—
2. Jute fabrics	-0·6	—	53·3	2·7	21·6	2·7	54·4	2·7	32·2	2·7
3. Sacks and bags	10·7	3·0	14·0	0·9	14·3	1·6	2·7	0·2	10·4	1·0

TABLE 4.7 continued

Commodity	United States Effective rate	Ratio to nominal tariff	EEC Effective rate	Ratio to nominal tariff	Sweden Effective rate	Ratio to nominal tariff	Japan Effective rate	Ratio to nominal tariff	Average Effective rate	Ratio to nominal tariff
Sisal and products										
1. Raw sisal	0·0	—	0·0	—	0·0	—	0·0	—	0·0	—
2. Cordage	10·3	2·9	30·6	3·0	32·2	3·1	28·1	2·9	25·3	3·0
Iron and products										
1. Iron ore	0·0	—	0·0	—	0·0	—	0·0	—	0·0	—
2. Pig iron	0·0	0·0	3·5	0·9	−4·3	—	2·9	1·5	0·5	0·3
3. Steel ingots	62·2	9·9	1·1	0·3	41·1	10·8	16·6	2·6	30·3	5·9
4. Mill products	−4·8	—	11·5	2·1	12·6	2·5	20·5	2·3	10·0	1·7
5. Special steel items	6·3	1·6	19·5	2·6	8·6	1·7	8·6	1·1	10·8	1·8
Copper and products										
1. Copper ores	0·1	—	0·0	—	0·0	—	0·0	—	0·0	—
2. Unwrought copper	11·2	4·9	−5·6	—	−1·2	—	43·1	6·2	11·8	5·1
3. Copper wrought	5·4	1·3	10·5	1·3	2·2	1·1	34·9	2·0	13·2	1·7
Aluminium										
1. Bauxite	0·0	—	0·0	—	0·0	0·0	0·0	—	0·0	—
2. Alumina	0·0	0·0	11·1	2·0	0·0	0·0	0·0	0·0	2·8	2·0
3. Unwrought aluminium	6·0	1·5	5·6	1·0	0·0	0·0	11·4	1·1	5·8	1·1
4. Wrought aluminium	11·5	1·9	29·3	2·3	5·3	2·7	29·0	2·1	18·8	2·2
Lead and products										
1. Lead ores	6·0	—	0·0	—	0·0	—	0·0	—	1·5	—
2. Unwrought lead	42·7	5·1	33·8	4·7	0·0	0·0	29·4	4·5	26·5	4·8
3. Wrought lead	17·7	1·7	7·7	1·2	0·0	0·0	30·8	2·1	14·1	1·8

Zinc and products										
1. Zinc ores	12·0	—	0·0	—	0·0	—	0·0	—	3·0	—
2. Unwrought zinc	2·5	0·4	13·4	2·3	0·0	0·0	14·8	2·3	7·7	1·6
3. Wrought zinc	-0·3	—	13·0	1·6	0·0	0·0	30·8	2·1	10·9	1·7
All items										
Stage 1	3·9	—	2·9	—	0·7	—	2·7	—	2·6	—
Stage 2	14·7	2·0	38·8	3·6	8·4	2·6	30·8	3·0	23·4	3·0
Stage 3	20·6	2·7	15·7	1·6	15·5	2·8	27·3	2·0	19·8	2·1
Stage 4	8·0	1·0	20·1	2·0	11·3	1·9	21·3	1·9	15·2	1·7

[1] Leather products including shoes.
[2] Includes crude and refined oils.
[3] Includes cotton blends and other types of clothing.

Source: Data adapted from Alexander J. Yeats, 'Effective Tariff Protection in the United States, the European Economic Community, and Japan', *Quarterly Review of Economics and Business* (Summer 1974), p. 45 and UNCTAD, *The Kennedy Round Estimated Effects on Tariff Barriers* (New York: United Nations, 1968), pp. 209–13.

However, while these other factors may produce increases in total effective protection from all sources, the general pattern is for effective *tariffs* to register a decline as one moves from the primary to intermediate stage items and then hold fairly steady.[23]

EVALUATION OF POTENTIAL TRADE FLOWS

While the preceding analysis demonstrates that products of export interest to developing countries face what appear to be imposing tariff barriers, it tells nothing about the value of trade which might occur if these restrictive measures were removed. To evaluate the magnitude of these potential trade flows, a partial equilibrium model was used to simulate the effect of removal of trade barriers for a selection of products. While results from such an analysis must be interpreted with some qualifications, the approach does provide a useful approximation as to the potential order of magnitudes involved.

The model employed for analysing the influence of trade restraints can be developed as follows.[24] If the existing nominal rate of protection t for a product were reduced to zero, this would allow the domestic price of imports (P') to decline by,

$$dP'/P' = t\varepsilon/(\varepsilon + t\varepsilon + \eta) \qquad (4\text{--}12)$$

where η and ε represent import demand and supply elasticities. Similarly, the duty-free price (P) will rise by,

$$dP/P = t\eta/(\varepsilon + t\varepsilon + \eta) \qquad (4\text{--}13)$$

due to increased costs associated with the larger foreign output. As a result, the percentage increase in import volume following elimination of t becomes,

$$dM/M = t\eta\varepsilon/(\varepsilon + t\varepsilon + \eta) \qquad (4\text{--}14)$$

while the corresponding change in value is indicated by,

$$dV = Vt\eta[1 + \varepsilon + t\eta\varepsilon(\varepsilon + t\varepsilon + \eta)^{-1}](\varepsilon + t\varepsilon + \eta)^{-1} \qquad (4\text{--}15)$$

Table 4.8 shows the results, both in terms of total value and percentage increase in imports, when equation 4–15 was used to estimate the effect of EEC protection for ten broad product groups in which the LDCs have export interests. To assist in evaluating these figures, total 1971 imports are shown along with imports originating in developing countries.

TABLE 4.8 Simulation of the Effect of Removing EEC Trade Barriers on Products of Export Interest to Developing Countries

SITC	Product name	1971 imports ($000)[1]		Nominal protection[2]	Estimated increase in imports with removal of protection[2]	
		All sources	Developing countries		Value ($000)	%
01	Meat products	768026	338151	60	548058	71·4
02	Dairy products	143458	6087	190	263206	183·5
03	Seafoods	497363	101452	22	103461	20·8
046	Flour of wheat	1762	1	65	573	32·5
048	Bakery products	13203	79	50	5809	44·0
05	Fruits and vegetables	1799080	926681	30	312340	17·4
072.3	Cocoa products	41003	38852	15	3812	9·3
421	Fixed vegetable oils	331560	110554	10	21046	6·3
612	Leather	15753	4186	7	1083	6·9
65	Textiles	1033001	337367	10	120819	11·7
	Total above	4664209	1863410		1380207	

[1] Excludes intra-trade.
[2] Includes the effects of tariffs, levies, *taxes compensatoires*, and other special charges. Not included are *ad valorem* equivalents for quotas, subsidies, or other forms of trade barriers.

Source: Alexander J. Yeats, 'Effective Protection for Processed Agricultural Commodities: a Comparison of Industrial Countries', *Journal of Economics and Business* (Fall 1977), p. 37.

TABLE 4.9 Estimated Increase in Industrial Country Imports of Selected Products Following Reductions in Trade Barriers

Country	1971 Imports ($000)[1] All sources	1971 Imports ($000)[1] Developing countries	Estimated increase in imports with removal of protection[2] Value ($000)	Estimated increase in imports with removal of protection[2] %
EEC	4662209	1863410	1380207	29·6
Japan	1287541	632144	193865	15·1
Norway	272077	28010	35966	13·2
Sweden	727104	65628	151625	20·9
United States	4253982	1578189	614816	14·5
Total above	11202913	4167381	2376479	21·2

[1] Import values for the product groups identified in Table 4·7. Figures for the EEC exclude intra-trade.
[2] Estimated effect of removal of tariffs, levies, and other special charges.

Source: Alexander J. Yeats, 'Effective Protection for Processed Agricultural Commodities: a Comparison of Industrial Countries', *Journal of Economics and Business* (Fall 1977), p. 37.

On an overall basis, removal of the EEC trade restraints would result in imports rising approximately 30 per cent above 1971 levels. Items registering the largest potential increases, both on an absolute and a percentage basis, are meats, fruits and vegetables, and dairy products. The first two groups are of special importance to developing countries since they currently supply 40 to 50 per cent of the EEC import requirements and should be able to maintain, or increase, these margins for any expansion of demand.[25] Assuming that developing countries just maintained existing shares for these ten product groups, removal of the artificial trade barriers should result in LDCs' increasing export earnings by approximately 500 million dollars above 1971 levels.

Table 4.9 summarises results when the same simulations were run for other industrial nations. Shown here are the overall 1971 imports of these ten product groups, imports from developing countries, and the estimates of import expansion that would accompany removal of each country's tariff barriers.

Aside from the European Community, which offers the greatest potential for increased trade both on an absolute and percentage basis, all other industrial countries appear able to absorb an import expansion of at least 10 per cent or more. Again the real importance of the industrial country tariff barriers can be assessed by noting their probable effect on LDC export earnings. If developing countries just maintained existing market shares, a trade expansion of the magnitude indicated in Table 4.9 would raise their export earnings by about $800 million for the 10 basic product groups. The significance of this figure can be assessed by noting that the value of this lost trade is approximately equal to 10 per cent of the total development assistance commitments of all OECD member states in 1971.[26]

5 Nontariff Barriers Facing Developing Countries

While the preceding analysis demonstrated that the potential exists for a substantial expansion of developing country exports if trade barriers were liberalised, there are a variety of other restraints whose influence appears to be at least the equal of tariffs. For example, evidence suggests that agricultural exports from developing countries are often severely curtailed by complicated systems of nontariff barriers (NTBs) in industrial markets. Specifically, a recent study of the EEC system found that domestic farmers were protected from foreign competition by at least 15 different kinds of nontariff measures ranging from global or bilateral quotas to production subsidies and variable import levies. Similarly, in the area of textiles, where developing countries are acknowledged to have a real comparative advantage in production, developed countries have effectively limited imports through complex systems of quotas and other forms of export restraints. In fact, evidence exists that as tariffs are lowered in international forums such as the Kennedy Round, industrial nations are turning more heavily to nontariff barriers to insulate domestic producers from foreign competition.

Unlike tariffs, however, the trade effects of nontariff barriers may be difficult to evaluate within reasonable limits. Part of the problem is that NTBs take a variety of different forms, few of which may be directly comparable. Also, considerably less comprehensive information is available on the existence or application of NTBs than is the case with tariffs. Tariff schedules are published in detail by government and international agencies, so data on the level and structure of these charges are easily accessible for inspection and analysis. However, no readily available or strictly comparable source of information exists for systematic comparisons of nontariff trade barriers. Those inventories which international agencies or national governments have attempted to compile are often incomplete and are usually several years out of date.

104

However, the real problem associated with empirical evaluation of nontariff barriers is that often it may be very difficult to assess potential trade which would occur if a quota, export restraint, prohibition or similar measure operating directly on import volumes were removed. Similarly, for those NTBs like variable levies, advanced deposit requirements and standards which operate directly on producer costs, it is often difficult to measure the increase in landed foreign prices, and the curtailment of domestic demand which is due to the operation of these measures. In the case of tariffs, these price-cost elements are apparent since the import duty is directly expressed as a percentage of foreign price, or *ad valorem* equivalents can be calculated. However, most estimates of the price effects of nontariff barriers can only be approximated within wide ranges so conclusions as to the restrictive effect of these measures are frequently subject to dispute.

While there admittedly are problems in analysis and interpretation, this chapter examines evidence concerning the influence of nontariff barriers on developing country exports. To develop a background for this analysis, discussion is devoted to empirical procedures employed for evaluation of NTBs, as well as a useful classification scheme for these measures. A section analyses the effects of protection in industrial country agricultural sectors since considerable information on these nontariff restraints has become available. Marshalling other data, an attempt is made to evaluate the importance of various types of NTBs on manufactures exported by developing countries. For those cases where sufficient information is available, an effort is made to estimate the value of LDC trade which would occur if the nontariff trade restraints were removed.

A DEFINITION OF NONTARIFF BARRIERS

In previous economic analyses of nontariff barriers, various definitions have been advanced. For example, Baldwin (1970, p. 5) suggests that a nontariff trade distorting policy is 'any measure (public or private) that causes internationally traded goods and services, or resources devoted to the production of these goods and services, to be allocated in such a way as to reduce potential real world income'. Potential real world income is further defined as that level attainable if resources and outputs were allocated in an economically efficient manner. While the definition has intuitive appeal, there are obvious difficulties associated with practical applications. Specifically, it requires knowledge of the level of potential real world income or, as a minimum, the directional movement in actual income associated with alternative policy measures. While there may be agreement on the directional movement for measures such as a rigorously enforced quota, whose objective is protection of domestic producers, there are other instances where the issue is less clear. For example, would removal of health and sanitary standards applied to agricultural products result in an increase or decrease in world income if the resulting expansion in imports was accompanied by a reduction in community health standards? While the question can be resolved in theory, an answer may be unobtainable in practice.

In search of a more workable definition, Ingo Walter (1969) starts with the proposition that, in the broadest sense, nontariff barriers to international trade encompass all private and governmental policies and practices that serve to distort the volume, commodity-composition or direction of trade in goods and services. Walter recognises that this is a weak operational definition, however, in that it hinges on a fine judgement as to what constitutes a trade distortion. For example, in day-to-day operations firms influence the volume and composition of trade by various actions which affect supply or demand conditions. Measures aimed at lowering production costs or prices, or increasing product differentiation through style changes or advertising, may reduce imports if practised by import competing firms, or increase foreign sales when implemented by exporters. Yet most economists would not classify such policies as nontariff barriers since they are not assumed to convey any unfair competitive advantage. At the same time, it is recognised that firms engage in practices such as dumping or predatory pricing. Most economists would seem to agree that these practices should be classified as nontariff distortions due to their intent. Government policy measures may influence the volume and composition of trade flows, sometimes as a remote side effect not connected with the primary purpose of the action. However, in other cases a specific policy measure may be aimed directly at modification of an existing pattern of international trade.

In part, the definitional difficulty for a nontariff barrier can be resolved by adopting Walter's suggestion and classifying measures on the basis of their apparent *intent*. The United Nations Conference on Trade and Development has found this approach particularly fruitful and has adopted a three-tier classification scheme for NTBs which is primarily based on the purpose or intent of individual measures. According to the UNCTAD schema, nontariff barriers are classified under one of the following headings; commercial policy measures designed primarily to protect domestic producers from foreign competition (type I barriers), measures designed to deal with problems not directly related to commercial policy, but which have been used on occasion to intentionally restrict imports or stimulate exports (type II), and measures applied with little or no intent to protect domestic industry, but which can have certain spill-over effects in the foreign trade sector (type III measures). Each of these three categories is further subdivided into a group A or B classification. The former operate primarily through quantitative restraint of trade, while the group B measures operate on production costs and prices. In attempts to assess the frequency of application and types of products to which these restraints are applied, UNCTAD (December 1969) has adopted the following classifications for individual policy measures:[1]

Type I—Commercial policy measures designed primarily to protect import-competing suppliers from foreign competition, or to assist exporters in expanding foreign markets:
Group A: Measures operating through quantitative restraint of trade:
1. Import quotas: globally administered including unspecified import quotas.
2. Import quotas: selectively or bilaterally administered.[2]
3. Licensing: discretionary and restrictive.
4. Licensing: liberal, including licensing for statistical purposes.
5. Export restraints of a voluntary nature, imposed by trading partners, both bilateral and multilateral.
6. Import prohibitions: embargoes.
7. Import prohibitions: selective with respect to origin.
8. State trading.
9. Domestic procurement practices by public units.
10. Domestic content and other mixing regulations.[3]
Group B: Measures operating primarily through costs and prices:
1. Variable levies or supplementary import charges, including minimum price regimes.
2. Advanced deposit requirements.
3. Anti-dumping and countervailing charges.
4. Credit or other restraints on imports through the financial sector.
5. Tax benefits for import-competing industries.
6. Direct or indirect subsidisation of import-competing industries, including credit subsidisation.

7. Special discriminatory internal transport charges.

Type II—Measures designed to deal with problems not directly related to commercial policy questions, but which are from time to time intentionally employed to restrict imports or to stimulate exports.

   Group A: Measures operating through quantitative restraint of trade:
   1. Communication-media restrictions.
   2. Quantitative marketing restraints.
   Group B: Measures operating through costs and prices:
   1. Packaging and labelling regulations, including mark-of-origin rules.
   2. Health and sanitary regulations and quality standards.
   3. Safety and industrial standards and regulations.
   4. Border tax adjustments.
   5. Use taxes and excises.
   6. Customs clearance and related practices.
   7. Customs valuation procedures and related practices.
   8. Customs classification procedures and related practices.[4]

Type III—Measures consistently applied with little or no intent to protect domestic industry, but which unavoidably produce certain spill-over effects in the trade sector.

   1. Government manufacturing, sales and trading monopolies covering individual products.
   2. Government structural and regional development policy measures.
   3. Government balance of payments policy measures.
   4. Variations in national tax systems.
   5. Variations in national social insurance and related programmes.
   6. Variations in allowable depreciation methods.
   7. Government financed research and development, and technology spill-overs from defence and other programmes.
   8. Scale effects induced by government procurement.
   9. Variations in national weights and measures.
   10. Discriminatory external transport charges.

EFFECTS OF NONTARIFF BARRIERS

While the precise pattern of effects resulting from application of a nontariff barrier will vary among the different types of measures, it is still possible to indicate the general consequences of these restraints' effects on the importing and exporting countries' balance of trade, level of aggregate demand, and other income and employment variables. However, in assessing the consequences of a nontariff barrier, a distinction should be made between those measures which operate primarily through quantitative restraint of trade (group A), as opposed to group B measures which influence relative prices and costs.

Starting first with group A measures, a quantitative restraint such as a quota reduces imports of a particular good into the implementing country with the result that the domestic market is cleared at a higher price and lower volume than would occur in the absence of the barrier.[5] The artificially raised price and reduced foreign share of the market leads to an increase in domestic production, which in turn attracts resources into the protected industry. If the economy was operating at or close to full employment, increased production of the import-competing good necessitates reduced output in other sectors. However, if the economy was operating below full employment, a net increase in output, real income, and employment could result. However, this would be accompanied by higher consumer prices which represent real income transfers to domestic producers and those traders able to operate under the quantitative restriction. For a country imposing such a restraint one should therefore expect, as a first approximation, some shift in industrial production toward the import competing industry and its service sectors, higher prices for domestic buyers with lower consumption of the protected good, some loss in overall production efficiency and consumer welfare, and the initial prospect of higher national product if unemployment previously existed. Since the quantitative restraint would have a limiting effect on imports, there should also be an initial improvement in the national trade balance.[6]

However, if the protected industry produces inputs for other domestic firms, further repercussions on prices and output could offset some of the favourable primary effects. Specifically, the initial improvement in the trade balance could be eroded if resulting increases in user prices and costs jeopardise their export performance. Other possible repercussions could be felt in third markets since barriers imposed by one country tend to force exporters to focus on other potential markets. If this search for new export outlets threatens to disrupt import-competing producers in the markets now under pressure, there may be a call for the establishment of additional quantitative barriers. Thus, the use of such restrictions as commercial policy measures may expand to the detriment of all exporting nations.

It should also be noted that there are important distinctions between the economic consequences of a tariff as opposed to an NTB in the form of a quota on foreign goods.[7] Under a tariff, the domestic price of an item cannot differ from world prices by more than the amount of the duty. If producers attempt to raise prices above this level, unlimited quantities of the product can be imported by anyone willing to pay the tax for the foreign good. Thus, starting from a situation where a tariff is in effect, any increase in domestic demand can be satisfied by imports without a price increase. Neither domestic production, nor its costs in terms of misallocated resources, need rise and reduce further the optimal consumption mix of foreign and domestically produced goods. This need not be the case with a quota since there is no such upper limit to domestic prices. Since an upward quantity adjustment is not possible for imports, any increase in domestic demand necessitates increases in domestic prices and production. These changes further raise the social costs of protection through misallocation of additional factors of production, and even less optimal foreign-domestic good consumption patterns.[8]

The influence on exporting nations
Imposition of a quantitative restraint lowers earnings and production of foreign exporting firms. While an attempt may be made to direct some of the surplus production to third markets, or to shift to higher unit value items in lines covered by the restraint, the net effect is still likely to be lower output, employment and export revenues. As production is curtailed in response to the reduced demand for exports, repercussions are felt in other parts of the economy. For example, there may be important linkage effects which reduce output and employment in industries servicing the export sector. Some estimates suggest the potential magnitude of these linkage effects may equal the direct production or employment loss in the export sector. The reduction in foreign exchange earnings, which may constitute central bank reserves, can force the authorities to follow more restrictive monetary policies, which further contracts income and employment.

Longer-term implications of the restraints are likely to be even more serious for the developing countries. Instead of allowing trade to be determined along the lines of comparative advantage, quantitative restraints direct capital and labour into alternative sectors where their contribution to growth and development may be considerably lower. The fact that industrial countries apply these measures so heavily on labour intensive industries in which LDCs have a comparative advantage certainly is a factor hampering their efforts to diversify away from traditional primary goods exports. Since primary product prices are generally more volatile than those of manufactures, the quantitative restraints work to maintain the vulnerability of LDCs to severe fluctuations in export earnings, with the adverse consequences of this instability for growth and development planning. Finally, the uncertainty associated with the use of quotas or other similar restraints may provide an important disincentive for new investment in productive capacity in developing countries. Since LDC producers do not know what future administrative actions will be taken to limit their penetration of foreign markets, they may restrict new plant and equipment expenditure below potential levels due to the threat of new import controls being established.[9]

Measures influencing price margins

Nontariff barriers which influence foreign price margins operate somewhat differently, although the economic effects may be similar. This type of measure can be analysed by taking an example where a variable charge is applied to imports which is designed to raise landed prices of the foreign product to a level equal to or higher than that of the domestically produced item. By itself, this action would tend to reduce the share of imports in total consumption, increase prices, profits, production and employment in the import competing industry, and generally result in aggregate economic and structural effects similar to those associated with quantitative restrictions. However, one difference is that the government may collect the variable import charge equalling the domestic-world price differential. In the case of the quantitative measures, this price differential accrues to private traders in the form of monopoly profits.

An additional feature of restraints that operate on price-cost margins is that these measures are often coupled with subsidies to import competing suppliers paid out of revenues collected through the import levy. The system therefore produces a two-fold trade restrictive effect whereby domestic producers are actually subsidised by more efficient foreign units. It should be noted that it does little good for foreign exporters to lower offer prices, since the variable import charge will be raised to compensate for the reduction. Since the system effectively removes the threat of foreign competition, its efficiency and welfare consequences are similar to those of the quantitative restrictions.

However, in the case of the *fixed* nontariff import charges, advanced deposit requirements, subsidisation of domestic producers and similar measures, the consequences may be different. As with tariffs, the foreign suppliers may overcome these restrictions by lowering offer prices so the landed price in the consuming country remains essentially unchanged. Further, the impact of these measures on exporting country producers may be moderated if importers and internal wholesalers agree to reduce profit margins. The end result may be that exporters are relatively unaffected, with employment and structural effects being less severe. At the same time, however, the exporting country probably will experience a decline in its terms of trade and a deterioration in its trade balance.

MEASUREMENT OF NONTARIFF BARRIERS

As shown by the preceding analysis, nontariff barriers may take a variety of forms which restrain trade by either establishing quantitative limits on its flow, or raising price-cost margins of foreign firms. It was also shown that individual restraints could be classified on the basis of intent. While type I measures are directed primarily at modification of actual trade patterns, type III restraints are concerned with other problems, but can have spill-over effects on trade. Between these two are the type II measures which are not strictly intended for trade control, but are from time to time employed to restrict imports or stimulate exports.

Due to the wide variety of nontariff barriers, the problem of empirically measuring their trade effects is difficult. However, several empirical procedures for evaluating the importance of NTBs have been developed and tested empirically. This section examines the advantages and shortcomings of these procedures, and also evaluates the evidence from each concerning the effects of NTBs on developing country trade.

The UNCTAD inventory approach

In its third session, the United Nations Conference on Trade and Development's Committee on Manufactures requested that the UNCTAD Secretariat initiate a series of investigations concerning the impact of nontariff restrictions on the trade of developing countries. Specifically, the Committee requested that UNCTAD,

> . . . make studies based, to the extent possible, on information from developing countries about specific cases of difficulties experienced as a result of nontariff barriers and to analyse the possibilities for the reduction of such barriers. The order of priority for such studies

should be based on the *frequency* [author's italics] with which the particular types of barriers are mentioned.

In partial response to the Committee's request, the Secretariat prepares and continually updates a detailed inventory of nontariff barriers affecting the trade of LDCs with the following industrial nations: Australia, Austria, Belgium, Canada, Denmark, Finland, France, Federal Republic of Germany, Ireland, Italy, Japan, Luxembourg, Netherlands, Norway, Sweden, Switzerland, United Kingdom and the United States. This inventory, generally available at the four-digit BTN level or lower, describes the nature of the NTB(s) applied, the industrial nation imposing the restriction, and other pertinent information relating to the influence of the barriers on potential trade flows. Basic data for these files have been supplied by individual developing countries, after verification by the GATT, and from internal records available at UNCTAD and GATT. In an attempt to ensure that the records are current, additions and deletions are made after periodic consultations with individual member states. All data are stored in machine-readable form for rapid access and use in connection with other data files available at UNCTAD.

Table 5.1 illustrates the type of information which can be derived from this data base. The left-hand columns of the table identify different four-digit BTN products which have been drawn for illustrative purposes. Using the EEC, Japan, Norway, Sweden and the United States as examples, the entries in the body of the table indicate the types of nontariff restraints developing countries have encountered (in addition to tariffs) in efforts to penetrate these markets.[10] Among other factors, the table indicates the surprising variety of NTBs which are applied to this common list of products in the five markets. For example, LDCs have primarily encountered variable import levies in exporting these products to Sweden, and to a lesser extent in the EEC, while the major complaints for Japan centre on state trading and discretionary licensing. In contrast, the United States primarily employs quotas or voluntary export restraints to control these products. The table also illustrates the phenomenon of 'stacking' nontariff barriers which has been a source of complaint among developing countries. Thus, for products like meat, fresh or pickled vegetables in the EEC, or fresh fish in Sweden, up to five different types of NTBs have been applied to a single product line in an effort to closely control imports.

The UNCTAD inventory provides a concise easily accessible source of information on the types and frequency of nontariff restraints applied

TABLE 5.1 Summary of Nontariff Barriers Applied by Industrial Countries on Imports of Selected Agricultural Commodities

BTN code	Product description	Nontariff trade barriers imposed by				
		EEC*	Japan	Norway	Sweden	USA
01-02	Bovine animals, live	VL		DL/GQ	VL	TQ
01-03	Swine	VL		DL/GQ	VL	TQ
02-01	Meat and edible offals	R/MP/P/ST/GQ/VL	DL/HS	DL/MP	VL	R/HS
02-06	Bacon, ham, and pigmeat	VL	DL/HS	DL/MP	VL	HS
03-01	Fish, fresh or frozen	BQ	DL		L/MP/TC	HS
03-02	Fish, processed		DL		L/TC	HS
03-03	Shell fish		DL			
04-03	Butter	VL	ST	DL	VL	Q/HS
04-04	Cheese and curd	VL	DL	DL/GQ	VL	Q
04-06	Natural honey	L		DL		
07-01	Fresh vegetables	SR/MP/BQ/GQ/VL		DL/SR/MP	VL	HS
08-01	Tropical fruits	R/DL/GQ				
08-02	Citrus fruits		DL			
08-04	Grapes, fresh or dried	SR/DL				
08-11	Fruit, preserved	R	DL	DL		
10-01	Wheat and meslin	VL	ST/CA	ST	VL	Q/CA
10-02	Rye	VL		ST	VL	
10-03	Barley	VL	ST	ST	VL	
10-04	Oats	VL		ST	VL	
10-05	Maize	VL		ST	VL	
10-06	Rice	VL	ST		VL	
11-01	Flour	VL	DL/CA	ST	VL/TC	Q/CA
11-02	Cereal groats and meal	VL	DL	ST	VL/TC	Q

16-01	Sausages	VL	DL		VL	
16-02	Prepared or preserved meat	VL	DL	DL	VL	
17-01	Beet and cane sugar	VL	DL		VL	Q
17-02	Other sugars	VL		DL/GQ	VL	Q
20-01	Pickled vegetables	L/Q/BQ/GQ	HS	DL		
20-02	Preserved vegetables	L/Q/BQ/GQ	DL/GQ	VL		HS
20-03	Preserved fruit	L				
20-05	Jams and jellies	BQ/DL/VL	DL	DL		
20-07	Fruit and vegetable juice	L/BQ/GQ/DL	DL	DL/GQ		
22-05	Wines	MP	ST	ST	ST	
22-06	Vermouths		ST	ST	ST	
24-01	Tobacco, unmanufactured	ST				
24-02	Cigars and cigarettes	ST/R				
41-02	Bovine leather		DL			
41-03	Sheepskin leather		DL			
53-01	Wool, greasy					
53-06	Combed wool	DL/GQ				XR
55-01	Raw cotton					Q
55-05	Cotton yarn					XR

* Restrictions imposed in whole, or in part, by EEC member countries.

Key: BQ = bilateral quota; DL = discretionary licensing scheme used to control imports; HS = special health and sanitary prohibitions; CA = commodity agreements to restrict imports; XR = voluntary export restraints; SR = seasonal restrictions on imports; R = various trade restrictions; TQ = tariff quota; GQ = global quota; ST = state trading; VL = variable levy; TC = special compensatory taxes; MP = minimum import price system; L = licensing of importers; P = import prohibition.

Source: Alexander J. Yeats, 'Effective Protection for Processed Agricultural Commodities: a Comparison of Industrial Countries', *Journal of Economics and Business, 29* (Fall 1976), p. 39.

to developing countries' exports. In this respect, it has proved most helpful to the LDCs in planning new export ventures since it shows what artificial protectionist measures will be encountered in potential export markets. The inventory has also been used by developing country representatives to the recent multilateral trade negotiations since it provides negotiators with summary information on the trade barriers facing their country's products.[11] In addition, it is also useful as a source of data for derivation of supplementary statistical information which can be employed for comparative analysis of NTBs in different industrial countries.

One such measure derived from the NTB inventories are frequency indices showing the per cent of tariff lines in major product groups covered by nontariff restraints. Specifically, this measure (F_j) is defined by,

$$F_j = \frac{N_r}{N_j}.100 \qquad (5\text{--}1)$$

where N_r is the number of commodities subject to reported NTBs within a given product class, and N_j represents the total number of commodities in the class. A second way to assess the importance of nontariff barriers in the protectionist profiles of various countries is to estimate the proportion of total imports in each commodity group subject to these restraints. This NTB coverage measure (C_j) is defined as,

$$C_j = \frac{M_r}{M_j}.100 \qquad (5\text{--}2)$$

where M_r represents the value of imports in each commodity group subject to NTBs, and M_j represents the total value of imports in product group j.[12] The values of C_j show the percentage of imports entering the economy under NTBs in relation to total imports for the commodity group. Table 5.2 presents results when the NTB frequency index (F_j) and the import coverage index were computed for some of the industrial countries covered by the UNCTAD inventory.

According to the figures shown in Table 5.2, sectors emerging as the most heavily protected by nontariff restraints are agricultural products, beverages, tobacco, certain chemicals, pharmaceuticals, textiles and clothing, coal, and transportation equipment. In agriculture, where average import coverage ratios of 70 per cent are observed, the data reflect high frequencies of variable levy application in the EEC countries and Sweden, and state trading in Japan. In the United States, coverage

TABLE 5.2 Frequency and Coverage Indices for Nontariff Barriers Applied in Major Industrial Markets: One-digit and Selected Two-digit SITC Product Groups

SITC	Description	USA Freq.	USA Cov.	UK Freq.	UK Cov.	Japan Freq.	Japan Cov.	France Freq.	France Cov.	Germany Freq.	Germany Cov.	Sweden Freq.	Sweden Cov.	Mean[1] Freq.	Mean[1] Cov.
0	Food and live animals	16	30	22	43	60	54	49	68	56	80	61	67	39	52
00	Live animals	17	28	—	—	50	49	50	49	50	98	83	69	48	71
01	Meat	24	60	17	34	42	22	58	67	50	89	58	100	43	67
02	Dairy products	50	97	67	77	67	42	67	100	67	100	100	100	59	70
04	Cereals	14	2	50	95	79	99	93	99	100	100	77	49	65	75
05	Fruit	—	—	27	28	59	52	27	63	45	67	27	35	28	48
06	Sugar	33	89	17	99	67	30	67	98	67	100	67	62	44	52
1	Beverages and tobacco	27	42	23	14	55	98	45	100	53	99	31	80	29	56
11	Beverages	20	79	20	26	60	96	40	100	80	100	40	99	34	71
12	Tobacco	33	5	25	2	50	100	50	100	25	98	25	60	23	40
2	Crude materials	3	14	1	0	6	7	4	5	2	5	2	2	3	4
22	Oilseeds and nuts	11	1	—	—	22	67	—	—	—	—	11	9	9	10
26	Textile fibres	8	67	—	—	—	—	—	—	—	—	4	6	4	9
29	Crude materials, n.e.c.	—	—	—	—	—	—	40	45	20	49	—	—	11	14
3	Mineral fuels	6	25	25	25	18	30	46	52	5	25	—	—	9	15
32	Coal and coke	—	—	100	100	60	100	20	70	20	100	—	—	18	38
33	Petroleum	25	100	—	—	12	19	12	10	—	—	—	—	7	16
4	Animal and vegetable oil	25	41	—	—	14	3	19	25	19	15	—	—	7	10
41	Animal oils and fats	50	75	—	—	—	—	50	65	50	44	—	—	11	14
42	Fixed vegetable oils	—	—	—	—	42	9	8	10	8	2	—	—	7	11
5	Chemicals	51	47	—	—	7	33	18	24	5	13	4	5	7	13
51	Chemical elements	41	49	—	—	14	96	—	—	—	—	—	—	6	19

TABLE 5.2 continued

SITC	Description	USA Freq.	USA Cov.	UK Freq.	UK Cov.	Japan Freq.	Japan Cov.	France Freq.	France Cov.	Germany Freq.	Germany Cov.	Sweden Freq.	Sweden Cov.	Mean[1] Freq.	Mean[1] Cov.
54	Medical products	63	38	—	—	14	100	14	100	—	—	—	—	9	20
56	Mfg. fertilisers	100	100	—	—	—	—	25	7	—	—	—	—	13	22
59	Misc. chemicals	60	38	—	—	20	23	20	11	20	18	20	11	14	10
6	Manufactured goods[2]	15	22	3	13	9	24	14	18	3	9	1	3	4	8
61	Leather manufactures	—	95	—	—	56	93	—	—	—	—	—	—	3	5
62	Rubber manufactures	20	25	—	—	—	—	—	—	—	—	—	—	6	14
65	Textile manufactures	14	25	5	35	11	45	70	75	16	69	5	25	12	30
67	Iron and steel	74	73	26	80	3	—	50	70	—	—	—	—	11	16
7	Machinery and transport	37	49	1	13	25	65	39	42	2	23	3	12	14	15
72	Electrical machinery	78	72	—	—	29	58	25	30	—	—	—	—	10	15
73	Transport equipment	24	73	4	39	16	65	88	94	8	70	8	35	28	26
8	Miscellaneous manufactures	28	31	1	0	16	5	9	15	4	7	4	4	12	8
84	Clothing	57	92	—	—	—	—	45	85	29	51	14	3	12	26
85	Footwear	25	16	7	3	7	35	14	16	—	—	—	—	13	12
86	Precision instruments	—	—	—	—	3	3	3	.2	—	—	—	—	4	11
89	Misc. manufactures	14	10	—	—	3	—	—	—	14	—	14	26	3	4
	Total imports	27	39	10	13	34	32	20	26	16	26	14	12	17	19

[1] Mean figures for the NTB frequency and coverage indices include data for Belgium, Denmark, Norway, Canada, Italy, Netherlands, Finland, Australia, and New Zealand.

[2] On 30 June 1968 the French government imposed quantitative restrictions on textiles, steel, various household appliances, tractors and automobiles. Frequency and coverage indices which include these restrictions were calculated by the author and have been incorporated in the table.

Source: Derived from Ingo Walter, 'Nontariff Protection Among Industrial Countries: Some Preliminary Evidence', *Economia Internazionale*

ratios of 60 to almost 100 per cent for meat and dairy products are primarily due to health standards, although a number of quotas are applied to items in these groups.[13] While the frequency and coverage ratios do not readily lend themselves to empirical analysis aimed at determining the resource costs associated with these barriers, supplementary studies suggest that these costs may be enormous. For example, Johnson (1967) estimated that if quotas were abolished for United States sugar imports, and the duty and excise taxes were also eliminated, the cost of sugar consumed in the United States would decline by $800 million. A second study by the UNCTAD Secretariat (March 1972) estimated that export gains for developing countries would be on the order of $17 billion a year if protection for agricultural products was removed in the industrial markets. From the viewpoint of United States producers, the European countries, quotas and other protectionist measures for coal are of special importance. Baldwin (1970, p. 36) estimates that the *ad valorem* equivalents of these restraints are equal to at least a 50 per cent duty for domestic producers, and result in a US export loss of about $2 billion a year.

Aside from agriculture, the textile sector is of prime importance to developing countries. Specifically, LDC exports of cotton textiles and clothing totalled $1·8 billion in 1965, or over 40 per cent of total manufactured goods exported by these countries. However, Table 5.2 shows that these products are also heavily covered by nontariff barriers. Many of the restraints are the result of the 1962 Long Term Arrangement Regarding International Trade in Cotton Textiles and its successor the 1974 Multifibre Arrangement (MFA). The 1974 arrangement continues a trend toward increasing protection for the industry as it has been considerably broadened to include all textiles and clothing. While the stated objective of these arrangements is to protect industrial markets from 'disruption', the exports of many developing countries have been severely constrained by the terms of these agreements.[14] For example, in the early 1970s the United States alone had over 20 bilateral agreements with individual developing countries to restrain textile exports. While it is difficult to translate the implications of these restraints into estimates of lost trade, the evidence suggests that the values involved may be staggering. For example, Baldwin (1970, p. 163) estimates that the United States' effective protection through tariffs and NTBs for broad and narrow fabrics in 1972 stood at close to 90 per cent, while that for apparel and fabricated textiles ranged between 35 and 45 per cent. An alternative set of estimates based on domestic-world price differentials suggests that the *ad valorem* equivalents for these textile

TABLE 5.3 Developing Country Export Values Subject to Various Forms of Nontariff Barriers in the European Economic Community, Japan and the United States in 1974 (values in $m)

| Exporting country | 1974 Exports subject to NTBs | | | | | Nontariff barrier coverage (%) |
	Export restraints	Licensing plus quotas	Variable levies	Total NTBs	Total exports	
Mauritius	8·5	22·8	109·8	141·1	155·3	90·9
Bahamas	0·0	708·4	0·0	708·4	971·9	72·9
Philippines	79·1	993·2	1·1	1073·4	1495·0	71·8
Hong Kong	1237·7	215·3	2·1	1455·1	2374·7	61·3
Ecuador	1·8	357·1	0·0	358·9	613·7	58·5
Panama	0·3	101·4	0·1	101·8	175·0	58·2
Costa Rica	11·5	163·1	1·8	176·4	311·1	56·7
Dominican Republic	5·6	259·5	31·8	296·9	546·9	54·3
Argentina	7·2	270·6	831·3	1109·1	2162·2	51·3
Pakistan	151·1	51·8	11·3	214·2	424·0	50·5
Malta	32·6	6·2	0·1	38·9	79·7	48·8
Haiti	47·6	7·0	0·0	54·6	114·2	47·8
Tunisia	40·3	78·9	114·0	233·2	495·7	47·0
Singapore	100·7	593·3	0·3	694·3	1574·8	44·1
Uruguay	1·4	12·5	33·7	47·6	117·2	40·6
India	249·9	521·3	7·7	778·9	2245·0	34·7
Peru	4·8	385·5	0·0	390·3	1267·3	30·8
Jamaica	8·6	59·0	29·5	97·1	350·4	27·7
Bolivia	0·5	67·7	0·1	68·3	253·4	27·0
Taiwan	656·6	298·5	0·0	955·1	3770·3	25·6
Republic of Korea	496·9	397·4	0·4	894·7	3535·7	25·3
Afghanistan	14·3	0·3	0·0	14·6	61·1	23·9

Egypt	27·6	98·1	5·0	130·7	550·7	23·7
Brazil	171·9	790·5	210·6	1173·0	5036·5	23·3
Nicaragua	2·1	36·9	0·1	39·1	193·0	20·3
Bangladesh	10·4	23·0	0·0	33·4	169·7	19·7
Colombia	66·9	95·9	16·2	179·0	914·9	19·6
Guatemala	2·0	64·4	12·1	78·5	402·2	19·6
Morocco	59·5	70·7	59·9	190·1	1045·6	18·2
Chile	0·1	252·3	0·1	252·5	1500·0	16·8
Lebanon	7·2	12·0	1·0	20·2	125·5	16·1
Mexico	240·7	365·1	8·5	614·3	4076·8	15·1
Israel	72·6	29·7	6·1	108·4	957·6	11·3
Thailand	33·8	61·8	24·8	120·4	1290·4	9·3
Cuba	0·1	0·7	50·3	51·1	554·1	9·2
Total of above	3851·9	7471·9	1569·8	12893·6	39911·6	32·3

Source: Computed from Appendix Tables 1 to 3.

restraints are on the order of 35 to 40 per cent in the United States and France, and about 15 per cent in Sweden.[15] Finally, an investigation by the UNCTAD Secretariat which employed the import elasticity of demand approach estimated that the differentials between external and internal prices resulting from quotas are likely to have reduced imports into the Federal Republic of Germany by 18 per cent, into Sweden by about 20 per cent, and into the United Kingdom by 22 per cent below the level which would have prevailed in the absence of quotas or licensing. These estimates were based on an estimated import elasticity of demand of 0·58, and on the assumption that import and export unit values are reasonable proxies for prevailing internal and external prices.[16]

Trade coverage by nontariff barriers
While the preceding analysis examined the frequency and coverage of products by nontariff barriers, a question of importance concerns the value of developing country exports which are subject to these measures. For an assessment, a correspondence was established between 1974 LDC exports to industrial countries and the UNCTAD records of nontariff barrier application. Table 5.3 shows the value of exports from a sample of 35 individual developing countries to the United States, EEC, and Japan, and also indicates coverage by four major types of NTBs; export restraints, quotas, licensing, and variable levies. Since it was desired to observe the incidence of NTBs on countries relying on primary product or manufacturers exports, the major petroleum exporting countries were excluded from this analysis. Appendix tables 1 to 3 provide a further breakdown of NTB coverage on individual developing country exports.

As shown in Table 5.3, nontariff barriers are applied to almost $13 billion, or about one-third of these countries' total exports. However, there is considerable variation on an individual country basis. Mauritius has over 90 per cent of its exports (primarily sugar) covered by NTBs, while Thailand and Cuba have less than 10 per cent coverage. Also, the types of NTBs primarily applied vary considerably from country to country. Hong Kong has about $1·2 billion, or 50 per cent of its total trade subject to export restraints, while variable levies are applied to almost 40 per cent of Argentina's exports. Overall, licensing and quotas are the most prevalent type of NTBs facing these countries covering almost $7·5 billion, or about 20 per cent of total exports, while export restraints are applied to slightly less than $4 billion. Since this selection of countries was randomly drawn, and also includes many of the major

LDC exporters, the aggregate coverage ratio of 32·3 per cent is probably a reliable approximation to total non-petroleum exporting LDC trade subject to these four types of nontariff barriers.[17]

Overall, what evidence emerges from the NTB inventories concerning the application of nontariff restraints in industrial markets? In a number of different studies, investigators have come to the following conclusions. First, nontariff barriers are generally concentrated in industrial or agricultural sectors which may be considered politically or economically sensitive in that they have high inputs of low skilled labour. Second, correlations between frequency or coverage indices and nominal tariffs suggest that product groups enjoying a high rate of nontariff protection are often subject to relatively high tariffs. These findings indicate that tariffs and NTBs are frequently applied in a way that their individual protective effects reinforce each other. The fact that four types of NTBs: quotas, levies, licensing and export restraints, cover approximately one-third of developing country trade also accents the importance of these measures.

The pattern of results emerging from the NTB inventories have special implications for the developing countries. For example, in a recent study by Walter and Chung (1972) the authors note that nontariff barriers result in significant variations in their relative impact on foreign suppliers, particularly as between developed and developing countries. One reason cited for this regressive effect is that the NTBs tend to be applied most frequently to products in which the developing countries at present have or are establishing a comparative advantage, and because the impact of individual NTBs tends almost uniformly to bear more heavily on LDC suppliers. Results of a series of six product studies by Allen and Walter (1970) also conclude that there are disproportionate applications of such measures as quantitative import restrictions, liberal or quasi-automatic licensing procedures, public and quasi-public procurement, and indirect tax and border adjustments on developing country suppliers.[18] Indeed, the authors estimate that in the absence of NTBs on the groups studied, a 1968 LDC trade base of $486 million would have been 50 to 70 per cent higher. Although qualifying their results, Allen and Walter suggest that this range may be interpreted as an indication of the order of magnitude involved in estimates of the restrictiveness of NTBs, particularly in sectors such as agriculture, on the export performance of developing countries.

A CRITIQUE OF THE INVENTORY APPROACH

Since much of the discussion in this chapter, as well as previous investigations, has drawn heavily on the inventory approach to NTB analysis, it is useful to review some of the advantages and potential deficiencies of this procedure. Because an inventory, such as that maintained by UNCTAD, provides concise systematic records of the frequency and types of NTBs applied by industrial nations, there is no doubting the utility of maintaining these records. However, there are limitations to all NTB inventories which make it difficult to draw strong conclusions from these records. While the following comments focus on specific problems encountered with the UNCTAD data base, they are also relevant for other inventories such as that maintained by the United States International Trade Commission.

Definitional problems

A preceding section of this chapter suggested a definition and classification scheme in which NTBs were categorised by type, and by the mechanism through which they exercised their trade restrictive effect. A key point in this definition was that measures, to be classified as NTBs, must clearly *discriminate* against foreign producers and have an adverse differential effect on these units.[19] Since individual developing countries are employed as reporting units for the UNCTAD inventory, it is crucial that they employ a clear and consistent definition concerning nontariff restraints. However, after an item-by-item analysis of the entries, it seems that some irrelevant material may have been incorporated in the inventory.[20]

As a case in point, health and sanitary regulations are among the most frequently cited 'restraints' for United States imports of primary and processed agricultural products. The frequency with which this restriction is reported is largely explained by the fact that producers in LDCs do not prepare produce in accordance with minimum standards acceptable for the importing nation. Since they find their own products barred, this is reported in the inventory as a trade barrier.

The basic question is, of course, whether the regulations are being differentially enforced, i.e., whether they raise the costs of foreign producers relative to domestic units. Based on a detailed analysis of foreign and domestic requirements for numerous entries in the inventory, there appears to be little evidence for the differential cost hypothesis since foreign firms are merely being required to maintain the same standards domestic producers must satisfy before being permitted market access. While these regulations involve increased costs associated with compliance, these costs also fall on domestic producers so there is generally no differential adverse competitive effect for foreign producers.[21]

The whole question of differential costs is crucial to the definition of NTBs, yet this factor may have been neglected in some other entries in the inventory. For example, state trading is listed as an NTB for various products in Japan and several European countries, yet without evidence to the contrary there is no *prima facie* case for doing so. In fact, there may be reasons for arguing that state control of imports lowers costs of foreign firms since this procedure centralises and standardises the number and requirements of importing units. Furthermore, dealing with a state agency, instead of a large number of independent units, may lower costs through possible reductions in required sales and service personnel, centralisation of information on import requirements and prices, and standardisation of products. For many of the items involving state trading (alcoholic beverages, tobacco, and grains) domestic concerns are required to deal with the same organisation. Thus, without proof to the contrary, the crucial element of differential treatment or costs is missing.[22] Similar considerations may make some commodity agreements and related policy measures questionable as NTBs. While there is no doubt that such measures could be enforced in a manner that produces adverse cost differentials or discriminates in purchasing policy, detailed supporting evidence to this effect is generally not provided. Rather, these measures appear to have been almost automatically incorporated in the inventory once the practices have been identified.

The reporting units

Since data comprising the UNCTAD inventory are primarily supplied by developing countries, it is of paramount importance that: (1) LDCs have a clear and consistent notion of what constitutes a nontariff barrier, and (2) the LDCs are aware of the nature of the restriction responsible for limiting their penetration of industrial markets. While the first premise has been questioned, there is reason to believe that the second need not always hold.

With the wide variety of measures that can restrain trade, it is doubtful that an LDC, with imperfect knowledge of the industrial markets, will necessarily have the capability to identify the primary factors responsible for limiting market access. In some cases, the immediate and apparent barrier—say, packaging regulations—may be far less important than factors such as special tax concessions, subsidies to domestic producers, or differential transportation charges which, although hidden, may exert more of a prohibitive effect than the highly visible barrier. If the developing countries do not have accurate information concerning these internal measures, then the *apparent* reported NTB may only be a minor element in the total protection for a commodity. Further, without complete information concerning the internal domestic policies of industrial nations, LDCs may not be able to identify the nontariff measures which are in fact restricting their imports. In these cases, the trade barrier will not be included in the inventory simply because it was not visible to the reporting unit. As noted by the United States Tariff Commission (1974, p. 24), proper identification of nontariff restraints is a major problem in any attempt to construct an NTB inventory.

> Nontariff charges on imports were second only to quantitative restrictions in the number of complaints received in the Tariff Commission's survey of trade barriers. This is perhaps because, like quantitative restrictions, these charges are more highly visible and directly restrictive than many trade barriers.

Technical aspects

If an inventory of nontariff restrictions is to be used for current analysis of trade problems, practical considerations dictate that the information be up-to-date. However, unlike the case with tariffs, where data are usually current, verification, tabulation, processing and other prepara-tory requirements necessitate a delay before this information is available to analysts. For example, in preparing its NTB inventory the US Tariff Commission (1974, p. 49) admitted that,

> The period during which this report has been in preparation has been one of rapid and radical change in international trade, and upheaval in the monetary world. Since the beginning of 1971, Japan has dismantled or relaxed a large number of import and other restrictions which had been a source of aggravation in U.S. trade relations with that country. The United States found itself placing a temporary surcharge on virtually all dutiable imports, and later quotas on exports of products which it had vigorously promoted in foreign markets for many years. Important agreements controlling world trade in textiles were negotiated. The United States removed long-standing limitations on its imports of petroleum. In a research task of

the magnitude necessary for this report, it was simply not practical to continuously update and assemble information in order to reflect all the numerous changes in the trade barriers being catalogued.

Since some nontariff restraints have the characteristic of changing frequently, reliance on an NTB inventory may unduly focus on measures applied two or more years in the past. Experience with the UNCTAD inventory over the 1970s suggests that this is the approximate interval by which the data lag behind the current situation.

An additional problem is that there are normally difficulties associated with the coverage of any inventory. For example, UNCTAD tabulates only about ten broad types of NTBs. Such measures as production subsidies, differential exchange controls, border and use taxes, marketing restrictions, as well as the whole range of restrictive business practices, are not catalogued due to lack of information. It therefore seems possible that the limited listing of NTBs may give a misleading picture of the *overall* distribution of nontariff restraints or their frequency of application.

A final problem centres on the fact that there is no *a priori* basis for believing that any tabulation, coverage, or frequency index of nontariff barriers offers insights into the actual trade restrictive effects of these measures. Yet this question is crucial if trade negotiators are to establish priorities for removal of different restraints. Frequency or coverage indices need not prove adequate for this task since the overall *ad valorem* equivalents for several NTBs may be less than that of a single restriction whose effect is almost prohibitive. However, if recorded frequency of application or coverage is not directly related to incidence, then the inventory approach has the potential to misdirect attention from areas where NTBs exert their most restrictive effect on trade flows. The conclusion which emerges is that supplementary information on the *restrictiveness* of NTBs must be generated to properly evaluate information in the inventories. A forthcoming section argues that international price differentials hold considerable promise as such supplementary measures.

AGRICULTURAL PROTECTION: AN EMPIRICAL ANALYSIS

In contrast to the deficiencies of the inventory approach for evaluating nontariff barriers, there are certain product-sectors where more appropriate empirical procedures have been employed. One such area is agriculture where a considerable body of quantitative information has become available. Using this data, this section focuses on the extent and magnitude of agricultural protection in industrial countries. Particular attention is devoted to the European Economic Community's protectionist policies since these measures have been the subject of considerable controversy in recent multilateral trade negotiations.

The Common Agricultural Policy

The EEC's Treaty of Rome created the Common Agricultural Policy as a vehicle for achieving the specific objectives set forth in Articles 38–40: to create a common market in agricultural products, increase agricultural efficiency, provide a fair standard of living for the agricultural community, stabilise markets, ensure security of supply, maintain reasonable prices for consumers, and develop world trade harmoniously. To achieve these ends, an intricate system of protectionist devices and production aids has evolved over the last decade. This system, which now covers more than 90 per cent of total EEC, agricultural output, involves a mass of market regulations, including schemes for internal price support, external protection measures (e.g., tariffs and levies) and production subsidies.[23] However, none of these measures need operate independently. For example, the degree of external protection required to keep domestic prices competitive with world prices varies inversely with the support provided by production subsidies.[24]

While regulations differ according to commodities, the basic philosophy of the Common Agricultural Policy regarding internal price support and external protection has evolved out of the 1962 regulations for marketing of grains. The three key elements of this programme are as follows;

(a) A basic target price (P_t) is established each year in advance of the following crop year. This price is intended to serve as a guide for producers in allotting future acreage. Since transportation charges influence price differentials within the EEC, the target price is set as the delivered cost-insurance-freight price in Duisberg, Germany. This location was chosen since it represents the greatest grain deficit (i.e., production minus consumption) region in the EEC.

(b) An intervention price (P_i) is the price guaranteed to producers. More than 400 intervention and marketing centres have been established throughout the EEC, and these stand ready to accept all quantities of cereals offered at this floor price. While there is variation on a product-by-product basis, the intervention price is generally not more than 10 per cent below the target price.

(c) Threshold prices (P_h are used to insulate domestic EEC prices from fluctuations in world price (P_w) levels. The threshold price is equal to the basic target price minus transport costs from a fixed port of entry to the centre of largest deficit. Imports from non-EEC countries are then subject to a variable levy that equals the excess of the threshold price over the world price.

The interconnections between these various prices and the functioning of the levy system can be best expressed in symbolic form. In equation 5–4 below, the target price is established at a certain fixed level k. Equation 5–5 shows the relation between the intervention price and the target price, while equation 5–6 indicates that the threshold price is equal to the target price minus internal (EEC) transport charges. The key to the system, equation 5–7, shows that the variable levy fluctuates to maintain equality between world and domestic EEC prices.

$$P_t = k, \tag{5-4}$$
$$(P_i - 0 \cdot 1 P_t) \leqq P_i \leqq P_t \tag{5-5}$$
$$P_h = P_t - T_d \tag{5-6}$$

and,

$$L_i = P_t - (P_w + T_d) \tag{5-7}$$

where $L_i \leqq 0$.

Evaluation of the relationship shown in equation 5–7 indicates how variable levies operate to restrict demand for foreign agricultural products. By incorporating a variable charge (L_i) into the delivered price of imports, the system maintains foreign prices at or above those received by domestic producers. When levies are positive they hold demand for imported agricultural products below levels that would prevail in their absence.

While the above demonstrates how variable levies restrain import demand, these charges can also have an adverse destabilising effect on natural fluctuations in world agricultural prices. As indicated by equation 5–7, levies exercise this destabilising effect by moving counter to world price changes. As an illustration of the potential variability of import levies, Table 5.4 shows changes which occurred for some key agricultural products over the interval 1967–71. Thus, while the Common Agricultural Policy serves to ensure stability for domestic producers, it does so by augmenting the instability in foreign producers'

Table 5.4 Estimated *Ad Valorem* Equivalents of the European Economic Community's Variable Levies over the period 1967–71 (percentages)

Commodities	Ad Valorem *equivalent of variable levy*[1]			
	1967–8	*1968–9*	*1969–70*	*1970–1*
Soft wheat	90·7	95·4	114·4	89·3
Durum wheat	62·6	67·9	80·9	82·0
Rye	68·9	79·3	78·0	72·4
Barley	62·5	97·0	102·9	46·0
Oats	54·4	84·3	76·9	42·4
Maize	65·5	77·9	59·1	40·8
Sorghum	61·0	89·0	66·8	49·2
Rice, husked but not broken	18·0	38·1	85·5	110·2
Rice, broken	0·0	18·5	46·9	60·4
Raw sugar	—	232·4	169·2	110·0
White sugar	—	329·3	252·8	155·3
Olive oil	24·1	14·1	6·5	4·5
Pork	43·7	71·0	76·0	53·3
Eggs	34·2	52·0	53·2	37·2
Eviscerated chickens	22·9	30·6	29·9	23·5
Eviscerated turkeys	23·8	32·5	33·2	26·0
Butter	—	526·2	535·8	214·2
Fatted cattle	—	43·3	22·4	20·7
Calves	—	2·6	0·0	1·1

[1] Yearly averages of levies expressed as percentages of average c.i.f. import prices. The yearly averages relate to the period 1 August–31 July, except for rice (1 September–31 August), sugar (1 July–30 June), and olive oil (1 November–31 October).

Source: Calculated from the EEC, *Marchés Agricoles*, various issues.

prices by increasing the inelasticity of world demand curves. The Common Agricultural Policy can have other disruptive effects on world trade flows. For those items produced in surplus, the CAP provides for disposal of the excess through export subsidies. Such disposal can displace exports from LDCs or other producer nations.

Variable levies: an empirical evaluation

A point which follows from the previous analysis is that the trade effects of variable levies are related to the ratio P_t/P_w. Thus, the higher the EEC target price is set above world levels, the greater the *ad valorem* incidence of levies on imports, and the larger the curtailment of potential import demand.

For information on these *ad valorem* rates, a General Agreement on Tariffs and Trade (1971) document was used. Essentially, this study approximated *ad valorem* rates for the variable levies (N_L) by tabulating revenues from these charges as a percentage of the total value of imports,

$$N_L = \Sigma L_i Q_i / \Sigma P_i Q_i \qquad (5\text{–}8)$$

where P_i and Q_i are prices and quantities of individual items imported into the EEC over the period 1969–70. In general, these ratios were computed for each six-digit BTN item to which a levy is applied. However, in some cases these import charges were set at levels sufficient to restrict trade with the result that an *ad valorem* incidence could not be estimated.

Table 5.5 illustrates the importance of variable levies for products classified in SITC 0 (food and live animals) and SITC 4 (animal and vegetable oils). Shown here is the percentage of trade in each two-digit SITC group covered by levies, as well as similar information on the tariff lines subject to these charges. For purposes of comparison, both the average *ad valorem* tariff and levy rate are shown, as well as their joint protective effect. Finally, EEC imports from developing countries are also shown for each two-digit SITC group.

Perhaps the most striking feature in Table 5.5 concerns the relative height of the average nominal tariff and average *ad valorem* equivalent of the variable levies. In SITC 0, for example, a nominal tariff of 18 per cent is coupled with levies which average about three times this figure. Only in the case of SITC 06 (coffee, tea and spices) is the incidence of variable levies less than that for tariffs. The primary reason for this departure is a tariff that averages 50 per cent. Much the same picture concerning the relative importance of these import charges is observed in SITC 4 (animal and vegetable oils), where average tariffs of approximately 8 per cent are coupled with levies of 24 per cent.[25] On an overall basis, these groups enjoy protection of about 60 per cent from tariffs and levies, with roughly two-thirds of the total from levies.

A product-by-product comparison shows that total nominal rates of protection facing a large proportion of these agricultural products are extremely high. For example, when levies are combined with tariffs the nominal rate for dairy products and eggs is over 170 per cent. Cereals and preparations face a combined trade barrier of almost 70 per cent, while nominal rates of protection for meat and sugar are both about 50 per cent. While these figures pertain solely to the EEC, empirical studies for other European countries also show that *ad valorem* equivalents for variable levies may frequently exceed 50 per cent or more for meat, dairy and cereal products.[26]

TABLE 5.5 Estimated Rates of Nominal Protection for the European Economic Community's Agricultural Products from both Tariffs and Variable Levies

SITC	Description	EEC coverage by levies Tariff lines	1974 value of trade ($ m)	Nominal protection (%) Tariffs	Levies	Total	1974 Imports from LDCs ($ m)
0	Food and live animals						
00	Live animals	33·4	1828	11·8	18·2	30·0	37
01	Meat and meat preparations	39·5	188887	18·1	30·4	48·5	523
02	Dairy products and eggs	29·4	892	18·4	152·9	171·3	2
03	Fish and fish preparations	0·0	0	12·8	—	12·8	298
04	Cereals and preparations	41·9	355330	15·2	52·1	67·3	698
05	Fruits and vegetables	8·2	91936	16·4	37·1	53·8	1927
06	Sugar and honey	38·5	97075	53·1	12·0	65·1	804
07	Coffee, tea and spices	6·9	0	10·8	51·0	61·8	2834
08	Feeding stuff for animals	8·4	11	5·4	56·0	61·4	788
09	Miscellaneous food preparations	13·4	8	19·2	47·3	66·5	23
1	Beverages and tobacco						
11	Beverages	0·0	0	27·0	—	27·0	127
12	Tobacco manufactures	0·0	0	61·4	—	61·4	340
4	Animal and vegetable oils						
41	Animal oils and fats	9·6	14	3·5	31·8	35·3	58
42	Processed vegetable oils and fats	15·8	16640	11·4	39·2	50·6	1111
43	Processed animal oils and fats	11·2	0	7·5	1·1	8·6	21

Source: Alexander J. Yeats and Gary P. Sampson, 'An Evaluation of the Common Agricultural Policy as a Barrier Facing Agricultural Exports to the European Economic Community', *American Journal of Agricultural Economics* (February 1977), p. 102.

While the beverage and tobacco group is not subject to levies, protection from tariffs has been substituted. For example, tobacco manufactures face an average tariff of over 60 per cent, while a nominal rate of 27 per cent is applied to beverages. In assessing this latter figure it should be noted that transportation costs for such items may also constitute a high percentage of product price. Thus, tariff protection for bulky, low-value products need not be set as high as for other items since freight costs provide a natural barrier. The overall impression that emerges from Table 5.5, however, is that artificial protectionist measures such as tariffs and levies have been set at very high levels and constitute an imposing barrier to LDC trade in agricultural products.[27]

Effective protection of agricultural products

While the previous analysis provided an overview of the coverage and importance of variable levies, it told nothing about the influence of these charges on the protection of value added in a production process. Yet, as Chapter 4 demonstrated, this may be of key importance since it indicates the extent to which the foreign (LDC) producers must operate with direct costs lower than their EEC counterparts in order to penetrate this market.

Table 5.6 shows the estimated effective protection rates for these agricultural products and also indicates nominal rates of protection. To assist in evaluating these results, ERP estimates derived separately from tariffs and levies are given, as well as that for their combined effect. In addition, the table shows average nominal and effective rates for these products.

Perhaps the most striking feature in Table 5.6 concerns the relative importance of tariffs and levies as sources of protection against imports. For the nine farm-gate products, an average tariff rate of 14 per cent already presents an imposing trade barrier, yet the additional nominal protection from levies (45 per cent) is roughly three times this figure. Much the same pattern is observed for the processed agricultural products as an average tariff rate of 18 per cent is combined with a nominal rate for levies of 75 per cent. Only in one case out of the twenty-three products with joint coverage (meal and groats) is the nominal tariff rate higher. Altogether, the evidence from these comparisons suggests that variable levies are a far more important source of protection for agricultural products than current MFN tariffs.[28]

Similar conclusions concerning the relative importance of tariffs and levies emerge from comparisons of the effective protection rates. For the farm-gate products an average effective tariff rate of 30 per cent is

Table 5.6 Comparison of Nominal and Effective Rates of Protection for Selected Agricultural Products in the European Economic Community

Description	Nominal rate (%) Tariffs	Levies	Effective rate (%) Tariffs	Levies	Total
Farm gate products					
Oats	13·0	84·2	25·8	177·9	203·7
Rye	16·0	75·8	32·1	160·0	192·1
Wheat	20·0	73·0	40·6	154·1	194·1
Rice	16·0	34·5	32·1	72·8	104·9
Maize	6·0	34·1	10·7	72·0	82·7
Sheep	14·8	—	33·7	−42·7	−9·0
Swine	15·8	26·4	37·7	34·4	72·1
Poultry	12·0	15·9	25·5	3·8	29·3
Bovine animals	15·2	16·0	34·9	5·0	38·9
Meat products					
Bovine meat	20·0	64·2	38·2	215·2	253·4
Pig meat	20·0	30·4	36·7	52·9	89·6
Mutton	20·0	20·0	39·3	80·0	119·3
Poultry meat	18·0	23·3	38·5	51·9	90·4
Preserved fruits and vegetables	26·0	26·8	62·5	199·2	161·7
Grain products					
Corn flour	8·0	45·3	10·4	85·6	96·0
Wheat flour	25·0	76·4	98·9	206·8	305·7
Other flour	8·3	37·5	−2·8	41·9	39·1
Rolled cereal flakes	26·9	33·4	95·4	19·5	114·9
Meal or groats	23·0	17·3	75·6	−51·2	24·4
Roasted and puffed cereals	8·0	24·9	−14·9	−52·2	−67·1
Fodder	14·8	35·2	61·2	62·8	134·0
Macaroni and spaghetti	12·0	43·7	6·7	50·6	57·3
Dairy products					
Cheese	23·0	82·5	58·8	217·2	276·0
Butter	21·0	328·0	76·5	1244·2	1322·7
Condensed milk	21·3	98·5	44·3	290·1	334·4
Tobacco products	87·1	—	148·5	—	148·5
Leather products	7·0	—	21·4	—	21·4
Vegetable oils					
Soybean oil	11·0	—	148·1	—	148·1
Groundnut oil	7·5	—	92·9	—	92·9
Coconut oil	8·0	—	70·3	—	70·2
Average	18·2	56·1	49·3	134·1	158·1

Source: Alexander J. Yeats and Gary P. Sampson, 'An Evaluation of the Common Agricultural Policy', *American Journal of Agricultural Economics*, 59 (February 1977), p. 104.

coupled with effective protection of 63 per cent from levies. However, in the case of livestock, variable levies on grains and other basic feeds raise producer costs and reduce effective protection below corresponding levels for tariffs. A similar pattern emerges for some of the processed grains (i.e., meal and groats, puffed cereals, etc.,) where levies on inputs artificially inflate production costs. On an overall basis, effective protection from levies averages 134 per cent, roughly two-and-a-half times the effective tariff rate. However, certain key products such as meat, cereals, fruits and vegetables face an average effective protection rate of 150 per cent or more, with the major portion of this protection associated with variable levies.[29]

Application of other nontariff restraints
While the preceding sections empirically evaluated trade barriers posed by the EEC's tariffs and variable levies, there are a variety of other nontariff trade restrictions applied to agricultural imports by the Community. Unfortunately, it has been difficult to quantitatively assess the influence of these measures since *ad valorem* equivalents have not yet been calculated. However, a tabulation does show the variety of protectionist devices used to control imports.

Using information drawn primarily from the UNCTAD nontariff barrier inventory, Table 5.7 shows the types of NTBs applied to these processed agricultural products or their inputs. The impression that emerges from this tabulation is that an extensive system of controls has been established to regulate or limit foreign competition for domestic producers. While variable levies are applied to fourteen of these three-digit SITC product groups, the table shows that quotas or other quantitative restrictions are used with an almost equal frequency. Seasonal prohibitions are also employed to bar imports of certain commodities in periods when the domestic crop is being harvested. Table 5.7 also shows that special licensing arrangements are used for controlling imports of nine of the three-digit products, while state trading is employed for regulating imports of certain meat and cereal products.

TRADE EFFECTS OF AGRICULTURAL PROTECTION

Due to the comparative advantage developing countries have in the production of many agricultural commodities, recent studies at UNCTAD and the United Nations Food and Agricultural Organ-

TABLE 5.7 Nontariff Trade Barriers Facing Agricultural Exports to the European Economic Community

SITC	Description	Nontariff trade restraint[1]
001	Live animals	PHS, R, SP
011	Meat, fresh chilled or frozen	HS, PHS, DL, GQ, R, MP, ST, VL, SP
013	Meat in airtight containers	HS, PHS, R, DL, VL, SP
022	Milk and cream	VL
031	Fish and fish preparations	SP, Q, BQ
041	Wheat and meslin unmilled	VL, SP
042	Rice	VL, SP
043	Barley unmilled	VL, SP
044	Maize unmilled	VL, SP
045	Other cereals unmilled	VL, SP
046	Meal and wheat flour	VL, SP
047	Meal and cereal flour	VL, SP
048	Cereal preparations	VL, SP, ST, HS
051	Fresh fruit and nuts	HS, GQ, BQ, SP, R, SR, DL, SR
052	Dried fruit	DL, HS, Q
053	Preserved fruit	BQ, Q, HS, DL, GQ, VL, SP
054	Preserved vegetables	SP, BQ, DL
055	Vegetable roots and tubers	SP, HS, BQ, GQ
061	Sugar and honey	VL, SP, PHS, L, HS, BQ
071	Coffee	SP
072	Cocoa	SP
073	Cocoa food preparations	SP, HS, BQ, LL, DL
074	Tea and maté	SP
081	Feeding stuff for animals	VL, SP
099	Food preparations, n.e.s.	SP, L, BQ, DL
112	Alcoholic beverages	R, SP, HS, ST, DL, LL
122	Tobacco manufactures	DL, GQ, SP
422	Fixed vegetable oils	SP
431	Processed oils	SP, R, DL

[1] Restrictions applied in whole or in part to the SITC group. The key to these symbols is as follows: PHS, HS = prohibitions due to health and sanitary reasons or health and sanitary regulations; SP = special import preferences for states associated with the EEC; Q = quotas (method unspecified) or bilateral quotas; GQ = global quotas; DL, LL = discretionary or liberal licensing of imports; L = import licensing (method unspecified); VL, MP = variable levy or other minimum import price restriction; R, SP = restrictions (method unspecified) or special seasonal restrictions; and ST = state trading.

Source: Alexander J. Yeats and Gary P. Sampson, 'An Evaluation of the Common Agricultural Policy', *American Journal of Agricultural Economics* (February 1977), p. 107.

ization (FAO) have attempted to project the changes in LDC trade and economic activity which would occur under alternative levels of protection in industrial markets. While uncertainties as to the exact nature of supply and demand responses to price changes make the results highly tentative, the findings are useful in that they provide a guide to potential orders of magnitude involved.[30]

The effects of simulating the removal of agricultural protection on world market prices for key agricultural products are summarised in Table 5.8. These results suggest that world prices would increase for all items due to higher demand, but the largest increases (over 50 per cent) are projected for sugar and rice. Increases of between 20 to almost 40 per cent are estimated for wheat, coarse grains, meat (except pork), poultry and milk, but vegetable oils and pork are expected to increase by only about 10 per cent. On a regional basis, removal of the high rates of domestic protection should result in lower consumer prices in Europe and Japan, with prices rising by 16 to 24 per cent in the United States, Australia and New Zealand. To a large extent the price increases in these nations, and the developing countries (up 4 per cent), are associated with the predicted export expansion as low cost producers strive to satisfy demand in previously protected markets.

The higher world prices for agricultural commodities would further stimulate production and exports in those developing countries with a positive trade balance in these items.[31] According to the UNCTAD-FAO model, the export gains to LDCs as a group are likely to be on the order of $17 billion per year, which corresponds roughly to 20 per cent of nonpetroleum exports. Additional export earnings of this magnitude would produce a considerable stimulus to development programmes, and to the improvement of general living standards. Table 5.9 also shows that developed countries (primarily the United States, Australia, Canada and New Zealand) would increase export earnings by about $18 billion, while the trade of the socialist countries would rise by about $3 billion.

The UNCTAD-FAO econometric model is also capable of estimating feedback effects from the liberalisation of agricultural protection on gross domestic product. According to these estimates, removal of agricultural protection would increase total (world) GDP by about $84 billion which is about a 2 per cent increase over recent levels. Nearly half this gain ($37·6 billion) is expected to accrue to the developing countries, with this increase representing about a 5 per cent expansion of domestic product. Thus, liberalisation of agricultural protection in industrial countries would produce extensive beneficial economic

TABLE 5.8 Estimated Price Effects of a Hypothetical Removal of Agricultural Protection (percentages)

Producer region	Wheat	Rice	Coarse grains	Sugar	Vegetable oils	Beef and veal	Mutton and lamb	Pig meat	Poultry	Milk	Average
World market price	28	64	24	54	11	20	32	10	28	37	29
Domestic prices:											
Developing countries	0	23	4	29	9	13	–17	10	–2	–36	4
Oceania	28	–32	24	54	11	20	32	10	–46	37	34
United States	29	–7	25	–17	11	20	7	10	24	–17	16
European Community[1]	–47	–22	–21	–24	–27	–40	–54	10	–45	–18	–19
Other West Europe	–14	–13	–20	–15	7	–29	–16	–17	–17	–12	–5
Japan	–54	–75	–58	–46	–38	2	–32	–13	28	–22	–32

[1] Excludes the United Kingdom.

Source: UNCTAD, *Agricultural Protection and the Food Economy*, Research Memo. No. 46 (Geneva: United Nations, 30 March 1972).

TABLE 5.9 Estimated Economic Effects of a Removal of Agricultural Protection in Industrial Markets ($000 million)

Country group	Total GDP	Value added in agriculture	Agricultural export earnings
World	84·3	65·4	38·5
Developed countries	26·4	19·0	18·0
Low-cost producers[1]	13·4	na	10·1
High-cost producers[2]	12·0	na	7·8
Developing countries	37·6	27·7	17·2
Socialist countries	20·3	18·7	3.3

[1] Australia, Canada, Denmark, Ireland, New Zealand, South Africa and the United States.
[2] Western European countries excluding Denmark.

Source: Data derived from UNCTAD, *Agricultural Protection and the Food Economy*, Research Memo. No. 46 (Geneva, 30 March (1972)).

effects in LDCs, which could act as a stimulus to development and growth.

THE EVIDENCE FROM PRICE DIFFERENTIALS

As noted, international comparisons of trade restraints are complicated by the problem that these barriers take different and not easily comparable forms. However, as an approximation of their magnitude a GATT panel of experts headed by Gottfried Haberler suggested that 'the degree of protection can be roughly judged by the extent to which the price paid to the producer exceeds the world price for importers'.[32] While it is acknowledged that there are difficulties associated with differences in supply and demand elasticities, the effect of subsidies, differentials in national tax schemes, etc., several researchers have found the GATT approach provides a useful vehicle for quantifying international trade restrictions.[33]

While most previous studies have relied on general import statistics for computation of domestic-world price comparisons, these data sources suffer from the deficiency that it is impossible to accurately determine the portion of the observed differential attributable to quality and other non-price factors. In large part, this deficiency can be rectified by drawing on a closely controlled sample of international price statistics of the sort compiled by Business International. Since this data source provides cross-country price information for close to 90 individual items, whose characteristics have been clearly specified before drawing the sample, it appears unlikely that observed price differentials should be strongly influenced by product variation.

In making comparisons, the problem of how to derive the 'world price' for each product included in the sample arose. Following the procedure employed by Pryor (1966), the lowest price observed in the 15 developed countries included in the sample was used as a proxy for this variable. This approach means, therefore, that trade barriers are measured on a relative rather than an absolute basis. Nevertheless, the comparisons should not differ greatly from those derived on an absolute basis since several countries generally had low tariffs, and few apparent nontariff restrictions on sampled items.

While computed price differentials were used for the comparisons, it was felt appropriate to make several adjustments in the data. For example, cross-country price relatives will be influenced to the extent that different countries rely on sales, excise and other forms of direct taxation. Since these charges influence the overall level of a country's prices without having an adverse differential effect on foreign goods, an effort was made to estimate and remove the incidence of these taxes from the data. In addition, the nominal tariff for each item was subtracted with the expectation that the residual would reflect the influence of the country's nontariff trade restrictions.[34]

Empirical results

Table 5.10 summarises results from these international price comparisons for 21 two-digit BTN product groups which had important export positions for developing countries. Tariff averages have also been computed for each group so these figures could be compared with the price differentials. In addition, the table shows NTB frequency indices as well as averages for each data set.

In terms of overall results, Japan and Sweden have the highest price differentials (70 per cent), followed by France and the United States at 40 and 35 per cent respectively. However, these figures still incorporate the influence of international transportation charges which work to maintain price differences between markets. Using estimates of United States and German freight costs as a guide, it appears that the average relatives in Table 5.10 should be reduced by about 10 to 15 percentage points to arrive at a 'pure' NTB residual.[35] The resulting figures suggest, therefore, that the average *ad valorem* NTB for these products is in the

TABLE 5.10 Comparison of Nominal Tariff Rates, *Ad Valorem* Incidence and Frequencies of Nontariff Barriers Applied to Two-Digit BTN Groups; Selected Industrial Countries, 1973 (percentages)

		France			Japan			Sweden			United States		
			Nontariff barriers			Nontariff barriers			Nontariff barriers			Nontariff barriers	
BTN	Product group	Nominal tariff	Reported frequency	Price relative[1]	Nominal tariff	Reported frequency	Price relative	Nominal tariff	Reported frequency	Price relative[1]	Nominal tariff	Reported frequency	Price relative[1]
02	Meat products	15	100	67	13	17	161	0	83	133	7	50	54
03	Fish and seafood	10	33	34	8	100	72	0	66	64	1	100	78
04	Dairy products	18	83	15	35	50	10	0	17	23	10	66	0
07	Vegetables and products	12	66	30	12	17	72	7	—	80	13	100	50
08	Edible fruits and nuts	14	46	22	14	23	180	4	23	51	7	69	128
09	Coffee, tea and spices	10	—	83	6	—	155	1	—	100	1	30	38
10	Cereals	13	100	11	11	43	16	0	—	12	5	43	0
11	Mill products	21	100	40	25	44	158	0	100	85	8	33	57
15	Fats and oils	7	29	0	8	—	50	0	18	94	5	12	0
17	Sugar and products	38	20	9	66	20	68	18	80	51	6	80	23
18	Cocoa and products	12	17	0	16	—	157	5	∵	47	2	50	2
19	Cereal preparations	10	63	94	23	—	92	19	—	113	5	88	47
20	Vegetable preparations	23	86	63	23	57	76	11	14	54	13	86	3
22	Beverages	28	50	0	47	10	0	8	40	73	5	20	19
24	Tobacco and products	74	100	0	352	100	0	14	—	72	20	—	0
48	Paper and products	7	5	67	13	—	33	2	—	75	5	—	39
60	Knitted goods	13	100	92	16	—	44	15	100	15	28	100	61
61	Apparel	15	100	16	19	—	0	15	36	0	21	100	32
64	Footwear	17	—	28	18	17	11	14	—	62	15	—	70
82	Tools and cutlery	7	—	41	12	—	59	6	—	121	17	7	82
92	Instruments and recorders	6	—	25	10	—	32	7	—	41	6	—	0
	All item average	17	45	40	32	19	70	7	22	70	9	41	35

[1] Price relative after removal of *ad valorem* tariffs and taxes.

Source: Alexander J. Yeats and Vernon Roningen, 'Nontariff Distortions of International Trade: Some Preliminary Empirical Evidence', *Weltwirtschaftliches Archiv* (January 1977), pp. 616–17.

range of 20 to 25 per cent for the United States and France, and 50 to 60 per cent for Japan and Sweden.

Of course, there is considerable variation on a product-by-product basis. In France, an average trade-weighted price relative of 40 to 50 per cent for food and grains is almost entirely accounted for by transport charges and levies, while freight costs appear to account for almost all of the Japanese textile differential. However, even when a transport factor of 15 to 20 per cent is assumed for Japan's imports of foods and grains, an NTB residual of 70 to 90 per cent still exists. A residual of 35 to 45 per cent remains for apparel in both the United States and France, while this figure is about 15 per cent in Sweden. Table 5.11 presents estimates of NTB residuals after *ad valorem* tariff, tax, and transport components have been subtracted from the international price relatives.

NONTARIFF BARRIERS: A SUMMARY APPRAISAL

Although reliable empirical evidence concerning the influence of nontariff barriers on developing country trade is more difficult to secure than comparable information on tariffs, this chapter presented data from which summary conclusions could be drawn. From an analysis of NTB frequency and coverage indices, it was established that nontariff restraints are concentrated in specific industrial or agricultural sectors which might be considered politically or economically sensitive. Investigations also reveal positive significant correlations between NTB indices and nominal tariffs, which indicate that products enjoying high rates of tariff protection also have a high incidence of nontariff protection. Several studies also show that NTBs tend to be applied most heavily on products in which the LDCs have, or are establishing, a comparative advantage. The importance of only four types of nontariff barriers; quotas, variable levies, voluntary restraints, and licensing, was established by tabulations showing that these measures are applied to approximately one-third (by value) of exports from non-OPEC developing countries.

Attempts to project the potential volume of LDC trade which would occur in the absence of nontariff measures suggest that the losses to developing countries are staggering. A recent UNCTAD-FAO investigation indicated that removal of agricultural protection in industrial markets would increase LDC export earnings by about $17 billion, and that the gross domestic product of these countries would rise by 5 per cent. Studies by the UNCTAD Secretariat, as well as a

TABLE 5.11 Estimation of an NTB Residual through Removal of *Ad Valorem* Tariffs, Transport Costs, Taxes, and Variable Levies from International Price Relatives

		Estimated nontariff barrier *Ad Valorem* equivalent[1]			
BTN	Description	France	Japan	Sweden	USA
0	Food products[2]	35 (0)	90	50 (20)	25
1	Grains and products[3]	35 (0)	70	45 (10)	20
2	Beverages, tobacco, etc.	10 (0)	10	45 (35)	15
6	Apparel	35	5	15	40
	All items	30 (10)	45 to 50	60 (40)	25

[1] Figures in parentheses exclude estimated *ad valorem* equivalents for variable levies.
[2] Meat, fish, dairy and vegetable products.
[3] Excludes sugar and cocoa.

Source: Derived from Alexander J. Yeats and Vernon Roningen, 'Nontariff Distortions of International Trade: Some Preliminary Empirical Evidence', *Weltwirtschaftliches Archiv* (January 1977), p. 620

procedure involving decomposition of international price relatives, suggests that *ad valorem* equivalents for NTBs applied to textiles, clothing and shoes are of the same magnitude as those for agriculture. Using this information in connection with import demand elasticities suggests that the developing countries experience a further trade loss in the range of $15 to 20 billion. However, there are other highly protected product groups such as basic manufactures, instruments, electronic components, some steels and nonferrous metals, which are also of export interest to developing countries. Significant trade and development objectives would undoubtedly be realised if market access for LDCs were improved in these sectors.

6 Liberalisation of Tariff and Nontariff Barriers

Empirical analyses of existing tariff and nontariff barriers clearly establish that these artificial trade control measures have a major retardation effect on the exports of developing countries. Furthermore, evidence exists that these restraints are applied in a discriminatory manner against LDCs. Tariffs on developing countries' manufactured goods are typically higher than average in most industrial markets, and have been reduced less in multilateral trade negotiations. Similarly, the frequency of nontariff barrier application is often highest on goods which are of special interest to developing countries. Evidence also suggests that stacking, or multiple application of nontariff restraints, is frequently used to restrict imports from LDCs.

Due to the magnitude of the potential benefits which could accrue to developing countries, the Programme of Action for the Establishment of a New Economic Order calls for a major effort aimed at 'improved access to markets in developed countries through the progressive removal of tariff and nontariff barriers'. Improved market access is also a theme that runs through much of the recent thinking on development planning and policy. Indeed, it is acknowledged that liberalisation of trade restraints in industrial markets is a key precondition if LDCs are to achieve the Lima Declaration's target of 25 per cent of world industrial production by the year 2000. Removal of trade restraints is also a cornerstone of the Integrated Programme for Commodities which envisions both expanded LDC commodity trade and a shift in exports from primary to processed goods.

While there is general agreement on the need for improved market access for developing countries, the key question centres on how this is to be accomplished. This chapter considers measures which would work toward this end. For tariffs, solutions within the framework of the multilateral trade negotiations are discussed including the effects of alternative tariff cutting formulas. Programmes through which LDCs could lower the incidence of tariffs on their exports, such as the Generalised System of Preferences and Off-shore Assembly, are also evaluated. Action in the area of nontariff barriers is considered through measures to reduce the major trade restrictions facing developing countries' exports.

TARIFF REDUCTIONS IN INDUSTRIAL COUNTRIES

A primary objective of the Multilateral Trade Negotiations convened under GATT's auspices is to reduce industrial tariffs. However, there are various procedures whereby tariffs might be lowered. The general approach has been for negotiating parties to advance proposals or formulas for the reduction of import duties. These are then subject to study, discussion, and modification in an effort to reach agreement on the adoption of a general formula which is satisfactory to all parties.[1]

The economic implications of alternative tariff-cutting formulas can be assessed with standard partial equilibrium trade models. Assuming a constant foreign supply price, the domestic price of imports in the consuming market will be equal to the foreign price plus the tariff. If the foreign price is set equal to unity, the domestic price can be taken as one plus the *ad valorem* tariff. However, if import duties are reduced the percentage change in the consumer price can be expressed as a ratio of the change in the import tariff to a value of one plus the original duty. Assuming that the tariff originally was not prohibitive, this ratio approximates the extent to which the tariff reduction lowers the domestic price of imports.[2] One then needs to determine how responsive the quantity demanded will be to the price change in order to project the expected change in trade values. That is, one needs to know what the price elasticity of import demand may be and how responsive domestic supply is.

Empirical measurement of import demand and supply elasticities involves difficult statistical problems with the results subject to some margin of error. However, since numerous investigations have been conducted, a plausible range of demand elasticities for individual countries and commodity groups can be determined.[3] The estimation of supply elasticities is much less exact and there is little reliable information on this parameter. Nevertheless, if values can be approximated, it is possible to determine how imports would change in response to alternative tariff reductions, and what the effects on other economic variables should be. Given this information, one could assess choices among alternative tariff reduction formulas.[4]

Tariff reduction formulas

The simplest and most direct tariff cutting formula calls for a linear reduction of existing duties. Since this approach lowers all tariffs by the same percentage, high duties are reduced by a larger absolute amount than low tariffs. If t_0 is the initial MFN rate and t_1 is the duty after the tariff cut, the linear reduction formula can be expressed as,

$$t_1 = \alpha t_0 \qquad (6\text{--}1)$$

where α can range between zero and one in tariff cutting negotiations. However, since the United States delegation is not empowered to negotiate tariff reductions exceeding 60 per cent, values of alpha below 0·4 have not generally been considered for the Tokyo Round Negotiations. A modified version of this equation establishes a floor at 5 per cent. Lower tariffs would not be cut, nor would existing duties be reduced below the 5 per cent level.

As an alternative, several delegates to the negotiations have recommended that tariff harmonisation be given more attention. To accomplish this objective, the Japanese have proposed a formula which combines the features of *linear reduction with harmonisation*. This approach can be expressed as,

$$t_1 = \alpha t_0 + \beta \qquad (6\text{--}2)$$

where parameters alpha and beta would be subject to negotiation. Beta accomplishes harmonisation through larger percentage reductions on high than on low duties. The larger the parameters the smaller the absolute and percentage cuts in tariffs. However, the harmonisation objective is not as strongly fulfilled as it might be under some alternative formula since the new tariff rates are a linear function of the original duties.

The European Economic Community's proposal is specifically directed toward the problem of *tariff harmonisation*. This formula,

$$t_1 = t_0 - t_0^2/100 \qquad (6\text{--}3)$$

reduces each duty by a different percentage, with the largest percentage cuts borne by the highest tariffs. To achieve maximum benefits, the EEC suggests the formula be reapplied in three successive stages. In some cases, this proposal would produce a very different distribution of tariffs from that which originally existed since descending values for import duties will occur where current tariffs exceed 50 per cent.

Among other proposals the Swiss formula,

$$t_1 = \alpha \sqrt{t_0} + \beta \qquad (6\text{--}4)$$

has the maximum effect in reducing *tariff disparity* since the square root operation sharply lowers high tariffs. While the parameters are to be negotiated, values of 2 for alpha and 0·5 for beta have been discussed. When applied to duties under 30 per cent, this proposal produces deeper cuts than harmonisation equation 6–3, yet smaller than those associated with a 60 per cent linear reduction.

Another widely discussed formula is the Canadian three-part proposal which provides for elimination of import duties under 5 per cent, linear cuts on tariffs between 5 and 20 per cent, while rates above 20 per cent would be reduced to this maximum. One difficulty with this suggestion is that a linear formula which affords sizeable tariff reductions in the 5 to 20 per cent range will produce a discontinuity at 20 per cent. In other words, this proposal could create a gap in the tariff schedules with no duties between (say) 16 and 20 per cent.

To summarise the implications of these formulas, Figure 6.1 graphs the relations between current and new tariffs under proposals character-ised by equations 6–1 to 6–4. The values employed for these equations' parameters are in the range of those discussed during the Tokyo Round negotiations. To compare these results with achievements of the Kennedy Round, the relationship for a 40 per cent linear cut is also shown. While there were exceptions, this is approximately the average tariff cut achieved during the Kennedy negotiations.

While a tariff cutting strategy for developing countries depends on interrelations between the tariffs their exports face (both MFN and special preferences), the position of competitors, and the LDCs' capacity to increase production, depth of tariff cut constitutes a useful first approximation to a choice among alternative strategies. As indicated in Figure 6.1, the deepest MFN cuts in the 5 to 10 per cent tariff range are offered by the linear reduction formula followed by the proposal combining linear reductions with harmonisation (equation 6–2). Even with the 5 per cent floor, the linear cuts yield deeper tariff reductions than either the square root or staged-harmonisation formula.

In the middle range of tariffs between 10 to 25 per cent, the 60 per cent linear formula again produces the deepest reductions while the 40 per cent alternative is a relatively poor performer. At duties over 13 per cent, both the square root and linear reduction plus harmonisation

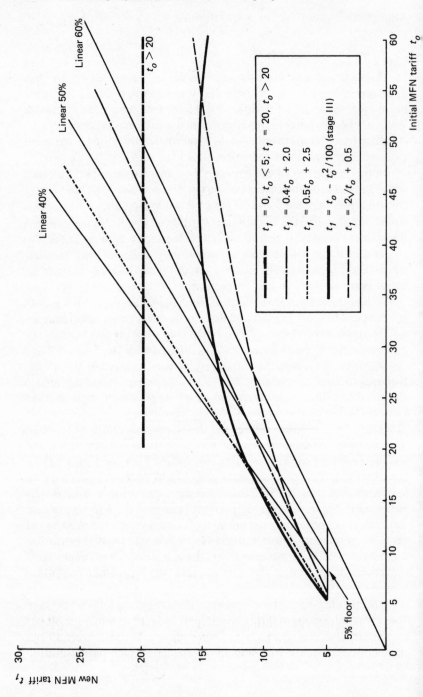

formula, yield deeper cuts, with the differential rising to 5 percentage points for tariffs of 25 per cent. Both these alternatives are also superior to a 50 per cent linear reduction when tariffs exceed 25 per cent, although the margins of difference are lower. Above 30 per cent the square root formula or the EEC harmonisation proposal offer the largest MFN cuts. The Canadian suggestion, that tariffs over 20 per cent be reduced to this level, yields smaller reductions than either of these alternatives, although it produces deeper cuts than the linear 60 per cent formula.

Table 6.1 attempts to determine if a clear-cut optimal choice for developing countries exists among the alternative tariff-cutting pro-posals. The table shows both the 1974 value of manufactures exported from a selection of developing countries to the United States, and the average (trade-weighted) MFN tariff applied to these products. To assess the implications of alternative tariff cutting formulas, new MFN rates are calculated when three different proposals—a linear 40 per cent cut without floor, linear reduction with harmonisation, and the square root formula—are applied to each country's tariff average. To assist in evaluating this information, the lowest resulting tariff among the three alternatives is marked with an asterisk.[5]

The results show the conflict of interest that can result among developing countries. At average tariffs as high as the 28·5 per cent rate facing Costa Rica's exports, the square root proposal is most attractive, producing a new average duty about 6 points lower than the linear 40 per cent formula. For countries facing average tariffs of under 10 per cent, however, the results are reversed with the linear formula offering the greatest margins. Countries in the middle range of tariffs, like Hong Kong, Taiwan, Singapore, etc., would find the linear reduction with harmonisation proposal yields the deepest cuts although the margins of difference are relatively small.

Aside from the disparity in individual developing countries' interests; there is a further problem complicating any choice among alternative tariff-cutting formulas. Since the early 1970s, industrial nations have extended preferential tariffs to LDCs with a view toward stimulating industrialisation in these countries. As such, any evaluation of tariff-cutting formulas must balance the possible adverse consequences of reductions in preferential tariff margins against the potential expansion due to lower MFN tariffs. Before turning to this complication, the implications and functions of these special preference programmes should be noted.

TABLE 6.1 Analysis of the Influence of Alternative Tariff Cutting Formulas on Average Import Duties for Manufactures Exported From Selected Developing Countries to the United States

Exporting country	1974 exports		Revised tariff with alternative formula[1]		
	Value ($m)	Weighted MFN tariff	Linear 40%	Linear reduction with harmonisation	Square root
Costa Rica	13·1	28·5	17·1	13·4	11·2*
Mauritius	1·0	27·7	16·6	13·1	11·0*
El Salvador	19·0	23·7	14·2	11·5	10·2*
Philippines	153·3	20·2	12·1	10·1	9·5*
Korea	897·4	18·5	11·1	9·4	9·1*
Thailand	43·4	18·1	10·9	9·2	9·0*
Taiwan	1301·5	16·7	10·0	8·7*	8·7*
Sri Lanka	1·9	16·3	9·8	8·5*	8·5*
Hong Kong	1148·2	15·4	9·2	8·2*	8·3
Dominican Republic	13·6	12·3	7·4	6·9*	7·5
Singapore	304·4	11·3	6·8	6·5*	7·2
Honduras	6·7	11·1	6·7	6·4*	7·2
Brazil	281·4	7·9	4·7*	5·2	6·1
Israel	195·2	7·3	4·4*	4·9	5·9
Mexico	1472·1	7·0	4·2*	4·8	5·8
Argentina	57·8	6·4	3·8*	4·6	5·6
Egypt	9·5	5·7	3·4*	4·3	5·3

[1] Linear 40 per cent formula without a 5 per cent floor. Values of alpha and beta are 0·4 and 2·0 respectively for the linear cut with harmonisation formula, while values of 2·0 and 0·5 have been used for the square root formula.

* Minimal tariff value among alternative formulas.

THE GENERALISED SYSTEM OF PREFERENCES

One of the major proposals advanced at the first meeting of the United Nations Conference on Trade and Development in 1964 was that developing countries should receive tariff preferences for their man-ufactured exports to industrial markets. The reasoning behind this suggestion was that if LDC exports faced lower duties than similar products from industrial nations, this would convey competitive advantages that could stimulate industrialisation and growth. As conceived by the United Nations, these Generalised System of Pre-ference (GSP) schemes should have three characteristics: (1) the preference should be global or *generalised* in favour of developing countries; (2) they should be extended without reciprocity; and (3) preferences should be non-discriminatory and not differentiate between individual developing countries. At present, all of the Organisation for Economic Cooperation and Development countries as well as some countries of Eastern Europe have initiated GSP schemes.

An attraction of the GSP concept is that it can exert a positive two-fold stimulus to developing country exports. First, preferences should have a *trade-diversion* effect. Specifically, favourable tariff margins can result in imports from non-beneficiaries being displaced by those from preference receiving countries. Secondly, *trade creation* results from the reduced tariffs on imports from beneficiary countries. Since lower tariffs reduce the landed price of imports, some domestic production is displaced in the preference granting country. The full magnitude of the trade creation and diversion effects depends on the depth of the preferential tariff margins and the extent of product coverage.[6]

While the developing countries had envisioned broad schemes with wide product coverage and few limitations, what emerged were programmes of narrow scope with numerous practical deficiencies. For example, not all manufactured goods qualify for special tariff treatment under the GSP. Japan and the United States have excluded textiles, while the EEC offers limited coverage if the exporting country abides by export restraints in the Multifibre Arrangement. Other important items omitted from most schemes are petroleum products, shoes, and industrial raw materials, while the United States also excludes watches, specialty steel products, and some items subject to escape clause action. Furthermore, most plans normally exclude processed agricultural products falling in BTN Chapters 1–25 so the GSP fails to cover this broad range of important developing country exports. Since a number of schemes have only been authorised to run for ten years, the time frame for the plans is also rather limited.

Another drawback is that most industrial countries place narrow limits on the value of imports qualifying for GSP treatment. Both the EEC and Japan classify manufactures into product groups and place ceilings on each group's imports qualifying for preferential treatment. After the ceiling is reached, additional shipments are taxed at the normal MFN tariff rate.[7] These provisions create considerable uncertainty about whether given shipments will qualify for GSP treatment since it is normally not possible to determine if these limits have been exceeded until the produce arrives in the export market. This uncertainty reduces the incentive for importers to switch to LDC suppliers since the tariff status of specific shipments cannot be determined precisely. The ceilings may also reduce the incentive for industrialisation which is a basic objective of the GSP. If new investment is undertaken, the resulting output expansion may exceed the group ceiling so additional exports would be taxed at the standard MFN rate.[8]

Aside from ceilings on products and suppliers, certain low income countries are exempted from benefits of the GSP. For example, neither Greece, Spain, nor Portugal, nor member countries of OPEC qualify under the United States programme. Special restrictions also apply to Hong Kong's exports under the Japanese scheme, while the EEC does not grant preferences to the Mediterranean countries or Taiwan. The introduction of the GSP raised another problem for the EEC since members of other special preference systems (i.e. signatories of the Yaoundé and Arusha Conventions plus Tunisia and Morocco) might have found their preferences eroded. However, the EEC excluded the main exports of these countries from its GSP with the result that only 5 or 6 per cent of the associate's trade was affected. Appendix Table 1 shows individual developing countries' exports under the special preferences.

Special rules of origin are another factor limiting the effectiveness of the GSP. In general, these regulations were introduced to guarantee that developing country exports gaining preferential treatment are produced, or substantially transformed in the LDCs, rather than transhipped from excluded sources. These rules of origin limit the amount of imported materials and components that can be embodied in products qualifying for special treatment, and may result in *de facto* elimination of preferences for particular products. For example, under the EEC rules, radios must be produced with locally made transistors. Since few developing countries produce transistors, this eliminates radios from the preference system. Under US regulations, preferential imports must embody 'domestic processing costs plus locally produced materials and components' which exceed 35 per cent of the export value of an item. Such a requirement results in the elimination of items produced under a technology and marketing operation embodying high indirect processing costs such as administrative overheads, selling commissions, executive salaries and profits.[9]

With the various exclusions and limitations, as well as the complex rules of origin, the Generalised System of Preferences has had only a modest expansionary influence on developing country trade. For example, Table 6.2 compares the total value of 1974 exports to the United States, Japan and the EEC by major groups of developing countries with these nations' shipments under the GSP and other special preferences.[10] In addition, a similar tabulation shows a breakdown of these totals in terms of primary product exports (excluding petroleum) and manufactured goods. The average tariff on the GSP products has also been computed to assess the restrictiveness of import duties on the preferential shipments.

On an overall basis, approximately 15 billion dollars, or 10·8 per cent of developing country exports, enter these industrial markets under tariff lines covered by preferences. However, this percentage is somewhat misleading due to the influence of petroleum products which do not normally benefit from preferential access. Preferential entry is intended to almost 30 per cent ($13·7 billion) of the non-oil imports, which represents about 21 per cent of the developing countries' primary product shipments and 46 per cent of their manufactures. However, even though these goods receive preferential rates over other exporters, Table 6.2 shows that the actual tariffs on these products may still constitute a barrier to trade. For example, primary products exported to the European Economic Community under preferences face tariffs which average 7 per cent, while shipments from the fast growing LDC exporters, and developing countries with over $400 per capita GNP, face a rate of about 8·5 per cent. Only in the United States is a zero preferential tariff rate applied to all primary products and manufactures imported under the system.

While the total value of imports covered by the Generalised System of Preferences may appear impressive, a key question concerns the value of *new* trade created by the system. As previously noted, the trade expansion effects of the GSP may be constrained by quotas, ceilings and other limits. Also, Table 6.2 shows that some of the preferential trade flows still face import tariffs in Japan and the European Economic

TABLE 6.2 Imports under the Generalised System of Preferences and other Preference Systems in the EEC, Japan and the USA in 1974 (values in $ billion)

| Export product—LDC group | Total imports from developing countries | | | Imports under preferences | | | | | | |
| | | | | USA | | Japan | | EEC | | |
	USA	Japan	EEC	Value	GSP Rate	Value	GSP Rate	Value	GSP Rate	Special Pref. Rate
All products										
Total developing countries	36·94	32·00	69·03	3·10	0·0	2·49	2·6	9·28	2·1	0·5
Petroleum exporters	17·35	21·72	47·11	0·02	0·0	0·13	3·4	1·50	0·6	0·1
Others	19·59	10·28	21·92	3·08	0·0	2·36	2·5	7·78	2·5	0·6
Fast growing exporters	7·25	2·84	3·58	1·79	0·0	1·27	3·6	1·92	0·6	2·2
Others	12·34	7·45	18·34	1·29	0·0	1·09	1·2	5·86	3·7	0·4
GNP per capita over $400	5·61	0·94	3·92	0·52	0·0	0·13	0·8	1·19	5·0	0·0
$200 to $400 GNP	5·41	5·34	9·99	0·62	0·0	0·82	1·0	3·06	4·1	0·4
Under $200 GNP	1·33	1·17	4·44	0·19	0·0	0·20	2·3	1·61	1·9	0·0
Least developed	0·44	0·17	1·15	0·05	0·0	0·01	2·7	0·46	2·7	0·0
Primary products excl. petroleum										
Total developing countries	10·25	8·42	13·45	1·27	0·0	0·89	1·6	4·68	7·0	0·7
Petroleum exporters	1·22	1·39	1·52	0·01	0·0	0·12	3·6	0·38	4·6	0·2
Others	8·83	7·02	11·94	1·25	0·0	0·77	1·3	4·31	7·3	0·8
Fast growing exporters	1·78	0·69	0·68	0·42	0·0	0·09	5·2	0·31	8·5	3·6
Others	7·06	6·33	11·27	0·83	0·0	0·69	0·8	4·00	7·2	0·5
GNP per capita over $400	1·96	0·72	2·95	0·28	0·0	0·03	1·5	0·59	8·6	0·1
$200 to $400 GNP	4·43	4·73	6·08	0·49	0·0	0·66	0·7	2·46	6·1	1·1
Under $200 GNP	0·67	0·88	2·23	0·06	0·0	0·06	0·4	0·94	6·5	0·0
Least developed	0·27	0·10	0·77	0·03	0·0	0·00	3·2	0·36	5·1	0·0

Manufactured products									
Total developing countries	7·70	1·98	5·15	1·83	0·0	1·58	3·1	3·42	0·1	0·0
Petroleum exporters	0·14	0·03	0·37	0·00	0·0	0·01	1·4	0·32	0·0	0·0
Others	7·56	1·95	4·78	1·82	0·0	1·57	3·2	3·10	0·2	0·0
Fast growing exporters	5·40	1·38	2·64	1·37	0·0	1·18	3·5	1·52	0·0	0·0
Others	2·16	0·57	2·14	0·46	0·0	0·39	2·0	1·58	0·4	0·0
GNP per capita over $400	0·79	0·16	0·63	0·24	0·0	0·09	0·6	0·43	0·0	0·0
$200 to $400 GNP	0·71	0·26	0·64	0·13	0·0	0·16	1·9	0·52	0·0	0·0
Under $200 GNP	0·66	0·15	0·88	0·08	0·0	0·14	3·1	0·64	0·7	0·0
Least developed	0·17	0·01	0·10	0·02	0·0	0·01	2·5	0·07	3·5	0·0

Source: Computed from Appendix Tables 1 to 3 and internal UNCTAD records.

Community which can constitute a trade barrier. These factors, combined with other restrictions such as the rules of origin, could seriously reduce the trade creation effects which were intended to benefit the developing countries. It is possible that little new LDC trade could result due to the restrictions, while the lower preferential tariff margins may be absorbed as windfall profits by importers.

Although there is some variance in the estimates, most empirical studies suggest that the LDC trade creation effects of the Generalised System of Preferences have been quite small. For example, a study by Clague (1972) estimated that the United States, European Economic Community and Japanese schemes result in an expanded value of LDC exports in the range of $300 to $400 million per year. A more recent analysis by Murray (1973) confirms the minimal effects of the system and concludes that the various institutional constraints reduce the actual trade expansion to around $100 million per year. Thus, the Generalised System of Preference schemes of the United States, European Economic Community and Japan have probably resulted in only a 1 or 2 per cent increase in these countries' nonpetroleum product imports from the developing countries.

OFF-SHORE ASSEMBLY

Aside from the Generalised System of Preferences, there is a second procedure whereby the LDCs can offset tariffs applied to their exports. Specifically, the assembly of components produced in industrial countries constitutes a large and rapidly growing segment of some developing countries' manufactured exports. This activity is encouraged by tariff provisions providing for duty free re-entry of domestically produced components which have been assembled abroad. Thus, if US cloth was exported to Mexico and tailored into clothing, the finished goods could be re-exported to the United States under tariffs which applied only to the value added component of the manufacturing process. These off-shore assembly provisions (OAP), plus the attraction of lower labour costs abroad, have provided a powerful incentive for the establishment of some processing industries in developing countries.

While the intent is similar, variations exist between OAP regulations in the United States and Europe. In the latter case, imported products must fulfil three conditions: they must be made from components exported by a domestic firm on its own account, the components must be processed abroad on account for the exporting firm, and the assembled items must be imported by the original firm. All types of finished goods, as well as forms of processing, are covered by the European OAP provisions.

In the United States, two distinct provisions provide for the import of domestically produced components under reduced tariffs. Tariff code 806.30, which deals with the off-shore assembly of certain metal products, is similar to the European provision except that it is limited to products returned to the United States for further processing. However, approximately 90 per cent of OAP shipments enter under US tariff code 807.00 which permits duty free re-entry of components that do not lose their physical identity in the assembled article. This provision is somewhat more liberal than that of the European countries since the import of components, assembly, and export of fabricated goods can be handled entirely on the account of foreign firms.[11]

Table 6.3 shows the value of off-shore assembly imports by West Germany, Netherlands and the United States as well as the growth rate over 1966–72. For comparison purposes, the rate of increase of non-OAP manufactured imports is given, as well as the percentage of OAP goods in the total. As the table indicates, the increase in off-shore assembly manufactures from LDCs has been very rapid with a compound growth rate equal to 60 per cent in the United States and 36 per cent in Germany. In the United States, OAP shipments actually accounted for 22 per cent of manufactured imports, with Mexico having 43 per cent of the total. About 50 per cent of United States OAP imports originated in South Korea, Hong Kong, Taiwan, and Singapore, while about 6 per cent came from various Caribbean countries.

Since both the Generalised System of Preferences and off-shore assembly provide a means for developing countries to reduce MFN tariffs on exports, comparisons between the two systems are inevitable. One major difference is that relatively few LDCs have been able to effectively utilise the OAP provisions since over 90 per cent of these United States imports originate in 5 advanced developing countries. The fact that Mexico has over 40 per cent of the OAP total indicates the potential importance of proximity to the major industrial markets. Since the attractiveness of the OAP provisions declines with increasing transportation costs, both for the import of components and re-export of fabricated goods, nearness to markets or efficient low-cost transportation is important. In addition, the range of products suitable for this type of manufacture is normally confined to items where unskilled labour is an important input, tariffs are relatively high, and *ad valorem* transportation costs are low. On the other hand, the GSP covers

TABLE 6.3 Imports under Off-shore Assembly Provisions of the Netherlands,
West Germany and the United States

Importing country and origin of imports	1972 value ($m)	OAP Imports % of manu- factured imports, 1972	Compound rate of increase 1966–72	Rate of increase of non-OAP manu- factured imports
Netherlands				
From non-EEC countries	101	3	28	8
From Eastern Europe	31	17	72	10
From non-European countries	16	2	39	2
West Germany				
From non-EEC countries	451	4	19	11
From Eastern Europe	126	17	84	19
From developing countries	156	10	36	11
From Yugoslavia	139	30	35	12
United States				
From all countries	3409	9	24	17
From developed countries	2377	8	18	17
From developing countries	1032	22	60	12

Source: J. M. Finger, 'Tariff Provisions for Offshore Assembly and the Exports of
Developing Countries', *Economic Journal*, 85 (June 1975), p. 366.

a greater range of products and has been utilised by a large number of
developing countries. As such, the benefits from GSP are considerably
broader while the off-shore assembly provisions have been utilised by a
relatively few developing countries for a rather narrow range of
products.[12] However, the OAP items can be exported without limit
while ceilings frequently reduce the effectiveness of the Generalised
System of Preferences.

TARIFF REDUCTIONS AND SPECIAL PREFERENCES

The systems of special preferences complicate the strategy of developing
countries *vis-à-vis* the multilateral trade negotiations. On the one hand,
substantial MFN tariff cuts have the potential to adversely influence

trade by eroding preferential margins. Hence, there may be negative trade effects for these items. However, it is likely that MFN cuts would cover a broader range of products and benefit some developing countries which are excluded from the GSP. Furthermore, MFN tariff reductions normally provide more favourable conditions of access for unlimited trade flows while GSP schemes generally place ceilings on the trade benefiting from preferences.

A key decision that must be made is whether LDCs should pursue a policy aimed at broad tariff cuts, or attempt to preserve preferential margins. This problem is complicated by the fact that the GSP schemes are relatively new and may evolve into a more important trade creation factor than current plans. However, many of the plans have been established with an official lifetime of ten years so there is no way of determining with certainty if they will be liberalised or terminated. Thus, in formulating a tariff strategy important assumptions must be made as to the future of the GSP. If the programmes were liberalised to include additional products of export interest to developing countries there would be important new trade benefits. However, if duties are reduced to a point where important preferential margins no longer exist, the future of the GSP concept becomes very limited.

While the issue is clouded by these uncertainties, some evidence indicates that developing countries are well advised to push for comprehensive MFN tariff cuts rather than attempt to preserve preferential tariff margins. For example, Table 6.4 summarises findings

TABLE 6.4 Projected Costs and Benefits of a 50 per cent MFN Tariff Reduction in the United States, the European Economic Community and Japan (annual trade flows in US $m)

| Cost or benefit for developing countries | Importing Market | | | |
	USA	EEC	Japan	Total
Cost due to erosion of preferential margins	−22·8	−9·1	−0·3	−32·2
Benefit from absence of value limits[1]	43·5	45·0	17·4	105·9
Benefit from broader product coverage[2]	17·6	2·3	7·0	26·9
Benefit to non-beneficiary LDCs	186·0	76·3	5·9	268·2
Net benefits	225·3	114·5	30·3	369·2

[1] Trade creation from MFN tariff cuts on products which do not receive GSP duty-free entry because of ceiling type limits.
[2] Trade creation from MFN tariff cuts on products not covered by the GSP schemes.

Source: R. Baldwin and T. Murray, 'MFN Tariff Reductions and Developing Country Trade Benefits Under the GSP', *Economic Journal*, 87 (March 1977), p. 41.

of a cost-benefit study which contrasted the positive effects of a 50 per cent MFN tariff reduction on developing countries' trade against adverse consequences resulting from erosion of preferential margins. According to these calculations, reductions in GSP margins would mean a trade loss of about $32 million. However, this would be more than offset by expanded MFN trade due to the absence of ceilings on this exchange ($105·9 million), as well as the broader coverage of products under MFN tariff cuts. The most important gains would be made by low-income countries currently excluded from GSP schemes. Overall, broad-based MFN tariff cuts should increase LDC annual trade by about $370 million over a policy aimed at maintaining existing GSP preferential margins.[13]

Given that an optimal trade policy for developing countries is based on pursuance of MFN cuts, the question remains as to a choice among the alternative tariff reduction formulas. As indicated, the potential for conflict of interests exists on this question since the position of LDCs facing high average tariffs may be quite different from that of the medium or low tariff countries. However, evidence suggests that the linear approach has advantages for the LDCs as a group. Experiments by UNCTAD show a 60 per cent linear tariff reduction with elimination of duties under 5 per cent consistently results in larger LDC trade-weighted tariff changes than any one of five alternative tariff cutting formulas. The results of a 50 per cent linear cut are also generally superior although the EEC harmonisation proposal is an attractive alternative. Below the 50 per cent level, the results are mixed with no one formula being clearly superior.[14]

REDUCTION OF NONTARIFF BARRIERS

Efforts to reduce nontariff barriers are complicated by the fact that procedures which have been established for liberalising tariffs are often not applicable. Negotiating reductions on a reciprocal basis may not be practical due to the number of types of NTBs, their diverse forms and relative importance among countries, and the difficulty in measuring their effect on trade. This latter consideration is of special importance since a linear reduction in nontariff barriers cannot be made without fairly precise estimates of the protection afforded by the restraints.[15]

The problems in negotiating reductions in nontariff barriers surfaced during the early stages of the Kennedy Round. Initially, it was decided that the subject of NTBs should be included along with tariffs. As such, one of the four principle subcommittees of the Trade Negotiations Committee was assigned the task of drawing up rules and methods to be employed for liberalising nontariff barriers, while a second was assigned the problem of nontariff restrictions in agricultural trade.[16] After several failures, efforts to formulate general guidelines were abandoned as negotiations shifted to a barrier-by-barrier approach. The final results were meagre with the only agreements being the GATT 'anti-dumping code' and the US offer to end the American Selling Price (ASP) valuation system in return for certain tariff concessions. The ASP agreement was later nullified by the United States Congress.

Since the conclusion of the Kennedy Round, successful efforts to reduce NTBs have been the result of the barrier-by-barrier approach. For example, the GATT Committee on Trade in Industrial Products finalised draft codes of conduct for import licensing, industrial standards, and customs valuation. However, the barrier approach can be frustrated by multiple NTBs on products since the remaining restraints can be adjusted to compensate for the restriction which was removed. In cases where this 'stacking' of NTBs is a problem, a sector or industry approach may be necessary.

The following discussion deals with proposals which have been advanced for reducing nontariff barriers on products exported by developing countries. Since it is thought that quantitative restrictions, variable import levies, licensing, state trading, government procurement, and standards are among the most important NTBs facing developing countries, the discussion focuses on procedures for liberalising these nontariff restraints.

Quantitative restrictions

A key first step toward the liberalisation of trade barriers facing developing countries rests on the principle of a 'standstill' on the imposition of new restraints or the extension of existing barriers. This principle was adopted by the first session of the United Nations Conference on Trade and Development and subsequently incorporated in the International Development Strategy for the Second Development Decade. The basic idea behind the standstill is to freeze barriers on LDC exports in order to halt the spread of protection against these products. By freezing protection levels, the standstill would provide the time and environment for orderly negotiations aimed at dismantling existing trade restraints.

To establish the dimensions of the problem, tabulations should be made of the value of trade subject to quantitative import restrictions.

Ideally, this effort could be incorporated in UNCTAD's data gathering activities on NTBs (see Chapter 5), and result in a periodic progress report on the dismantling of quantitative restraints. Such a report could be used in international forums to apply pressure on states which are lax in liberalising these restrictions. There is also considerable scope for intensification of policy efforts, both within and outside the multilateral negotiations, aimed at dismantling or securing progressive quota increases which could be of considerable benefit to LDCs. Such increases could be automatic (by fixed annual percentage increases), or by a schedule which retains some flexibility concerning the quota enlargements.[17] Related proposals suggest that unutilised quotas be eliminated, and that portions of annual quotas not utilised be extended to the next quota period.

Long-standing quota arrangements frequently tend to freeze newly industrialised states out of established markets. To enable these nations to expand and diversify their trade, immediate provisions should be made through the conversion of bilateral to global quotas. Discriminatory aspects of existing nontariff barriers must also be eliminated. Quantitative restrictions or licensing schemes are sometimes enforced in ways that result in LDCs' being treated less favourably than developed countries. As an individual step in the liberalisation of quantitative restrictions, such discriminatory features of country import classifications should be abolished.

Elimination of quantitative restrictions (i.e., ceilings) which interfere with Generalised System of Preference programmes should be given high priority. Since limited preferential tariffs are extended to many GSP products, the imposition of quantitative restrictions affords double protection, making it difficult for LDCs to expand exports. Extension of LDC preferential treatment to include quantitative restraints should be considered. The Tokyo Declaration calls for 'special and differential' treatment for developing countries as an integral part of the multilateral trade negotiations. One way this could be accomplished is through preferential treatment when existing quantitative restraints are enlarged. Indeed, the GSP principle could easily be extended to cover preferences for LDC exports facing nontariff barriers, just as the present system offers competitive tariff margins. Liberalisation of quantitative restraints may be handled more readily through such a procedure than by other commercial policy proposals.[18] Quantitative restraints are normally not administered in ways that treat all exporters equally, but are allocated according to considerations involving the volume or historical pattern of trade. When restraints are being relaxed, trade could be allocated preferentially to LDCs, possibly with the poorest countries receiving the greatest shares of the enlarged market.

A major effort should be made to negotiate a 'code of conduct' for quantitative restraints which would provide a framework and timetable for dismantling these barriers. Murray and Walter (1977, pp. 415–17) suggest that such a code be established under the auspices of GATT and cover the following points:

—The code should require that GATT be notified of all products to which individual developed countries apply quantitative restrictions, and provide for trade-policy sanctions against countries failing to supply complete information. Required data should include restraint levels, consumption, production, and employment information for the protected industry as well as the reason for the NTB's application. The code should stress that notification does not legitimise the use of these measures, or repeal the GATT regulations concerning their use.

—The code should include explicit recognition that these restraints are justified only as temporary measures to allow time for less costly adjustments. They should not provide permanent protection for an uncompetitive sector (such as textiles) or be used for long-term balance-of-payments problems. Consequently, countries which impose these restraints should be required to announce, at the time of introduction, a time-schedule for phasing out each quantitative restriction.

—Consultation procedures should be established for importing and exporting countries on matters relating to quantitative restraints. In addition, periodic reviews, possibly as a cooperative effort between UNCTAD and GATT, of individual countries' use of these measures should be undertaken and published. These reviews should be made with a view toward liberalisation, elimination, or replacement of existing quantitative restraints. A complaint procedure should be established whereby countries injured by these restraints can seek redress. Penalties should be established for failure to remove or liberalise existing restrictions according to established time-schedules.

—The country imposing the restraint should be obligated to introduce specific domestic measures to facilitate adjustments by the import-competing industries. Ideally, such measures should be designed to ease the transfer of resources from non-competitive industries. To guard against repeated use of restraints, rather than corrective policies, the code should prohibit the re-application of

NTBs on products previously protected without some minimum time interruption.

—General rules for special or differential treatment should be incorporated in any code on quantitative restraints. These should include a statement of intent to supply larger market shares to developing countries. The possible segmentation of LDCs by level of development, in order to allow different degrees of preferential treatment, and *automatic exclusion* of least developed LDCs from all provisions of quantitative restraints should be considered.[19]

Variable levies

Exporters of products covered by variable levies are adversely affected by the resulting price increases for their products in export markets, as well as the uncertainty created by the system. As shown in Chapter 5, *ad valorem* equivalents of these charges may exceed 100 per cent, so the price effects can be very important. Furthermore, frequent changes in the levies make it difficult to agree on export prices. The levies can also have destabilising effects on commodity prices since they make the EEC's and other European countries' demand curves for these items highly inelastic.

Since developing countries are generally acknowledged to have a comparative advantage in the production of commodities, liberalisation of protection afforded by levies is very much in their interests. Aside from the UNCTAD (June 1973) recommendation that developing countries be excluded from these charges, the following specific proposals have been made:

(a) Estimate *ad valorem* equivalents for levies by calculating unit differences between domestic and world prices and reduce these equivalents by fixed percentages over an agreed time schedule.

(b) Binding each levy to a maximum *ad valorem* incidence.

(c) Levy free, or entry at a reduced levy, subject to exporters observing a minimum c.i.f. price.

(d) Differentiation of the height of levies according to individual suppliers' offer price.

(e) Lengthening the interval between changes in values of a levy.

An objective assessment must conclude that proposals calling for the abolition of the levy system have few current prospects for success. Despite intense pressure from the United States, Canada, Australia, and other agricultural exporting nations during the Kennedy Round, the EEC failed to offer any significant liberalisation in its agricultural protection programmes. Since developing countries have much less political leverage, it is unlikely that they will be able to extract concessions on this point when the industrial nations could not.

As an alternative to doing away with the system, the suggestion that products be afforded levy-free entry if exporters observe minimum c.i.f. prices has a special appeal. Since differentials between foreign and EEC internal prices are now collected by Common Market authorities as levies, they represent lost revenues to LDC exporters. Under this proposal, foreign producers would act in conformity with EEC policy and observe unit export prices in line with the common agricultural policy target. Political pressure could be applied to the EEC for such a compromise since the level and stability of import prices would be in harmony with EEC agricultural objectives. Another attraction is that higher prices for LDC agricultural exporters could be an important source of new revenues for development finance. Differentiation of the levies' height according to the offer (production) price of individual suppliers could ease access to EEC markets for developing country exporters who are not low-cost producers. Finally, the recommendation that the levies be fixed for some minimum time interval might reduce some of the existing uncertainties concerning export prices.

A further problem concerns EEC practices for disposal of excess agricultural products in foreign markets. Under the high domestic prices prevailing in the Common Market, agricultural surpluses may be built up which are exported at subsidised prices. These shipments have displaced LDC producers in third markets. Due to the growing proportions of the problem, procedures are required whereby developing countries can secure compensation for market disruption caused by the EEC's disposal of agricultural surpluses.[20]

Import licensing

Licensing requirements may contain various elements that restrict imports. Since licensing is often used to control the volume of imports, many of the proposals for liberalising quantitative restrictions also apply to this NTB.[21] However, differential enforcement of licensing schemes, or complex bureaucratic requirements, can be a serious problem for developing countries. A working group of the GATT Committee on Trade in Industrial Products has prepared a draft text on proposals aimed at simplifying licensing requirements, while the OECD and other international organisations have prepared similar recommendations. The following suggestions are aimed at simplifying licensing requirements and guarding against differential enforcement of these measures. As such, they supplement other proposals for liberalising quantitative restrictions:

(a) Information concerning technical details and formalities for filing applications for licences should be published as far in advance as possible of any opening date for submission of applications. Also, upon request, information should be provided concerning all details of the administration of import restrictions, the import licences granted over a recent period, the distribution of licences among supplying countries, and the names of importing enterprises.

(b) Forms and procedures for application and renewal should be as simple as possible, while a reasonable period should be allowed for submission of licence applications.

(c) Licensing systems should not be designed or operated in a manner such as to prohibit or discriminate between sources of imports.

(d) Foreign exchange for the payment of imports subject to licensing should be available to licence holders on the same terms as to importers of goods not requiring import licences.

(e) The authority granting licences should take into account whether licences previously issued to applicants have been utilised. Also, licences should not be issued for goods in such small quantities as to make imports uneconomical.

(f) The validity of the licence should not be so short as to prevent imports from countries situated at a distance, taking into account transport and communications conditions.

(g) In the event of refusal, licence applicants should be informed of the reasons for refusal and should have the right to appeal. A reasonable allocation of licences to new importers should be made taking into account the desirability of issuing licences for goods in economic lots.

State trading and government procurement

As noted in Chapter 5, state trading *per se* may not be considered a nontariff barrier to trade. However, if applied in a discriminatory manner, state trading or government procurement can influence the volume and geographic distribution of imports. In the absence of some control, a state trading organisation could frustrate the intent of many GATT regulations without involving the government in overt violations. For example, such an organisation could discriminate between foreign sellers solely on the basis of source, or charge a resale mark-up on imports higher than that for comparable domestic products, thereby producing the same anticompetitive effect as a protective tariff. By limiting foreign purchases, it could also restrict the quantity of merchandise imported. Due to the potential for abuse, standards are needed to ensure that state monopolies do not discriminate between foreign and domestic goods, nor between sources of imports. This is in fact the intent of GATT regulations concerning state trading organisations.

The definition of state trading and applicable rules of behaviour are set forth in Article XVII of GATT, and in a note on the articles relating to quantitative restrictions.[22] The GATT rules consist of three obligations for state trading establishments: (1) the nondiscriminatory treatment of trade; (2) the limitation of implicit quantitative restrictions; and (3) the provision of information regarding products imported and exported by state enterprises.[23] The limitation on the implicit rates of protection, set forth in paragraph 4 of Article II, applies equally to import monopolies as well as state trading enterprises.

The GATT regulations concerning nondiscrimination may be met by conditions set forth in Article XVII, paragraph 1. Essentially, discrimination is prohibited by the stipulation that state trading organisations choose among foreign suppliers 'solely in accordance with commercial considerations'. Price protection for domestic products was proscribed by requiring that the resale mark-ups for imports must not exceed the country's tariff rate on the product if bound in the tariff schedule. Finally, commercial operations producing effects equivalent to quantitative restrictions are prohibited by the requirement that the organisation import sufficient quantities to satisfy full domestic demand.

From the viewpoint of developing countries, there are several limitations in current regulations governing state trading. While the GATT rules have theoretical appeal, there have been few practical tests of the enforceability of these articles. This may have been due to a preoccupation with tariffs and other trade barriers, but the accession of Poland and Romania to GATT should accent the need for viable regulations to deal with state trading organisations. While the *intent* of existing GATT rules seems sufficient to protect developing countries, formal procedures must be developed for the enforcement of these regulations.[24] Specifically, tests are needed to determine if GATT's 'commercial policy criteria' and rules on price mark-ups are sufficient to prevent state trading organisations from discriminating between foreign and domestic sources of supply, or establishing *de facto* quotas.

A more serious problem for LDCs stems from the fact that the major state trading countries are not covered by GATT regulations. As noted in Chapter 3, trade control measures by the USSR have adversely influenced both the level and structure of imports from developing countries.[25] Efforts should be made to formalise trade relations between centrally planned and developing countries in a protocol along the lines of the GATT regulations with a view toward expanding and diversifying LDC trade opportunities.

Government procurement practices can also lead to related problems of trade discrimination and distortion. Existing domestic regulations, procedures and practices involving government purchasing may hamper or distort international trade by favouring domestic over foreign producers. To control against potential abuses, codes of conduct have been proposed for government procurement operations. The following suggestions by Baldwin are illustrative of the points which should be covered in such a code.[26]

General Principles:

1. Government purchasing policies (including those of state-owned or state-controlled enterprises) should be based on the principle of nondiscrimination against foreign products and suppliers of foreign products.

2. Purchasing procedures should be set forth in a public code, designed and administered to assure nondiscriminatory treatment of foreign suppliers and foreign products in the solicitation of bids and the awarding of contracts.

3. Existing measures in conflict with these principles and their derogations should be phased out by multilateral agreement, and no new discriminatory or preferential measures should be introduced.

4. Confrontation, justification, and reporting procedures should be established to ensure that all signatories bring their procurement policies and procedures into conformity with the articles of the agreement.

Derogations:

5. Discrimination for reasons of national security or public health should not be greater than necessary to achieve the legitimate objectives of domestic purchases for these purposes.

6. Preferential measures introduced as parts of programmes to foster economic development in particular regions, to aid small or medium sized firms, or to assist new or ailing firms, should be temporary and limited in scope. These measures should have no more differential effect on foreign suppliers than on domestic suppliers who do not qualify for special assistance.

(a) Any preferences granted should take the form of a uniform percentage price differential.

(b) Countries adopting new or strengthening old preferential measures should make compensating reductions in other tariff or nontariff trade restrictions unless the measures can be justified as economically efficient. Countries should report periodically on the continued need for such measures and the progress made toward their eventual elimination.

7. Preferential measures designed to aid specific groups, such as handicapped persons, should be of very limited importance to trade.

Applications of General Principles:

8. Public bidding should be employed to the greatest feasible extent. Notices to bidders should be widely distributed and should be centralised in one national publication.

9. Where selective tendering is used, publicity efforts should be made, when appropriate, to ensure that all interested foreign suppliers have an opportunity to apply for inclusion on the selective list of bidders.

10. Single tendering should be used only when other procedures are clearly inappropriate or inapplicable—for example, when the contract is for classified matter, the demand for goods is urgent, there is only one supplier of the commodity, or the administrative costs of public bidding would be excessive compared to the value of the product.

11. Procurement notices should include sufficient information to enable suppliers to decide whether they are interested in bidding and should contain an address where detailed information can be obtained. The technical and time-limit requirements should not be such as to discriminate unnecessarily against foreign firms.

12. Residence within the purchasing country should not be a condition for bidding except when clearly needed for reasons of national security, public order, or public health.

13. Bids should be judged objectively on the basis of normal commercial considerations.

14. All bids under public and selective tendering procedures should be made public except where such action would clearly lead to the possibility of collusion among suppliers, would result in the disclosure of confidential information, or would result in significant administrative difficulties.

15. A rejected bidder should upon request be informed in sufficient detail why his bid was rejected.

Standards

Wide varieties of imported manufactures and semi-manufactures are subject to industrial and safety standards, packaging and labelling requirements, or health regulations. Although the intent of these measures is normally not protection of domestic industry, many are of specific concern to developing countries. Technical standards can lead to higher costs through the need to discover the appropriate regulations of the importing country, to demonstrate compliance with the standards, and to produce different varieties of the same product for various markets.[27] Moreover, certification and approval procedures may hamper access by foreign suppliers if the responsible body employs different enforcement procedures for foreign producers, charges prohibitive fees for testing and inspection, or delays granting certificates of conformity.

To alleviate many of the trade problems associated with standards, GATT has prepared a draft Code of Conduct for Preventing Technical Barriers to Trade. Essentially, this Code seeks to secure agreement of signatories on the following points:

(a) not to prepare, adopt or apply standards with a view toward creating obstacles to international trade;[28]
(b) to use *international* standards as much as possible;
(c) to provide information on standards;
(d) to provide technical assistance to developing countries to enable them to bring their exported products up to required standards.

Since developing countries frequently have serious problems in meeting all the diverse standards which exist in various export markets, a key provision of the code relates to the use of international standards:

Where mandatory standards are required and relevant international standards exist or their completion is imminent, adherents shall use them, or the relevant parts of them as a basis for the mandatory standards, except where such international standards or relevant parts are inappropriate for the adherents concerned.

The Code requires that adherents notify the GATT Secretariat of any changes in standards, test methods, quality assurance schemes, and take into account comments from other adherents. Section 16 of the Code provides for the establishment of an 'enquiry point' in each country to respond to questions concerning local standards.

Certain provisions of the Code are designed to assist the developing countries in meeting technical standards. Under Section 17, adherents to the Code are obligated to advise other signatories, 'especially developing countries', in the preparation of mandatory standards, and 'shall use all reasonable means within their power to arrange for co-operation between their standards and quality assurance regulatory bodies and those of developing countries'. Also, signatories are required to advise other adherents and consider requests for technical assistance regarding the establishment of regulatory bodies to oversee the Code's operation, and the establishment of procedures by which mandatory standards can best be met.

NONRECIPROCITY AND THE DEVELOPING COUNTRIES

While the previous discussion proposed a variety of trade liberalisation measures which could produce substantial benefits for developing countries, the problem of how these measures might be implemented was only briefly considered. In practice, there appear to be at least three different approaches that developing countries could take in pursuance of the these objectives.

First, there are areas where a coincidence of interest exists between developing and some developed countries on matters concerning trade liberalisation. For example, the United States, Canada, Australia and a number of other commodity exporting developed countries have a common interest with LDCs in reducing the highly restrictive agricultural protection systems which characterise most European countries and Japan. Similarly, developed and developing countries often share a common goal of securing viable international agreements or codes governing the use of trade restrictive measures such as quotas, export restraints, or standards. Where areas of joint interest occur, a combined negotiating position for LDCs and some industrial countries may be feasible. For example, Japan or the Common Market countries may be more responsive to demands for liberalised agricultural trade if faced with a joint front of developing and developed countries. Unfortunately, the two groups often view each other as adversaries on many issues and the cooperative approach has been little used in practice.

For several reasons, the political power of developing countries in international forums seems to have strengthened in recent years. The price and production policies pursued by the Organization of Petroleum Exporting Countries demonstrated how susceptible industrial countries may be to interruptions in supplies of raw materials. Aside from petroleum, LDCs are important producers of other commodities such as iron ore, bauxite, copper, manganese, tin, and rubber. Although the policy has some potentially important drawbacks, the LDCs' control of raw material production could be used to enhance these countries' negotiating position in the MTN. Another recent development is worthy of consideration. Several developing countries, like India, Korea, Mexico, Singapore, Hong Kong, and Brazil, have extended their range of manufactures and now produce high quality metals, machinery and other capital goods. Thus, other LDCs now have a choice between traditional suppliers of this equipment, or these newly industrialised developing countries. Trade relations between the producers of manufactures and other LDCs should be encouraged since this may convey a number of important benefits. Aside from lower prices as a result of increased competition, the potential loss of export sales could make the developed nations more receptive to the LDCs' trade liberalisation proposals.

In the current Tokyo Round, as well as in previous trade negotiations, developing countries have clung to the principle of nonreciprocity. Due to the nature of their internal development problems, the LDCs argue, it is not feasible to offer reciprocal tariff reductions in return for those of the developed countries. Since the LDCs were in fact trying to negotiate tariff cuts in their export markets without offering concessions in return, their bargaining power was, at best, very weak.

Several developments suggest that the developing countries should now re-examine this aspect of their approach to the multilateral trade negotiations. First, the fast-growing exporters of manufactures have reached a stage in their industrialisation where reciprocal tariff concessions could be used to enhance their bargaining position. Such an offer would undoubtedly be more attractive if these advanced LDCs were able to extend a common package of trade liberalisation proposals in the MTN sessions. Second, a study by Balassa and Associates (1971) demonstrated that the levels of protection in developing countries are often very high and may actually be working against industrialisation and growth. A realisation that such was the case led to Argentina's recent decision to make extensive unilateral cuts in the level and structure of its external protection. A review of other developing countries' protectionist profiles should be undertaken with a view toward identifying sectors where MTN concessions could be made, and where lower levels of protection would act as a stimulus to industrialisation and growth.

7 Shipping Problems of Developing Countries

Economists have long realised that access costs play an important role in limiting developing countries' exports to industrial markets. However, while most previous empirical studies aimed at evaluating these barriers have focused on artificial trade control measures such as tariffs, transportation costs pose a formidable restraint for some items. The neglect of transportation costs may have been due to a lack of available data on their incidence, or to the (erroneous) assumption that these charges are exogenous variables outside the direct control of policymakers. Another reason for the neglect may have been the presumption that the influence of transport costs, relative to tariff or nontariff barriers, is generally small.

Recent studies have indicated that many of these views concerning transport costs will have to be altered. For example, using a special United States Census Bureau sample, one study demonstrated that average *ad valorem* transportation and insurance costs for United States imports exceeds most-favoured-nation tariffs.[1] Furthermore, it was shown that the incidence of shipping costs is higher on goods exported by developing countries than on developed nations' exports. Several other studies have contested the view that transportation costs are not subject to some degree of policy control. The United Nations Conference on Trade and Development (1969) (1973c) has conducted inquiries into the liner conference rate-making process and concluded that shipping charges are essentially administered prices which can discriminate against weaker elements. Thus, policy measures designed to strengthen the bargaining position of developing countries relative to shipowners deserve attention. In addition, a study of Australian shipping costs by Sampson and Yeats (1977) has shown that a nation adversely located in relation to its major markets may have considerable latitude in offsetting transport costs by changing the composition of its exports. Finally, to the extent that transportation costs are inflated by

TABLE 7.1 World Seaborne Trade in 1965 and 1974 by Types of Cargo and Shares of Groups of Countries in Terms of Goods Loaded

Groups of countries	1965 Crude petroleum	1965 Petroleum products	1965 Dry cargo	1965 Total all goods	1974 Crude petroleum	1974 Petroleum products	1974 Dry cargo	1974 Total all goods
World total (millions of tons)	622·0	240·0	812·0	1674·0	1497·0	335·0	1433·0	3175·0
Percentage share of each category of goods in the total	(37·2)	(14·3)	(48·5)	(100·0)	(45·3)	(10·2)	(44·5)	(100·0)
				(percentages)				
World total	100·0	100·0	100·0	100·0	100·0	100·0	100·0	100·0
Developed market economy[1]	0·1	23·0	53·5	28·6	1·7	29·3	62·1	31·4
Southern Europe	—	0·3	2·4	1·2	n.a.	n.a.	n.a.	n.a.
Socialist countries	4·6	8·9	8·2	6·9	2·9	10·0	7·2	5·5
Developing countries	95·3	67·8	35·9	63·3	95·4	60·7	30·7	63·1
Africa	16·0	1·7	10·6	11·3	16·6	2·7	7·6	11·2
Asia	58·4	23·3	9·2	30·0	71·4	23·0	8·6	38·5
Latin America	20·9	42·8	15·4	21·6	7·4	35·0	13·8	13·1
Oceania	—	—	0·7	0·4	—	—	0·7	0·3

[1] Excludes southern Europe in 1965.

Source: UNCTAD, *Review of Maritime Transport, 1976* (TD/B/C.4/169) (Geneva: United Nations, 25 March 1977).

inefficient port facilities, or a failure to achieve existing economies of scale in shipping, the policy alternatives are obvious.

OCEAN TRANSPORT AND DEVELOPING COUNTRIES

As an indication of the dependence of developing countries on ocean transport, Table 7.1 provides a breakdown of the origins of world seaborne trade, in terms of tons loaded, in 1965 and 1974. As indicated, the LDCs originated over 60 per cent of total tonnage in both years with the share of developed market economy countries running at about 30 per cent.[2] However, the developing country figures are inflated by crude petroleum shipments where they accounted for about 95 per cent of total tonnage. Nevertheless, the developing countries register an impressive 31 per cent of total dry cargo loadings in 1974, even though this share fell about 5 points from the 1965 level. In large part, the decline relates to the worldwide recession in 1974–5 which had more of an adverse effect on LDC trade than on the processed goods exported by industrial nations.

While the preceding shows that developing countries account for a major share of the total tonnage entering seaborne trade, Table 7.2 examines the ownership of the world fleet which carries this cargo. Shown here is the registration of world shipping tonnage by country group in 1965 and 1974, as well as the percentage of the world fleet controlled by each group.[3] While a total figure is given for developing countries, a further breakdown is also provided by geographic region.

The figures shown in Tables 7.1 and 7.2 illustrate a source of one of the developing countries' major complaints concerning the structure and operation of world shipping: the great disparity that exists between the amount of cargo capacity required to transport goods from LDCs, and that actually owned and operated by these nations. While the developing countries originated over 63 per cent of the total tonnage entering world trade in 1974, the combined registration of their vessels was only about 6 per cent of the world fleet. The fact that such a significant portion of LDC trade must be carried in foreign-owned vessels has been the source of charges that the shipping services provided are often not directed toward the trade promotion and industrialisation objectives of these countries.

The liner conference system
To a great degree, the focus of developing country criticism has been

TABLE 7.2 Distribution of World Shipping Tonnage by Country Group of Registration in 1965 and 1974

Flag of registration in groups of countries	Tonnage (million grt)		Share of world tonnage (%)	
	1965	1974	1965	1974
World total	146·8	306·1	100·0	100·0
Developed market economy countries[1]	90·6	155·6	61·8	50·9
Open registry countries[2]	22·1	74·5	15·0	24·3
Southern Europe (excluding Cyprus)	11·8	30·8	8·0	10·1
Socialist countries	10·9	25·3	7·4	8·3
Developing countries excluding open registry	10·7	18·5	7·3	6·0
Africa	0·6	1·5	0·4	0·5
Asia[3]	5·5	9·9	3·8	3·2
Latin America[4]	4·6	7·0	3·1	2·3
Oceania	—	0·1	—	—
Other, unallocated	0·7	1·4	0·5	0·4

[1] Excludes southern Europe.
[2] Liberia, Panama, Cyprus, Singapore and Somalia.
[3] In 1974 India accounted for over 60 per cent of the Asian tonnage with a fleet of 3·5 grt. Korean registry was 1·2 grt while the Philippines had 0·8 grt.
[4] Primarily Brazil with 2·4 grt, Argentina with 1·4 grt, and Mexico, Venezuela and Peru with about 0·5 grt each.

Source: Data compiled from UNCTAD, *Review of Maritime Transport, 1974* (TD/B/C.4/125/Supp. 1) (New York: United Nations, 1975).

directed at the operation of the liner or shipping conference system which handles most of the nonpetroleum product trade between developing and developed countries. Stated simply, a liner conference is little more than an unincorporated association of ocean liner owners who have joined together in agreement to regulate competition among members, and prevent competition as far as possible from outside sources.[4] In normal practice, a liner conference covers only one leg of a voyage from a specific group of ports to another. For example, the North Atlantic Westbound Freight Association covers shipments from Ireland and the United Kingdom to the United States' Atlantic ports. In the reverse direction, the North Atlantic United Kingdom Freight Conference covers a somewhat different range from Atlantic ports in the United States north of Hampton Roads to the United Kingdom and Ireland. However, a shipping line which operates on many different routes is likely to be a member of a number of conferences. At present, approximately 600 liner conferences have been established over the world's major ocean trade routes.[5]

A liner conference generally limits competition among the individual lines which constitute its membership by practices which prescribe freight rates for most cargoes, and by restricting the capacity of individual carriers. In this respect, the conference operates as a quota cartel since it determines each member's frequency of sailing, and may also set limits on the carrying capacity of the vessels employed. Adherence to conference regulations is encouraged by a system of fines and the risk of a rate war should the agreement dissolve. Competition from tramps and other nonconference vessels is offset by a potential threat of service loss, and a system of preferential rates or rebates for those shippers who refrain from using other vessels. As a justification for the limits placed on competition, the conference members generally suggest that such measures are necessary if they are to maintain regularity of services at stable prices. In this respect, the rates of liner conferences are much more stable than tramp or charter rates which may fluctuate markedly with supply and demand conditions.[6]

Since liner conferences do have varying degrees of control over the routes they service, this has led to a number of specific complaints by both developed and developing countries concerning discrimination in terms of prices and service. For example, developing countries have charged that the operations and level of rates imposed by conference lines of traditional shipping nations deliberately favour their own exporters, or those of other industrial countries, to the detriment of the LDCs. Allegations of this sort have also been made by a number of high ranking United States government officials. For example, in a series of hearings on ocean freight rates, the Joint Economic Committee (1965, p. 1) of the United States Congress concluded:

The international ocean freight rate structure is weighted against United States exports. Our exports bear most of the cost of vessel operation, even in trades where imports approximate exports in value and quantity.

In finding number 3, the Committee also noted that a group of liner companies acting in concert can discriminate against nations by their operations, and by the structure of the charges they adopt:

Most ocean freight rates are set by steamship conferences whose basic purpose is to set freight rates and sailing schedules. But some go beyond price fixing and include pooling arrangements whereby each member is guaranteed a share of cargo or revenues. United States flag lines are outnumbered in all but 7 of the more than 100 active conferences involved in United States foreign trade. In substance foreign lines, some of which are government owned, determine freight rates, sailing schedules, and other conditions vital to the expansion of American commerce.

The Joint Economic Committee thus noted it was possible for a group of liner companies, acting as a conference, to set rates and operating conditions which discriminate between the various nations they service. In related complaints, the developing countries have charged that, due to their monopoly position, the conferences have been able to achieve unduly high profits on freight carried between developing and developed countries; profits which unfavourably influence the export performance and industrialisation prospects of the LDCs.[7]

Aside from the level of conference charges, rate structure comes in for frequent criticism. Allegations have been made that conference rates favour the export of primary goods from developing countries at the expense of semi-finished products or manufactures. Such discrimination can have serious detrimental effects on exports prices and performance. For example, UNCTAD (1969, p. 94) noted that an ocean freight rate which caused even a 2 per cent export price disadvantage for a particular product might inhibit growth of the producing industry, and have a retardation effect on the scale of production which could increase over time. Other complaints suggest that calls for establishment of promotional rates for manufactures or new export ventures are often ignored by the conferences with the result that LDCs feel that these organisations are insensitive to national development objectives.

Alleged discrimination against ports, or against incoming as opposed to outgoing traffic, has also been a source of numerous complaints against the liner conferences. These charges often suggest that discrimination against incoming as opposed to outgoing traffic artificially lowers raw material costs for industrial countries, but raises landed costs of machinery and capital equipment for LDCs.[8] Individual ports can be discriminated against, not only in comparison with other ports in the same country, but in relation to ports in another state. As an example of the first type, Harff (1970, p. 126) noted that sheet-iron shipped from New York via the Panama Canal to Buenaventura, Colombia, costs $16·20 per ton to transport, while the charge from Los Angeles was 90 per cent higher, even though the distance is considerably shorter and no canal duties have to be paid. Such differences in ocean freight rates can have profound implications for developing countries.

For example, Brazilian cotton producers have complained that their product was unable to compete with Mexico in European markets due to the higher ocean freight rates they were charged by the conferences. In addition, the Organization of American States has issued an even more sweeping indictment of conference rate practices, which reflects on the economic consequences of conference operations on the development prospects of the Latin American region:

> The freight rates adopted on inter-Latin-American maritime routes, the principal means of transportation in the region, often tend to discourage trade diversification because such rates are higher than those for similar products originating outside the area, thus weakening the competitive position of Latin American products.[9]

Studies of conference practices

While recent investigations of conference operations and rate-making procedures have considerably broadened knowledge of how these cartels function, they have not as yet produced general agreement concerning the validity of these allegations. However, most objective studies of liner conference freight rates have concluded that these administered prices may differ substantially from those charges which would be justified on a cost-of-operation basis, and that the practice of 'charging what the traffic will bear' is often a key determinant of rates.[10] Since the conferences have the capacity to set rates on an 'other-than-cost' basis, there is no guarantee that the revenue objectives of these organisations will coincide with industrialisation goals of developing countries. In fact, evidence is presented in a forthcoming section which suggests the existing structure of liner rates may differ radically from that which would promote industrialisation.

While charges of discrimination between ports, or between shippers on the basis of size, are more difficult to prove, there is some evidence that these complaints are also justified. For example, situations have been documented in which shippers' organisations were able to exercise countervailing power to offset unfavourable price policies of the conference.[11] Due to the potential benefits from these organisations, UNCTAD has taken an active role in efforts to organise shippers' associations for the promotion of common interests, and to give small operators countervailing power to the liner operations. Evidence of discrimination between ports is difficult to document since efficiencies of operation may vary, but it has been demonstrated that rate differences can cause sizeable revenue losses. For example, one study which examined transport cost differentials for 10 similar products shipped from Indonesian and Malaysian ports to the United States indicated that higher charges on Indonesian exports caused a foreign exchange loss of about $40 million a year.[12] While it was conceded that Malaysian ports operated with a higher degree of efficiency, competition from nonconference vessels was cited as an important factor accounting for this country's lower rates.

Since transport costs, and the operation of liner conferences, have become the subject of such controversy, this chapter examines evidence concerning the importance of freight costs on the export position of developing countries. After a theoretical analysis of the consequences of shipping costs for exporters and importers, attention is directed to empirical investigations of the level and structure of freight charges borne by developing countries. An effort is made to evaluate the findings concerning actual freight costs in relation to the industrialisation objectives of the developing countries. After an evaluation of various policy measures which have been proposed to lower freight charges, the chapter closes with an assessment of the role of freight costs as a barrier to developing country exports.

THE INCIDENCE OF TRANSPORT COST

While transport costs are formally paid by exporters when goods are sold on a cost-insurance-freight basis, and by the importer when purchases are made free-on-board, the party paying the freight bill is not necessarily the one who bears the transport cost. In actual practice, the exporter can be regarded as bearing freight costs if the delivered price in the *importing* market is unaffected by any changes in freight rates. Conversely, the importer may be regarded as bearing the cost of transport if the commodities' price in the *export* market would remain the same irrespective of changes in shipping costs.

These points can be illustrated through reference to simple supply-demand relationships. Figure 7.1a depicts a situation in which the delivered supply schedule SS for an exportable is completely inelastic with regard to price. In the absence of freight costs, the quantity ON would be consumed in the importing market at a price OP. Assuming that shipping costs of T per unit are introduced, it is apparent that they will not influence the market clearing price. Any attempt to add these charges to delivered prices, necessitating an increase from OP to OC, would be frustrated by a deficiency of demand relative to supply. As a

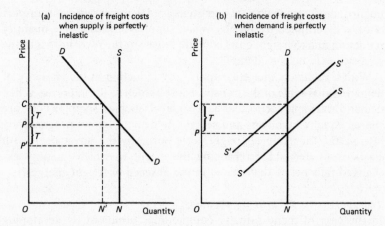

FIGURE 7.1 Analysis of the Relation between Supply and Demand Elasticities

result, excess supply forces the market clearing price back to OP, where the f.o.b. price received by exporters is OP'. Thus, in a situation where export supply is perfectly inelastic, the exporter bears the entire burden of freight costs.[13]

Figure 7.1b illustrates a situation where an inelastic demand curve for an exportable is matched with a less than perfectly inelastic supply schedule. In the absence of freight costs, quantity ON would clear the market at price OP. However, if freight costs of T per unit are again introduced, the supply schedule shifts leftward by an amount equal to the transport charge. Thus, SS represents the f.o.b. supply curve, while $S'S'$ is the delivered c.i.f. schedule.[14] In the equilibrium situation, the market is cleared at the same quantity (ON), but at a higher price OC with the increase borne by consumers. Therefore, when demand is perfectly inelastic the supply schedule does not influence who bears freight costs. In this situation, consumers in the importing market bear the full brunt of transportation costs or any changes in these charges.

In practice, completely inelastic demand or supply is seldom observed, and these limiting situations are employed solely to indicate tendencies for freight costs to fall on exporters or importers. In normal situations, the actual incidence of transport costs on buyers or sellers is determined by respective elasticities of demand or supply. When supply is relatively inelastic (the normal situation for many developing country products) the exporter bears the major part of the freight bill, and the price he receives falls below the 'zero transport cost' price by approximately the full extent of shipping costs. It also follows that the fall in quantity traded below that exchanged in the absence of transport costs is determined by supply. When supply is inelastic, the quantity reduction due to freight costs is small; however, the revenue loss to the exporter may be considerable.

With a relatively inelastic supply, any reduction in the elasticity of demand shifts some of the transport cost burden to the importer. When demand and supply schedules have equal elasticities, shipping costs are shared equally by buyers and sellers. As demand grows progressively less elastic, the share of freight costs borne by the buyer rises, with elasticity of demand determining the extent to which quantity exchanged falls below that traded in the absence of freight charges.

Transport costs for primary products
In the case of many primary commodities produced by developing countries, short-run supply is generally thought to be quite inelastic due to a variety of factors. For example, many of these items are highly perishable so exporters may be willing to absorb sizeable price fluctuations to clear markets. For non-perishable primary commodities, considerable time, and large capital investments, may be required before production capacity can be increased. Thus, a considerable delay may occur before a new mining capacity is developed, or plantation outputs of such items as rubber, tea, coffee, cocoa, etc. can be expanded. Although published estimates of demand elasticities for primary commodities are low, the demand schedules facing a given developing country are likely to be very elastic unless the country is an important source of supply, and the commodity has no close substitutes.[15] This, coupled with inelastic supply, means that developing country exporters normally bear the major burden of freight costs, and any increase in freight may be expected to produce equivalent declines in net export receipts. Stated differently, any increase in LDC freight costs, *ceteris paribus*, should have more of a depressant effect on exporters' prices than on raising the consumer price for these items.

Since transportation costs have the potential to be of such importance for developing country exporters, questions naturally arise as to the incidence and directional movements of these charges. Some evidence can be derived from United Nations sources which monitor freight costs for important primary products shipped along major conference line routes. Drawing on these data, Table 7.3 shows freight as a percentage of product price for shipments of rubber, tin, copra, hemp, jute, sisal, cocoa, tea, coconut oil, palm kernels and coffee over the period 1964 to 1975.

TABLE 7.3 The Ratio of Liner Freight Rates to Prices of Selected Commodities, 1964, 1970 and 1972–5

| Commodity | Liner route | 1964 | Freight as a percentage of product price | | | | |
			1970	1972	1973	1974	1975
Rubber	Singapore/Malaysia to Europe	8·0	10·5	15·4	9·2	11·0	18·5
Tin	Singapore/Malaysia to Europe	1·2	1·2	1·6	1·4	1·1	1·6
Copra	Philippines to Europe	11·0	14·0	22·1	9·3	n.a.	n.a.
Jute	Bangladesh to Europe	8·7	12·1	12·6	15·8	18·1	19·5
Sisal hemp	East Africa to Europe	8·4	19·5	18·1	10·0	7·3	12·8
Cocoa beans	Ghana to Europe	3·1	2·4	3·9	3·1	2·3	3·4
Coconut oil	Sri Lanka to Europe	8·8	8·9	14·5	n.a.	7·9	9·1
Tea	Sri Lanka to Europe	6·5	9·5	8·2	10·1	14·2	10·4
Coffee	Brazil to Europe	4·9	5·2	6·7	7·0	8·0	9·7
Palm kernels	Nigeria to Europe	9·5	8·8	16·9	7·2	9·6	25·5
Coffee	Colombia (Atlantic ports) to Europe	4·2	4·2	4·2	3·8	4·8	5·7
Cocoa beans	Brazil to Europe	8·6	7·4	10·7	6·9	6·1	8·2
Coffee	Colombia (Pacific ports) to Europe	4·5	4·5	5·0	4·3	5·4	6·3

Source: UNCTAD, *Review of Maritime Transport, 1976* (TD/B/C.4/169) (Geneva: United Nations, 25 March 1977), p. 60.

On a product-by-product basis, the freight ratios range from under 2 per cent for Malaysian tin shipments to a high of 25 per cent for palm kernels on the Nigeria-Europe route. Two other products, rubber from Malaysia, and jute from Bangladesh, have freight factors close to 20 per cent. Since the latter is undoubtedly characterised by inelastic supply and elastic demand, due to competition from synthetic and other substitutes, most of the burden of these high freight costs is undoubtedly reflected in depressed export prices.

Another fact emerging from these data is that sizeable year-to-year fluctuations have occurred in freight ratios for certain products. Freight factors changed by as much as 8 percentage points for sisal and 13 points for copra during 1972–3, while a 16 percentage point rise in the factor for palm kernels occurred over the 1974–5 period. Examination of the underlying data indicates that wide fluctuations in primary product prices were the main reason for these swings in freight ratios, as conference shipping rates advanced steadily on a secular trend.

Another, perhaps more disturbing fact emerging from these figures is that a general rise in freight factors seems to have occurred, although it is difficult to separate cyclical factors from trend. However, in every case except one (cocoa) the freight factors for 1975 rose above their 1964 base, often by considerable margins. For jute, rubber and palm kernels the ratios increased by more than 100 per cent, while *ad valorem* freight rates for coffee were 98 per cent above their earlier base. For the 12 commodities, an average increase of 62 per cent was experienced in freight factors, with Brazilian cocoa the only item to register a slight decline (down 4·7 per cent). One explanation for these relative increases in transport rates centres on the Organization for Petroleum Exporting Countries' Pricing policies which resulted in a four-fold increase in crude oil prices. Since shipping is a petroleum intensive operation, the increases in crude prices resulted in markedly higher bunker and liner operating costs, which were responsible for a dramatic upsurge in shipping rates over the period 1974–6.[16]

AGGREGATE TRANSPORT COSTS: AN EMPIRICAL ASSESSMENT

While the preceding analysis indicates that freight costs may comprise a high percentage of primary product prices, it tells nothing about the importance of these charges on aggregate trade flows, or on semi-finished goods and manufactures exported by developing countries.

However, a sizeable body of data on these charges has become available due to changes in the compilation of United States' import statistics. Specifically, in 1974 the United States initiated a system in which all imports were valued *jointly* at the point of exportation (free-alongside-ship), and also on a cost-insurance-freight basis. As such, the statistics provide information on international freight costs at a very low level of product detail.

According to United States' practices, the free-alongside-ship (f.a.s.) valuation represents the transaction value of imports at the foreign port of exportation and is based on the purchase price plus all charges incurred in placing merchandise *alongside* the vessel at the port of exportation. The c.i.f. valuation measures the value of imports at the first port of entry in the United States and includes all freight, insurance and other charges (excluding import duties) incurred in bringing the merchandise from the country of exportation and placing it alongside the vessel at the port of entry.[17] Taking the ratio of the c.i.f. to the f.a.s. import value thus provides a measure of the *ad valorem* incidence of international transport and insurance costs. Specifically, the formula used to estimate the *ad valorem* transport rate for product $j (R_j)$ was,

$$R_j = (V_c/V_f) - 1. \qquad (7\text{-}1)$$

where V is the c.i.f. or f.a.s. value of imports. The latter was placed denominator to make the *ad valorem* rates comparable to United States tariffs which are levied on an f.o.b. basis.[18]

Before proceeding, however, certain qualifications should be noted. While tariff rates are recorded in national schedules and, apart from preferential trading arrangements, apply to all exporters, a country's transport cost profile is more difficult to assess. The primary reason is that the *ad valorem* incidence of these charges is influenced both by the freight rate and the price of the internationally traded good. Both measures may be flexible and sensitive to short-term changes in supply and demand. Also, the *ad valorem* incidence of transportation charges may vary with the volume of shipments, if there are important scale economies, and a host of other related factors. Thus, estimates of transport profiles based on data from a given time period may be biased to the extent that prices or freight costs were atypical of their longer-term levels.

Transport costs of developing countries
For an initial assessment of the importance of international transportation costs, Table 7.4 has been prepared to show the incidence of these

TABLE 7.4 Analysis of the Incidence of Transportation Costs and Tariffs on
United States Imports from Developing Countries

Exporting country	*1974 Value of US imports ($m)*		*Nominal protection*		
	f.a.s.	*c.i.f.*	*Tariffs*	*Transport*	*Total*
Guinea	15·2	22·9	0·2	50·7	50·9
Afghanistan	3·9	4·8	5·1	23·0	28·1
Surinam	74·4	94·6	0·2	27·2	27·4
Morocco	19·3	22·4	8·9	16·1	25·0
Republic of Korea	1444·8	1583·7	15·1	9·6	24·7
Egypt	69·7	82·9	4·4	18·9	23·3
Hong Kong	1640·0	1778·5	14·2	8·4	22·6
Philippines	1083·9	1192·7	10·2	10·0	20·2
Liberia	96·4	115·7	0·1	20·0	20·1
Pakistan	60·7	67·7	8·4	11·5	19·9
Honduras	149·2	176·6	1·3	18·3	19·6
Bangladesh	68·0	81·2	0·1	19·4	19·5
Thailand	184·2	210·2	5·4	14·1	19·5
Costa Rica	168·5	195·5	3·2	16·0	19·2
Algeria	1090·5	1169·6	2·4	16·1	18·5
Iran	2132·2	2459·8	2·7	15·4	18·1
Sri Lanka	40·8	48·0	0·2	17·7	17·9
Saudi Arabia	1671·2	1926·5	2·4	15·3	17·7
Lebanon	29·9	32·0	10·5	7·0	17·5
India	559·5	635·2	3·4	13·5	16·9
Singapore	550·4	584·2	10·0	6·1	16·1
Malawi	10·4	11·6	4·1	11·5	15·5
Syria	2·1	2·3	5·6	9·5	15·1
Argentina	385·8	418·5	6·2	8·5	14·7
Panama	106·2	119·7	2·0	12·7	14·7
Nicaragua	97·4	108·4	2·9	11·3	14·2
Guyana	83·2	93·5	1·8	12·4	14·2
Tunisia	21·5	23·8	3·3	10·7	14·0
Ecuador	473·0	527·3	2·2	11·5	13·7
Indonesia	1688·1	1887·8	1·1	11·8	12·9
Paraguay	21·1	22·6	5·4	7·1	12·5
Brazil	1699·9	1853·2	3·4	9·0	12·4
Dominican Republic	473·3	502·5	6·0	6·2	12·2
Mauritius	31·8	34·9	2·2	9·7	11·9
Mozambique	44·9	50·0	0·3	11·4	11·7
Kenya	39·5	44·1	0·1	11·6	11·7
Uruguay	16·4	17·4	5·3	6·1	11·4
Gabon	162·3	178·7	0·8	10·1	10·9
Peru	608·7	650·4	3·9	6·9	10·8
Congo (Brazzaville)	2·2	2·4	1·1	9·1	10·2
Nigeria	3286·2	3541·1	2·3	7·8	10·1

TABLE 7.4 *continued*

| Exporting country | 1974 Value of US imports ($m) | | Nominal protection | | |
	f.a.s.	c.i.f.	Tariffs	Transport	Total
Guatemala	786·1	878·9	0·9	9·2	10·1
Venezuela	4671·1	5037·3	2·2	7·8	10·0
Ghana	125·5	136·8	0·6	9·0	9·6
Colombia	511·0	549·4	2·1	7·5	9·6
Angola	378·1	409·8	0·8	8·4	9·2
Tanzania	26·4	28·7	0·1	8·7	8·8
Malaysia	769·7	820·6	1·8	6·6	8·4
Ivory Coast	95·3	102·7	0·0	7·8	7·8
Chile	310·3	325·1	2·9	4·8	7·7
Uganda	66·9	71·9	0·0	7·5	7·5
Madagascar	60·0	64·3	0·1	7·2	7·3
Zaire	68·1	72·6	0·6	6·6	7·2
El Salvador	160·6	168·8	2·1	5·1	7·2
Sudan	26·8	28·3	1·6	5·6	7·2
Average			3·4	11·8	15·2

Source: Aggregate United States imports from developing countries were taken from United States Department of Commerce, *Highlights of U.S. Export and Import Trade* (Washington: Bureau of the Census, February 1975), pp. 88–90. Average tariff rates for aggregate LDC trade flows were computed from data given in UNCTAD, *Summary of Trade Barriers and Preferences Facing Individual Developing Countries in Major Developed Markets*, Research Memo. No. 57 (Geneva: United Nations, 10 May 1976).

charges on aggregate exports of 55 developing countries which traded at least $2 million worth of goods with the US.[19] The table shows both the total free-alongside-ship and cost-insurance-freight value of each country's exports, as well as the aggregate transport factor computed via equation 7–1. For purposes of comparison, the average tariff rate facing these aggregate trade flows has been computed, while the joint protective effect of tariffs and transport costs is shown. Finally, average tariff and transport factors for these developing countries is given to assist in evaluating the relative importance of these charges.

On an overall basis, average transport costs of 11·8 per cent are coupled with tariffs which are less than one-third this value. The relative importance of freight costs can also be appreciated by noting that in only five cases: Korea, Hong Kong, Philippines, Lebanon and Singapore does the *ad valorem* incidence of a country's transport costs fall below the corresponding tariff rate. Here, the normal transport-tariff relation is reversed due to a relatively high percentage of semifinished goods and manufactures in total exports. In other words, these five countries have reached a stage of development in which tariff barriers facing their manufactured exports exceed freight costs incurred by these relatively compact high-value items.

On a country by country basis, *ad valorem* costs range from a high of 50·7 per cent for Guinea down to about 4·8 per cent for Chile. In the case of Guinea, the 50 per cent freight factor is largely accounted for by a concentration of exports in bulky low-value items, such as bauxite and some scrap metal ores.[20] On the other hand, the low Chilean transport rate reflects a freight factor of 2·1 per cent for copper (about 70 per cent of total exports) where the development and efficient use of specialised carriers results in low *ad valorem* transportation costs. Freight factors of under 7 per cent for Zaire, Malaysia and Uruguay are, in part, accounted for by the use of bulk carriers to handle these countries' important metals trade.

Another factor stressing the importance of transport costs is that 12 of the 55 developing countries experienced freight factors of over 15 per cent of the f.a.s. value of exports, while 26 LDCs had aggregate transport rates exceeding 10 per cent. An analysis of disaggregate trade flows suggests that the transport ratios are primarily a function of the types of goods shipped, rather than the distance from the importing market. For example, Surinam's overall freight factor of 27 per cent is accounted for by a concentration of exports in low value scrap ores and aluminium (over 70 per cent of the total), while Afghanistan's overall 23 per cent freight factor is largely accounted for by *ad valorem* transport rates of 57 per cent for licorice root ($1·9 million in c.i.f. exports), although a rate of 6 per cent for hard-knotted floor coverings ($0·5 million in c.i.f. exports) acts as a moderating influence.

Transport costs for LDC products
Aside from the incidence of international transportation and insurance costs on aggregate trade flows, the influence of these charges on individual products exported by developing countries is of considerable importance. Analysis of the variation in transport costs over individual items can identify products which may be especially suitable for new export ventures due to relatively low freight charges. Conversely, identification of items where shipping costs constitute a high proportion of product price may indicate less desirable candidates for export industries if the supply and demand schedules are such that the major

portion of shipping costs will have to be borne by the exporter.

Table 7.5 provides information on the average *ad valorem* incidence of international transportation and insurance costs for a sample of approximately 50 three-digit SITC products exported by developing countries. These items were chosen randomly from an UNCTAD (1976, p. 180) tabulation of over 100 three-digit products which comprised the major LDC export items entering world trade. In computing both the average freight factor and the f.a.s. value of imports, Mexican trade was excluded due to the coincidence of this country's border with the United States. Thus, the figures reflect international freight costs that developing countries as a group must surmount in order to penetrate the United States market. To assist in making these comparisons, *ad valorem* transport rates for seven developing countries: Argentina, Brazil, Chile, India, Malaysia, Philippines and Taiwan, are shown to provide an indication of the potential variance in average freight rates.

On a product by product basis, the freight factors range from a high of over 50 per cent for SITC 276—crude materials (largely graphite, sodium chloride, asbestos, mica, fluorspar and barium) down to a low of under 2 per cent for tin and nonferrous base metals. In general, a number of items clustered at the low end of the scale are metals, or other primary commodities, for which bulk carriers or other specialised containers have been developed. In cases like coffee and cocoa, shipments from individual developing countries which are major suppliers are probably of sufficient size that substantial economies of scale in transport are experienced. However, even with these exceptions, the fact that more than one-third of the products had a freight factor of 15 per cent or more, coupled with a median freight rate of over 10 per cent, points to the importance of transport costs as a potential barrier to LDC exports.

Of course, the averages shown in Table 7.5 understate the importance of freight costs since they are biased in favour of countries better located to service the United States market. In other words, if penetration (i.e., freight) costs differ, one would expect that nations with lower transport costs should capitalise on this advantage to gain a larger market share. A more accurate indication of the potential importance of freight costs for some suppliers can be derived from the individual country statistics. For example, the overall freight factor of 40 per cent for iron ore conceals *ad valorem* transport costs of 77 per cent for Chile and 90 per cent for the Philippines. Similarly, an average freight factor of about 22 per cent for alcoholic beverages masks a 90 per cent freight rate for the Philippines exports and a 130 per cent rate for Brazil. While differences

TABLE 7.5 Estimated 1974 *Ad Valorem* Freight Rates for Developing Country Products Exported to the United States

SITC	Description	Ad valorem freight rate[1]							1974 f.a.s. imports[2] ($m)	Freight factor
		Argentina	Brazil	Chile	India	Malaysia	Philippines	Taiwan		
276	Crude materials, n.e.s.[3]	—	16·5	77·0	35·7	92·1	—	23·2	19·2	51·4
281	Iron ore and concentrates	—	39·9	69·8	—	—	76·8	—	339·1	40·4
242	Wood in the rough	—	—	—	—	57·1	89·3	—	5·4	34·7
641	Paper and paperboard	36·2	29·1	22·1	—	—	37·2	16·3	16·2	26·6
821	Furniture	16·1	15·5	—	40·5	16·6	51·2	20·7	61·4	23·3
052	Dried fruit	7·3	12·3	—	—	—	—	15·7	4·4	22·1
112	Alcoholic beverages	17·2	130·0	29·2	—	—	—	26·0	9·0	21·7
631	Plywood and veneers	—	16·5	—	34·9	23·2	91·8	16·6	264·6	20·6
341	Natural and manufactured gas	—	—	—	—	25·1	26·4	—	36·1	20·3
053	Preserved fruit	14·7	16·1	—	18·8	12·8	20·5	15·5	66·0	17·9
661	Lime and cement	12·7	13·1	—	43·9	—	—	11·6	25·6	17·6
074	Tea, crude or prepared	20·7	15·7	—	18·4	—	—	17·2	66·4	17·6
271	Crude fertilisers	—	—	8·7	—	—	—	—	18·3	15·9
697	Household equipment	28·2	14·3	—	17·6	—	—	16·6	50·0	15·9
812	Sanitary and lighting fixtures	—	26·8	—	18·8	—	44·1	12·4	17·5	15·8
292	Crude vegetable materials	17·6	13·8	7·6	13·4	9·2	34·1	22·3	138·7	15·1
642	Articles of paper	15·3	—	—	17·5	—	7·4	23·2	11·8	15·0
561	Manufactured fertilisers	—	17·4	6·1	27·4	—	—	12·2	10·8	13·4
651	Textile yarn and thread	8·4	11·4	—	26·9	—	10·9	14·5	19·6	13·0
081	Feeding stuff for animals	—	33·4	—	—	12·1	—	—	9·9	12·0
554	Soaps and detergents	—	—	—	—	—	—	—	0·4	11·6
678	Iron pipes and tubes	9·6	13·6	—	15·8	—	17·3	9·9	98·9	11·0
685	Lead	—	—	—	—	—	—	7·5	15·5	10·6
719	Non-electrical machinery	14·3	9·0	2·6	18·7	—	29·7	8·4	30·2	10·4

331 Crude petroleum	—	—	—	—	8·9	—	—	12924·7	10·2
291 Crude animal material	17·2	16·1	2·4	10·5	7·9	40·0	6·6	26·0	10·0
718 Machines for special industries	14·1	7·1	2·4	13·9	—	21·4	8·1	2·4	10·0
231 Crude natural rubber	—	8·4	4·7	10·2	8·8	10·4	—	516·4	9·9
121 Tobacco, unmanufactured	10·2	9·7	—	47·4	—	14·2	18·7	97·3	9·4
221 Oil seeds and nuts	—	9·4	—	—	9·9	6·3	16·1	24·5	8·9
262 Wool and animal hair	5·7	7·5	11·4	9·1	—	—	14·6	14·0	8·6
674 Steel plates and sheets	10·9	—	—	—	—	24·9	14·6	75·7	8·4
671 Pig iron	—	7·5	—	17·0	7·3	—	11·8	112·5	7·7
581 Articles of plastic	—	12·0	—	—	—	—	11·2	13·4	7·4
686 Zinc	6·4	8·3	17·4	9·3	—	8·4	26·4	40·9	7·1
061 Sugar and honey	—	5·9	—	8·0	7·7	—	—	1921·4	6·9
071 Coffee	4·6	5·2	—	9·4	—	—	4·8	1467·1	5·8
611 Leather	—	—	—	—	—	—	6·4	53·2	5·6
684 Aluminium	—	5·4	—	—	8·9	2·9	—	45·6	5·3
072 Cocoa	5·0	4·1	—	—	—	—	—	394·6	5·2
013 Meat in airtight containers	3·6	4·7	—	10·1	—	—	—	157·9	4·8
211 Hides and skins	8·7	—	—	—	—	—	—	55·6	4·5
421 Other fixed vegetable oils	6·8	5·1	—	10·4	5·0	2·7	—	5·4	4·4
422 Fixed vegetable oils, n.e.s.	—	—	—	6·8	—	—	—	449·8	3·9
682 Copper	—	1·5	2·1	—	1·6	—	1·1	443·4	2·3
687 Tin	—	4·0	0·7	—	—	—	3·5	269·5	1·5
689 Misc. nonferrous base metals								36·4	1·2

¹ Computed for shipments which exceeded $50,000.
² Total imports from developing countries excluding Mexico.
³ Primarily Graphite, Sodium chloride, Asbestos, Mica, Fluorspar and Barium.

of these magnitudes are undoubtedly due to variations in commodity composition as well as locational factors, they nevertheless do indicate the potential range of transport costs for some LDC products.

Transport costs and tariffs: a case study for India
Since the transportation cost averages shown in Table 7.5 have the potential to understate the importance of shipping costs for some developing countries which are not favourably located in relation to the United States market, a more detailed analysis was made for India. India was selected for further study due to its obvious importance among developing countries, with a 1970 population of well over 0·5 billion people. Also, India exports a wide range of primary and manufactured goods to the North American market so the potential exists for observing the incidence of transport costs on a variety of products at different stages of fabrication. While the analysis concentrates on India, it is expected that other highly populated nations in South Asia such as Bangladesh, Pakistan and Sri Lanka should face approximately the same transport profiles for common exports.

Table 7.6 shows the average incidence of freight charges on each three-digit SITC product which accounted for over one million dollars in trade. Altogether, these 45 product groups had a combined (f.a.s.) value of over $500 million or 85 per cent of India's 1974 United States exports. To assist in evaluating these data, the table also shows the average transport factor on United States imports from all sources (i.e., both developed and developing countries). Comparison of these figures with the transport rates for India shows the differential this country must pay due to its adverse location relative to some competitors. Finally, to assist in assessing the relative importance of tariff and transport costs on India's exports, both median and average values for these charges have been computed.

On an overall basis, the median transport value for these 45 product groups (14·2 per cent) is more than double that for the current United States MFN tariffs. Much the same picture concerning the relative importance of transport costs versus tariffs emerges from comparison of the average *ad valorem* incidence figures. For the product groups shown in Table 7.6, an average transport factor of 13·6 per cent combines with an average tariff rate of 7.5 per cent. When measured by averages, the spread between transport and tariff charges becomes 7·9 per cent as opposed to a difference of 6·1 per cent for the median figures.

Of course, there is considerable variation in the rates on a product by product basis. For example, woven textile products (SITC 653), India's largest single three-digit export product, experience approximately equal (20 per cent) transport and tariff barriers. It is also interesting to note that the existing transport differential between Indian exporters and their competitors (20 versus 5·8 per cent) is one of the largest observed in the table.[21] Much the same pattern exists for the other textile or related products, as India normally faces an adverse transport cost differential of up to 18 percentage points (SITC 651). The fact that India is able to compete in the North American market in the face of such transport costs may be generally attributed to the fact that its low unit labour costs enable exporters to absorb this differential.

Aside from the incidence of transport costs on the textile and fabric products, the highest recorded *ad valorem* shipping rates appear for the metals and metal ores group. For example, ores of nonferrous base metals (SITC 283) have a transport factor of 52·8 per cent, the highest recorded *ad valorem* rate for the 45 three-digit SITC items.[22] Furthermore, metal scrap, iron and steel castings, iron and steel bars, etc., also register transport factors of 20 per cent or more. Four other non-textile or non-metal groups; footwear, wood manufactures, other crude materials and leather, have rates in this range. Since India's competitors have significantly lower freight rates for these items, the data suggest that growth in some export markets may be limited if these estimated transport factors reflect actual costs of shipment, as opposed to an arbitrary rate structure by the conferences.

THE STRUCTURE OF FREIGHT COSTS

The preceding analysis demonstrated that international transport costs can assume imposing proportions, averaging over 50 per cent for some items, and constitute a serious barrier to LDC penetration of export markets. It was also suggested that the supply and demand elasticities for many of these developing country exports are such that the burden of freight costs falls primarily on exporters. The result is that shipping costs probably constitute a serious drag on export growth and foreign exchange earnings.

Aside from absolute levels, the structure of transportation costs for developing country products can be of key importance. For example, in Chapter 4 it was observed that tariffs in industrial countries typically tend to increase, or escalate, with the degree of product processing. It was also suggested that the net effect of these escalated tariff structures was to maintain LDCs as exporters of primary products. Since bulk, or

TABLE 7.6 Evaluation of the *Ad Valorem* Incidence of Most-Favoured-Nation Tariffs and International Transportation Costs on India's Exports to the United States

SITC	Description	Average Ad valorem transport rate for US imports (%)	Ad valorem Incidence on Indian Export to the US (%)			1974 F.A.S Imports from India ($000)
			Transport costs	Nominal tariffs	Total	
653	Woven textile fabrics	5·8	20·0	19·4	39·4	136093·3
652	Woven cotton fabrics	5·4	8·7	21·1	29·8	45374·0
841	Clothing	8·0	15·9	22·1	38·0	39354·2
667	Pearls and precious stones	0·5	0·8	2·5	3·3	36495·9
051	Fresh fruit and nuts	12·7	6·4	6·4	12·8	34658·9
061	Sugar and honey	6·8	9·3	4·3	13·6	32512·5
292	Crude vegetable materials	12·0	13·4	2·7	16·1	28550·4
031	Fresh and preserved fish	7·0	12·6	0·5	13·1	28334·0
657	Floor coverings	8·7	14·0	7·0	21·0	16027·0
075	Spices	8·9	12·6	0·6	13·2	12615·8
656	Articles of textile materials	8·2	11·1	18·6	29·7	10800·5
074	Tea and maté	15·9	18·4	0·0	18·4	8640·4
071	Coffee	5·4	8·0	0·0	8·0	7481·0
011	Fresh or frozen meat	10·5	15·6	6·8	22·4	6324·3
611	Leather	4·9	9·4	4·8	14·2	6161·3
032	Fish in airtight containers	5·6	12·6	4·7	17·3	4661·9
697	Household equipment of base metal	12·2	17·6	8·2	25·8	4602·1
693	Wire products and fencing grills	9·8	14·2	7·3	21·5	4380·3
673	Iron and steel bars	12·0	20·1	5·7	25·8	4201·7
851	Footwear	9·2	25·3	8·8	34·1	3941·4
695	Hand tools	6·7	6·7	8·0	14·7	3524·3
671	Pig iron	7·9	17·0	2·0	19·0	3523·8

422	Other fixed vegetable oils	4·0	10·4	7·3	17·7	3161·0
897	Jewellery	3·9	13·7	14·9	28·6	3113·2
681	Silver and platinum	0·5	2·1	0·1	2·2	2850·0
651	Textile yarn and thread	8·6	26·9	14·8	41·7	2729·0
663	Mineral manufactures, n.e.s.	7·0	8·1	8·6	16·7	2472·0
694	Nails, screws, nuts and bolts	7·3	17·0	5·9	22·9	2359·0
654	Lace and embroidery	5·7	9·1	18·4	27·5	2344·7
632	Wood manufactures, n.e.s.	8·6	28·4	5·7	34·1	2313·3
291	Crude animal materials, n.e.s.	11·0	10·5	2·1	12·6	2243·9
512	Organic materials	8·3	7·9	11·8	19·7	2095·8
276	Other crude materials	12·8	35·7	2·9	38·6	1909·6
729	Other electrical machinery	3·2	9·7	7·1	16·8	1891·4
612	Leather manufactures	6·2	21·1	5·0	26·1	1822·1
831	Travel goods and handbags	10·2	17·1	17·3	32·4	1649·5
698	Metal manufactures, n.e.s.	6·8	16·8	8·1	24·9	1635·9
284	Nonferrous metal scrap	3·8	37·8	4·6	42·4	1549·3
896	Antiques and works of art	1·0	9·3	1·4	10·7	1382·2
679	Iron and steel castings	7·8	28·5	8·2	36·7	1134·0
283	Ores of nonferrous base metals	16·5	52·8	1·1	53·9	1086·8
599	Chemical materials, n.e.s.	7·1	17·1	6·8	23·9	1054·5
655	Special textile fabrics	9·7	16·1	15·3	31·4	1046·2
678	Iron and steel tubes	10·9	15·8	7·2	23·0	1036·5
263	Cotton	4·6	17·8	3·1	20·9	1030·4
	Median *ad valorem* rate	7·8	14·2	6·4	20·6	
	Average *ad valorem* rate	7·4	13·6	7·5	21·1	
	Average rate for all exports[1]		13·8	5·9	19·7	

[1] Total Indian exports including products not shown in this table.

Source: Alexander J. Yeats, 'A Comparative Analysis of the Incidence of Tariffs and Transportation Costs on India's Exports', *Journal of Development Studies*, 14 (October 1977), 97–107.

stowage factors, generally decrease while product value increases, some economists have assumed that the incidence of transport costs would decline as one moved to higher stages of fabrication. However, it should be recognised that the processing function can render goods more fragile, difficult to handle, or subject to pilferage. All of these factors could lead to higher freight costs. It has also been noted that liner conference freight rates are administered prices which can discriminate against weaker elements. If these charges are in fact levied on an other-than-cost basis it could be another reason why actual freight rates fail to behave in the anticipated manner.

Using the stage of processing scheme developed in Chapter 3 in connection with the US import data, it is possible to observe the behaviour of shipping costs over products involving different degrees of fabrication. Before proceeding, it should be noted that there are special difficulties associated with attempts to evaluate the transportation cost profile of products composing a processing chain. For example, distance may have an important influence on the transport cost profile of different commodities and countries. Specifically, a nation which is far removed from its export market should, *ceteris paribus*, experience higher transport costs than one which enjoys a more favourable location. As such, simply calculating the average *ad valorem* transportation rate for United States imports of products at various stages of processing may not yield a reasonable approximation to the experience of individual countries if the *mix* of exporting countries changes at each stage.

To rectify this potential problem a two-stage procedure was used. First, overall *ad valorem* freight rates were calculated for all United States imports comprising different stages of the processing chains irrespective of the countries of origin at each level of fabrication. This procedure permitted an evaluation of the way in which transport costs influence the competitive position of processing industries in the United States. Next, similar ratios were derived (where possible) for specific countries in order to evaluate the behaviour of freight charges when the mix of exporting nations is held constant. Analysis of these data should indicate the extent to which the structure of ocean freight rates stimulates, or retards, the growth of processing industries in primary product-producing countries.

Table 7.7 provides summary data on the tariff and transportation cost profiles of the major developing country processing chains. Shown here are average *ad valorem* rates for each processing stage, as well as the percentage point change in freight and tariff charges. While these figures

TABLE 7.7 Nominal Tariffs and Transportation Costs for United States Imports: Data Presented by Stage of Processing

Commodity group		Stage of processing				Percentage point charge[1]	
		I	*II*	*III*	*IV*		
Leather	Tariffs	1·1	4·7	7·7	14·0	12·9	
	Transport	3·9	4·5	6·2	9·1	5·2	(5.0)
	Total	5·0	9·2	13·9	23·1	18·1	(17·9)
Wood products[2]	Tariffs	0·0	0·3	8·1	6·7		
	Transport	2·9	6·7	16·2	8·6	5·7	(5·3)
	Total	2·9	7·0	24·3	15·3	12·3	(12·0)
Textiles[3]	Tariffs	5·8	8·3	14·2	19·1	13·3	
	Transport	9·5	11·5	5·9	8·8	−0·7	(−1·5)
	Total	15·3	19·8	20·1	27·9	12·6	(11·8)
Rubber	Tariffs	0·0	4·6	—	—	4·6	
	Transport	9·9	15·6	—	—	5·7	(24·6)
	Total	9·9	20·2	—	—	10·3	(29·0)
Food processing	Tariffs	5·4	6·1	—	—	0·7	
	Transport	17·6	9·0	—	—	−8·6	(1·2)
	Total	23·0	15·1	—	—	−7·9	(1·9)
Metals	Tariffs	0·9	4·3	7·8	3·8	2·9	
	Transport	24·1	6·3	2·0	11·2	−12·2	(−7·4)
	Total	25·0	10·6	9·8	15·0	−10·0	(−4·4)
All commodities	Tariffs	3·5	4·4	11·6	18·2	14·7	
	Transport	14·0	8·6	8·0	9·2	−4·8	(−0·4)
	Total	17·5	13·0	19·6	27·4	9·9	(14·3)

[1] Figures in parentheses show changes in freight factors for specific countries.
[2] Includes paper and paper products.
[3] Excludes jute and sisal.

Note: Averages shown in this table have been computed using weights based on developed country imports from LDCs. For actual trade vales used in these computations see UNCTAD, *The Kennedy Round Estimated Effects on Tariff Barriers* (New York: United Nations, 1968), pp. 214–16.

Source: Alexander J. Yeats, 'Do International Transport Costs Increase with Fabrication? Some Empirical Evidence', *Oxford Economic Papers*, 29 (November 1977), 458–71.

have been derived from aggregate United States import statistics, with no attempt to hold the mix of exporting countries constant, data in parentheses show similar information for United States imports from specific developing countries.

On an overall basis, the structure of transportation costs appears to somewhat intensify the competitive pressures on United States processing concerns. For the all commodity average, freight rates decline almost 5 percentage points from the first stage (14 per cent) to just over 9 per cent for the final stage of fabrication. However, the decline is minor compared with the corresponding increase in tariffs from 3·5 to 18·2 per cent.

The influence of tariffs and transport charges thus produces a series of joint import costs which rise fully 10 percentage points over the four processing stages. However, it should be noted that there are instances where transportation costs behave quite differently than indicated by these overall figures. For leather, wood, and rubber freight costs clearly rise with the stage of processing and reinforce the protective effect of the graduated tariffs.

Table 7.7 also presents evidence that the apparent decline of transport rates evidenced in the aggregate trade statistics is largely the result of shifting sources of supply for United States imports. When similar transport cost figures are computed for shipments from specific developing countries the nominal freight factors fall by only 0·4 per cent. Within the levels of accuracy of the data employed in this study such a figure indicates essentially unchanged nominal shipping costs. However, this overall result is heavily influenced by metals shipments where transport costs do de-escalate considerably. Without the influence of metals in the overall average, nominal transportation rates for shipments from specific countries would show some increase as one moved to higher levels of fabrication.

An important question centres on the reason(s) why transportation costs behave as evidenced in Table 7.7. As noted, some processed products have a tendency to be more difficult to handle, more fragile, and also subject to higher insurance costs. All of these factors could contribute to increased freight rates for processed products. A high ratio for the volume of primary to processed goods shipments might also lead to rising shipping costs for some items if there are important economies of scale in transport. Technological innovations probably have also influenced the structure of freight costs. For example, over the last few decades considerable advances have been made in the transport of primary commodities (i.e., development of bulk carriers, mechanised loading and unloading procedures, etc.) and transport rates for many of these items have been continually lowered. While containerised shipping seems to offer considerable potential for reducing freight costs of processed goods, these advances may not have been as widely adopted or kept pace with improvements in the transport of bulk commodities.

While the preceding discussion notes that actual cost differentials in the handling and transport of processed commodities may be an important factor influencing the structure of freight rates, an alternative explanation might focus on an (alleged) arbitrary structure of shipping charges imposed by liner conferences. Investigations by Heaver (1973) and Fashbender and Wagner (1973) have suggested that a key element influencing liner rate structures is the practice of 'charging what the traffic will bear' or subsidising shipments of primary products through higher rates on processed goods. If the freight factors revealed in Table 7.7 do reflect such practices, then the rate-setting objectives of the liner conferences run counter to the development plans of LDCs. Frequently, these countries are attempting to shift the processing function for raw materials within their national frontiers. However, if the freight rates for fabricated goods are artificially inflated, this may retard the growth of processing industries—or at least remove the natural incentive that declining transport costs would provide.

THE POTENTIAL FOR FREIGHT COST REDUCTIONS

The preceding analysis demonstrated two important points concerning the influence of transport costs on developing country trade. First, freight costs may be quite high, averaging as much as 50 per cent of some commodities' f.o.b. export value. However, information on India's transport cost profile showed that shipping costs for a nation not favourably located in relation to its export markets may be considerably above the average charges. It was also demonstrated that freight rate structure is important, often rising with increased fabrication. The conclusion which follows is that shipping costs can have important retardation effects on both the volume and types of goods exported by developing countries. Obviously, it behoves the LDCs to take advantage of available measures for reducing freight costs.[23]

Technological factors in transport

While a thorough technical evaluation of potential measures for reducing freight costs is beyond the scope of this book, previous studies provide an indication of the potential magnitude of saving which could be involved. For example, one analysis suggests that there may be scope for substantial reductions in shipping costs for manufactures through the use of containers. By packaging manufactured goods in specially built steel containers, a homogeneous cargo is produced which, given appropriate equipment, can be loaded or unloaded in a fraction of the time required at present.[24] Since a large portion of shipping costs are incurred in port, containerisation could make a substantial cut in freight costs possible. An UNCTAD (1966, p. 26) estimate suggested that, on routes where containers could be used, freight rates might be reduced by as much as 25 per cent. While it is acknowledged that a sizeable initial investment in containers and port handling equipment could be required, the increase in efficiency for some congested ports like Bombay, Calcutta, Lagos, etc., should well justify these expenditures.

The move to larger vessels, or specialised containers, also holds considerable promise as a means of reducing shipping costs. For example, the Japanese lowered transport costs per metric ton of iron ore imports more than 30 per cent over the last decade in spite of an increase of over 50 per cent in the nautical mileage covered by these shipments.[25] A primary reason for this saving was the development of large bulk carriers and compatible loading and unloading facilities. A similar strategy may produce benefits for developing countries. Furthermore, in the liner trade, considerable savings can often be realised by rationalising the arrival and departure times of vessels. In the case of certain commodity shipments, savings can be achieved by consolidating small liner consignments to the point where charter or contract methods can be adopted. Consolidation of shipments can also have special advantages if it makes the use of larger vessels possible. For example, UNCTAD (1969, p. 74) suggests that the carriage of dry cargo, in a 10000 dwt vessel on a round-trip voyage of 2500 miles, costs $1.30 per ton, whereas the cost would be $0.56 per ton in a ship of 50000 dwt. The move to larger carriers would therefore reduce transport costs by more than 50 per cent.

For certain products, the question of transport subsidies offers intriguing possibilities. A study by Prewo and Geraci (1977) indicates that transport elasticities (i.e., the ratio of the percentage change in export revenues to the percentage change in freight costs) are frequently greater than unity. If products are characterised by constant or falling returns in production, it follows that a combination of transport subsidies and export tax revenues may work to the benefit of both domestic exporters and the government.

Finally, a key issue is the whole process by which ocean freight rates are determined. In the bulk trades, port modernisation and the use of larger vessels should automatically result in reduced transport costs; but this need not follow for liners where cost saving measures may merely result in higher profits for shipowners.[26] Policies are needed to ensure that the savings are passed on to exporters in the form of lower freight rates. Since liner conference charges are administered prices, serious attention should be given to measures aimed at strengthening the bargaining position of exporters. These measures might well include the formation of active commodity exporter groups, backed by direct government participation in the rate-setting negotiations when necessary.

Appendix
Trade Barriers Facing Individual Developing Countries

by Andrzej Olechowski

Tables in this Appendix show trade barriers facing individual developing countries which export at least $100 million to the major industrial country markets: the European Economic Community, Japan and the United States. This information is based on an aggregation of detailed tariff line data which has been grouped by exporting country, and by three major commodity classifications: all goods, primary products (SITC 0 to 4 plus 67 and 68) and manufactures (SITC 5 to 9 minus 67 and 68).

The 1974 trade data shown in these tables were drawn from national customs statistics while matching information on tariffs, nontariff barriers and preferences was tabulated from various GATT, UNCTAD and official national sources. The tariff averages show post-Kennedy Round Most-Favoured-Nation (MFN) rates, with specific duties having been converted to *ad valorem* equivalents by taking the ratio of these charges to the unit value of imports.

The detailed description of the tables is as follows.

The first column, *Source and kind of imports*, identifies the exporting developing country as well as the product group for which the tabulations are made.

Columns two and three under the heading *Total imports* show the value of imports from each developing country and corresponding weighted average tariff rate. These averages were obtained by weighting tariff-line level rates by the value of the imports to which they apply. In tables for the United States and Japan, these average rates have been derived for the total trade shown in the 'value' column, while in the case of the European Economic Community the calculations exclude trade covered by variable levies. This omission was necessitated by the fact that some imports into these markets under MFN or preferential tariffs are also covered by variable levies, or variable components, for which an *ad valorem* equivalent could not be derived.

Trade figures under *Imports subject to MFN* show values of imports not subject to any (special or generalised) preferences, although they may be covered by nontariff restraints. Average tariff rates shown in this section were computed using two alternative procedures: the first being a simple average based on tariff line information, while the second employs weights derived from the value of imports to which these tariffs apply. (See Chapter 4 for a discussion of problems and biases in tariff averaging.)

Estimated values of imports eligible for Generalised System of Preferences are shown in the section *Imports under GSP*. Due to the lack of current information on actual imports under these schemes, approximations have been made by applying information on products currently eligible for preferential treatment to the 1974 import data. Therefore, these figures show the value of trade which could have benefited from the GSP if the 1977 schemes had been operating in 1974. All values represent *maximum* estimates. In cases where preferences applied only to part of a tariff-line, import values for the whole line were included due to a lack of available lower-level trade data. Furthermore, these estimates account for beneficiary exclusions, but do not include the effect of ceilings, maximum amount, or other similar limitations. Average GSP tariff rates shown in this section were obtained using the same procedure as that employed in estimating trade-weighted MFN averages.

Data presented in the section *Other preferences* were computed using the same method employed to derive estimates for imports under the GSP. These preferences are granted by the European Economic Community to former colonial associates and certain Mediterranean States. Average preferential tariffs applied to these shipments were computed using trade-weighted tariff-line data.

The final section on *Imports subject to NTBs* shows estimated values of imports subject to four major types of nontariff barriers: (1) export restraints, (2) licensing (discretionary, liberal or automatic), (3) global and other quotas (with the exception of bilateral quotas), and (4) variable levies. In deriving these figures, data limitations again necessitated the assumption that all trade in a tariff-line covered by a reported NTB was subject to the restraint. However, in the case of the European

Economic Community, when a NTB is applied by only a portion of the member states the trade coverage was approximated using import weights derived from four-digit Brussels Tariff Nomenclature (BTN) totals for the countries applying the restraint. This procedure was necessary since tariff-line statistics are not available on a country basis within the European Economic Community.

APPENDIX TABLE 1. Trade Barriers Facing Individual Developing Countries in the EEC

Source and kind of imports	Total imports		Imports subject to MFN			Imports under GSP		Other preferences		Imports subject to NTBs ($m)		
	Value ($m)	Weighted average rate	Value ($m)	Average rate Unweighted	Weighted	Value ($m)	Weighted rate	Value ($m)	Weighted rate	Export restraints	Licensing plus quotas	Variable levies
Algeria												
All goods	2537·7	0·0	2331·9	2·1	0·0	0·4	4·9	183·4	0·3	4·6	932·0	6·5
Primary products	2514·3	0·0	2328·2	2·5	0·0	0·4	4·9	163·6	0·3	0·0	924·9	6·5
Manufactures	23·5	0·0	3·7	0·0	0·0	0·0	0·0	19·8	0·0	4·6	7·1	0·0
Angola												
All goods	228·4	1·2	208·8	2·1	1·2	3·6	1·7	0·0	0·0	0·0	13·1	0·0
Primary products	227·2	1·2	208·1	1·9	1·2	3·0	2·0	0·0	0·0	0·0	13·0	0·0
Manufactures	1·2	0·7	0·6	3·5	1·3	0·6	0·0	0·0	0·0	0·0	0·1	0·0
Argentina												
All goods	1561·2	4·2	417·6	5·0	3·1	259·7	6·0	0·0	0·0	5·2	170·3	831·3
Primary products	1443·4	4·5	369·3	4·6	2·7	190·7	8·1	0·0	0·0	0·0	131·8	830·9
Manufactures	117·9	2·7	48·3	6·1	6·0	69·0	0·0	0·0	0·0	5·2	38·5	0·4
Bangladesh												
All goods	101·5	3·0	69·1	3·2	1·6	32·4	5·9	0·0	0·0	9·9	23·0	0·0
Primary products	61·5	1·2	61·3	0·3	1·2	0·2	3·1	0·0	0·0	0·0	0·0	0·0
Manufactures	40·0	5·6	7·8	6·5	4·3	32·2	5·9	0·0	0·0	9·9	23·0	0·0
Bolivia												
All goods	117·8	0·1	116·8	4·6	0·1	0·9	0·2	0·0	0·0	0·3	0·1	0·1
Primary products	116·6	0·0	116·4	2·2	0·0	0·1	1·5	0·0	0·0	0·0	0·0	0·1
Manufactures	1·1	3·8	0·4	9·3	12·0	0·8	0·0	0·0	0·0	0·3	0·1	0·0
Brazil												
All goods	2707·9	2·7	2130·3	5·1	2·3	301·8	5·4	0·0	0·0	118·7	53·2	210·6
Primary products	2376·7	2·2	1914·0	3·6	1·6	188·4	8·6	0·0	0·0	0·0	16·2	209·1
Manufactures	331·1	5·8	216·2	8·1	8·8	113·4	0·0	0·0	0·0	118·7	37·0	1·5
Cameroon												
All goods	419·7	0·0	109·0	0·4	0·0	0·0	0·0	310·7	0·0	4·7	24·7	0·0
Primary products	405·0	0·0	109·0	0·5	0·0	0·0	0·0	296·0	0·0	0·0	23·1	0·0
Manufactures	14·7	0·0	0·0	12·4	9·9	0·0	0·0	14·7	0·0	4·7	1·7	0·0
Chile												
All goods	795·4	0·1	755·7	5·0	0·1	9·5	5·0	0·0	0·0	0·1	0·9	0·1
Primary products	788·8	0·1	750·0	5·0	0·1	8·6	5·5	0·0	0·0	0·0	0·9	0·1
Manufactures	6·5	0·3	5·7	5·1	0·3	0·9	0·0	0·0	0·0	0·1	0·0	0·0

APPENDIX TABLE 1 continued

Source and kind of imports	Total imports		Imports subject to MFN			Imports under GSP		Other preferences		Imports subject to NTBs ($m)		
	Value ($m)	Weighted average rate	Value ($m)	Average rate Unweighted	Weighted	Value ($m)	Weighted rate	Value ($m)	Weighted rate	Export restraints	Licensing plus quotas	Variable levies
Columbia												
All goods	367.1	6.4	294.1	4.3	6.4	50.2	6.4	0.0	0.0	34.1	30.4	16.2
Primary products	307.1	6.8	252.9	3.3	6.4	31.5	10.3	0.0	0.0	0.0	23.5	16.2
Manufactures	60.0	4.7	41.2	5.8	6.9	18.7	0.0	0.0	0.0	34.1	6.9	0.0
Congo												
All goods	202.2	0.0	184.4	0.3	0.0	0.0	0.0	16.8	0.0	0.1	56.1	1.0
Primary products	188.5	0.0	183.8	0.4	0.0	0.0	0.0	3.7	0.0	0.0	56.0	1.0
Manufactures	13.7	0.0	0.6	0.0	0.0	0.0	0.0	13.1	0.0	0.1	0.1	0.0
Costa Rica												
All goods	141.7	8.8	45.7	4.8	6.7	94.2	9.9	0.0	0.0	0.1	92.7	1.8
Primary products	140.7	8.9	45.6	5.2	6.7	93.2	10.0	0.0	0.0	0.0	92.7	1.8
Manufactures	1.0	0.6	0.1	3.7	6.6	0.9	0.0	0.0	0.0	0.1	0.0	0.0
Cuba												
All goods	110.4	10.4	36.9	5.0	3.0	20.8	23.5	0.0	0.0	0.1	1.1	50.3
Primary products	102.6	12.0	29.5	5.2	3.7	20.4	24.0	0.0	0.0	0.0	1.1	50.3
Manufactures	7.8	0.0	7.4	4.1	0.0	0.4	0.0	0.0	0.0	0.1	0.0	0.0
Ecuador												
All goods	141.2	7.2	69.7	4.1	4.7	69.4	9.8	0.0	0.0	0.2	67.1	0.0
Primary products	140.6	7.3	69.5	2.8	4.7	68.0	10.0	0.0	0.0	0.0	67.0	0.0
Manufactures	1.6	1.1	0.2	7.8	7.4	1.4	0.0	0.0	0.0	0.2	0.1	0.0
Egypt												
All goods	312.9	1.0	193.0	4.0	0.3	0.1	1.3	113.5	2.3	27.5	43.4	5.0
Primary products	277.1	1.2	188.3	4.9	0.3	0.1	1.3	82.5	3.1	0.0	39.9	5.0
Manufactures	35.8	0.0	4.7	0.0	0.0	0.0	0.0	31.0	0.0	27.5	3.5	0.0
El Salvador												
All goods	116.7	6.1	112.9	2.4	6.0	3.7	10.3	0.0	0.0	1.0	0.5	0.1
Primary products	113.0	6.0	110.6	0.7	5.8	2.3	16.8	0.0	0.0	0.0	0.1	0.1
Manufactures	3.7	9.4	2.3	5.4	15.2	1.4	0.0	0.0	0.0	1.0	0.4	0.0
Gabon												
All goods	588.2	0.0	551.4	0.0	0.0	0.0	0.0	36.8	0.0	0.0	153.7	0.0
Primary products	567.7	0.0	551.4	0.0	0.0	0.0	0.0	16.3	0.0	0.0	153.0	0.0
Manufactures	20.5	0.0	0.0	0.0	0.0	0.0	0.0	20.5	0.0	0.0	0.7	0.0

Ghana												
All goods	301·7	0·0	67·5	0·3	0·0	0·0	0·0	233·8	0·0	0·1	1·4	0·0
Primary products	288·3	0·0	65·5	0·3	0·0	0·0	0·0	222·4	0·0	0·1	0·3	0·0
Manufactures	13·4	0·0	2·0	0·0	0·0	0·0	0·0	11·4	0·0	0·1	1·1	0·0
Guatemala												
All goods	150·1	3·9	130·0	2·3	3·4	12·6	7·3	0·0	0·0	0·5	4·4	12·1
Primary products	148·1	3·9	128·8	2·0	3·4	14·2	6·4	0·0	0·0	0·0	4·0	12·1
Manufactures	2·0	0·1	1·2	3·6	0·2	0·0	0·8	0·0	0·0	0·5	0·3	0·0
Hong Kong												
All goods	1490·3	13·3	1311·6	7·5	15·1	0·2	176·3	0·0	0·0	749·4	200·8	2·1
Primary products	33·3	2·1	27·0	3·7	1·1	9·1	4·0	0·0	0·0	0·0	0·7	2·1
Manufactures	1456·9	13·6	1284·6	10·1	15·4	0·0	172·3	0·0	0·0	749·4	200·1	0·0
India												
All goods	1033·8	4·5	791·8	4·3	5·1	1·5	166·8	0·0	0·0	179·3	121·5	7·7
Primary products	526·6	2·9	420·5	3·0	2·8	3·7	30·9	0·0	0·0	0·0	2·5	7·7
Manufactures	507·3	5·8	371·3	6·3	7·6	1·0	135·9	0·0	0·0	179·3	119·0	0·1
Indonesia												
All goods	545·1	1·7	452·1	4·0	1·4	3·0	84·6	0·0	0·0	0·5	3·6	0·5
Primary products	513·1	1·8	437·3	3·1	1·5	3·7	67·4	0·0	0·0	0·0	0·2	0·4
Manufactures	32·0	0·2	14·8	6·0	0·5	0·0	17·1	0·0	0·0	0·5	3·4	0·0
Iran												
All goods	8072·8	0·3	8008·0	5·0	0·3	0·8	64·2	0·0	0·0	194·1	3046·7	0·6
Primary products	7859·2	0·1	7821·4	3·3	0·1	1·4	37·3	0·0	0·0	0·0	3045·7	0·4
Manufactures	213·7	8·3	186·6	8·2	9·5	0·0	26·9	0·0	0·0	194·1	1·0	0·2
Iraq												
All goods	3131·1	0·0	3128·2	2·5	0·0	0·1	2·5	0·0	0·0	0·2	1241·3	0·5
Primary products	3130·5	0·0	3128·1	2·1	0·0	0·1	1·9	0·0	0·0	0·0	1241·3	0·5
Manufactures	0·6	0·5	0·1	4·5	3·0	0·0	0·5	0·0	0·0	0·2	0·0	0·0
Israel												
All goods	613·1	2·1	226·6	6·2	1·9	0·0	0·0	364·5	2·3	46·7	24·7	6·1
Primary products	356·9	3·7	128·8	7·1	3·3	0·0	0·0	206·1	4·0	0·0	8·8	6·1
Manufactures	256·3	0·0	97·9	1·0	0·0	0·0	0·0	158·4	0·0	46·7	16·0	0·0
Ivory Coast												
All goods	882·7	0·0	318·4	1·2	0·0	0·0	0·0	564·2	0·0	3·3	45·9	0·1
Primary products	863·9	0·0	318·2	1·4	0·0	0·0	0·0	545·6	0·0	0·0	44·1	0·1
Manufactures	18·8	0·0	0·2	0·0	0·0	0·0	0·0	18·5	0·0	3·3	1·8	0·0

Appendix Table 1 continued

Source and kind of imports	Total imports		Imports subject to MFN			Imports under GSP		Other preferences		Imports subject to NTBs ($m)		
	Value ($m)	Weighted average rate	Value ($m)	Average rate Unweighted	Weighted	Value ($m)	Weighted rate	Value ($m)	Weighted rate	Export restraints	Licensing plus quotas	Variable levies
Jamaica												
All goods	117.9	0.0	6.8	0.2	0.0	0.0	7.9	109.7	0.0	0.2	20.4	29.4
Primary products	68.3	0.0	6.4	0.3	0.0	0.0	7.9	60.5	0.0	0.0	20.2	29.4
Manufactures	49.7	0.0	0.4	0.0	0.0	0.0	0.0	49.3	0.0	0.2	0.2	0.0
Kenya												
All goods	235.4	0.0	74.9	1.0	0.0	0.7	8.0	158.0	0.0	0.9	3.6	1.8
Primary products	225.5	0.0	73.0	1.2	0.0	0.7	8.0	149.9	0.0	0.0	0.9	1.8
Manufactures	10.0	0.0	1.9	0.0	0.0	0.0	0.0	8.1	0.0	0.9	2.7	0.0
Republic of Korea												
All goods	543.5	11.5	430.4	8.0	13.7	84.7	0.6	0.0	0.0	207.6	90.8	0.4
Primary products	100.1	3.3	39.6	4.0	4.6	32.2	1.6	0.0	0.0	0.0	5.4	0.4
Manufactures	443.3	12.9	390.8	10.8	14.6	52.5	0.0	0.0	0.0	207.6	85.4	0.0
Kuwait												
All goods	3718.5	0.1	3598.3	3.1	0.1	120.2	0.0	0.0	0.0	0.0	1409.5	0.0
Primary products	3708.5	0.1	3598.0	2.3	0.1	110.5	0.0	0.0	0.0	0.0	1409.4	0.0
Manufactures	10.0	0.0	0.3	4.4	1.7	9.7	0.0	0.0	0.0	0.0	0.1	0.0
Liberia												
All goods	381.1	0.0	370.4	0.0	0.0	0.0	0.0	10.7	0.0	0.0	1.5	0.0
Primary products	364.8	0.0	354.7	0.0	0.0	0.0	0.0	10.0	0.0	0.0	0.3	0.0
Manufactures	16.3	0.0	15.6	0.0	0.0	0.0	0.0	0.7	0.0	0.0	1.2	0.0
Libya												
All goods	5553.4	0.0	5475.0	5.9	0.0	78.4	0.0	0.0	0.0	0.0	2181.2	0.1
Primary products	5550.8	0.0	5474.8	4.1	0.0	75.9	0.0	0.0	0.0	0.0	2181.0	0.1
Manufactures	2.6	0.5	0.2	11.1	6.3	2.4	0.0	0.0	0.0	0.0	0.2	0.0
Madagascar												
All goods	129.8	0.0	38.4	0.2	0.0	0.0	0.0	83.1	0.0	6.4	6.2	8.3
Primary products	114.2	0.0	37.3	0.2	0.0	0.0	0.0	68.6	0.0	0.0	2.0	8.3
Manufactures	15.6	0.0	1.1	0.0	0.0	0.0	0.0	14.5	0.0	6.4	4.2	0.0
Malaysia												
All goods	1055.4	1.8	770.7	4.6	1.1	275.5	3.9	0.0	0.0	16.9	5.0	0.7
Primary products	957.8	1.2	714.9	3.2	0.1	234.2	4.6	0.0	0.0	0.0	0.2	0.1
Manufactures	97.6	8.2	55.7	7.4	14.2	41.3	0.0	0.0	0.0	16.9	4.8	0.6

	1	2	3	4	5	6	7	8	9	10	11
All goods	143·1	0·0	138·4	0·0	0·0	0·0	7·0	4·5	0·1	1·7	0·2
Primary products	142·9	0·0	138·4	0·0	0·0	0·0	7·0	4·3	0·0	1·7	0·2
Manufactures	0·2	0·0	0·0	0·0	0·0	0·0	0·0	0·2	0·1	0·0	0·0
Mauritius											
All goods	123·4	0·0	1·3	0·0	0·0	0·0	7·0	108·8	7·6	3·7	109·8
Primary products	112·9	0·0	1·1	0·0	0·0	0·0	7·0	98·4	0·0	0·8	109·8
Manufactures	10·6	0·0	0·2	0·0	0·0	0·0	0·0	10·4	7·6	2·9	0·0
Mexico											
All goods	409·6	3·5	271·2	4·7	3·8	121·8	2·9	0·0	41·2	25·3	8·5
Primary products	265·3	3·8	228·4	3·6	2·6	20·2	17·6	0·0	0·0	4·2	8·5
Manufactures	144·4	3·1	42·8	6·4	10·4	101·6	0·0	0·0	41·2	21·0	0·0
Morocco											
All goods	993·1	1·0	534·9	3·2	0·3	5·0	7·8	314·6	59·5	68·6	59·9
Primary products	893·4	1·2	529·5	3·6	0·3	5·0	7·8	220·2	0·0	55·0	59·9
Manufactures	99·7	0·0	5·3	0·0	0·0	0·0	0·0	94·4	59·5	13·6	0·0
Mozambique											
All goods	188·5	2·3	136·4	4·1	2·2	5·1	4·3	0·0	0·2	0·6	19·1
Primary products	186·0	2·2	134·9	3·7	2·1	4·1	5·4	0·0	0·0	0·4	19·1
Manufactures	2·5	3·9	1·5	6·7	6·6	1·0	0·0	0·0	0·2	0·2	0·0
Netherlands Antilles											
All goods	181·2	0·0	24·0	0·0	0·0	0·0	0·0	157·1	0·0	9·8	0·0
Primary products	147·3	0·0	7·4	0·0	0·0	0·0	0·0	139·9	0·0	9·4	0·0
Manufactures	33·9	0·0	16·7	0·0	0·0	0·0	0·0	17·2	0·0	0·4	0·0
Nigeria											
All goods	4566·8	0·0	4396·4	0·0	0·0	0·0	0·0	169·6	0·9	1658·9	0·0
Primary products	4547·3	0·0	4395·3	0·0	0·0	0·0	0·0	151·2	0·0	1656·2	0·0
Manufactures	19·5	0·0	1·0	0·0	0·0	0·0	0·0	18·5	0·9	2·8	0·0
Pakistan											
All goods	291·7	4·9	168·9	5·2	7·4	95·9	0·4	0·0	128·2	36·5	11·3
Primary products	89·1	1·1	53·5	2·2	0·5	8·7	4·7	0·0	0·0	0·8	11·3
Manufactures	202·6	6·0	115·4	8·7	10·6	87·2	0·0	0·0	128·2	35·7	0·0
Peru											
All goods	383·1	0·7	329·6	4·6	0·6	6·8	5·1	0·0	4·0	2·9	0·0
Primary products	374·7	0·5	325·1	2·8	0·4	2·9	11·9	0·0	0·0	1·1	0·0
Manufactures	8·5	6·2	4·6	8·3	11·4	3·9	0·0	0·0	4·0	1·8	0·0
Philippines											
All goods	309·1	1·5	215·1	4·6	0·9	79·1	3·1	0·0	5·6	1·6	1·1
Primary products	272·6	1·0	201·4	2·0	0·1	56·2	4·3	0·0	0·0	0·3	1·1
Manufactures	36·5	4·5	13·7	8·6	12·1	22·8	0·0	0·0	5·6	1·3	0·0

APPENDIX TABLE 1 *continued*

Source and kind of imports	Total imports Value ($m)	Weighted average rate	Imports subject to MFN Value ($m)	Average rate Unweighted	Weighted	Imports under GSP Value ($m)	Weighted rate	Other preferences Value ($m)	Weighted rate	Imports subject to NTBs ($m) Export restraints	Licensing plus quotas	Variable levies
Qatar												
All goods	1028·8	0·0	1025·5	5·3	0·0	3·3	0·0	0·0	0·0	0·0	408·2	0·0
Primary products	1025·4	0·0	1025·4	3·5	0·0	0·0	0·0	0·0	0·0	0·0	408·1	0·0
Manufactures	3·4	0·0	0·0	5·7	2·6	3·3	0·0	0·0	0·0	0·0	0·1	0·0
Saudi Arabia												
All goods	12961·1	0·0	12825·3	3·9	0·0	135·7	0·0	0·0	0·0	0·0	5084·4	0·0
Primary products	12949·4	0·0	12822·4	3·8	0·0	126·8	0·0	0·0	0·0	0·0	5084·0	0·0
Manufactures	11·8	0·1	2·9	4·1	0·4	8·9	0·0	0·0	0·0	0·0	0·4	0·0
Senegal												
All goods	288·1	0·0	151·3	0·1	0·0	0·0	0·0	136·6	0·0	1·0	15·6	0·0
Primary products	280·4	0·0	146·9	0·2	0·0	0·0	0·0	133·3	0·0	1·0	15·1	0·0
Manufactures	7·7	0·0	4·4	0·0	0·0	0·0	0·0	3·3	0·0	1·0	0·5	0·0
Singapore												
All goods	414·6	6·9	293·6	4·8	9·3	119·6	1·0	0·0	0·0	32·2	29·9	0·3
Primary products	126·6	2·4	107·9	3·3	1·9	17·3	7·2	0·0	0·0	0·0	1·5	0·3
Manufactures	288·0	8·8	185·7	7·4	13·6	102·3	0·0	0·0	0·0	32·2	28·4	0·0
Sri Lanka												
All goods	154·9	4·2	111·4	3·1	5·4	42·3	1·0	0·0	0·0	0·6	2·6	0·0
Primary products	143·0	4·5	102·7	2·3	5·8	39·2	1·0	0·0	0·0	0·0	0·2	0·0
Manufactures	11·9	0·5	8·7	4·7	0·7	3·1	0·0	0·0	0·0	0·6	2·4	0·0
Sudan												
All goods	171·2	0·0	155·9	0·5	0·0	0·0	0·0	12·6	0·0	0·1	3·1	2·6
Primary products	170·7	0·0	155·9	0·5	0·0	0·0	0·0	12·1	0·0	0·0	2·9	2·6
Manufactures	0·5	0·0	0·0	0·0	0·0	0·0	0·0	0·5	0·0	0·0	0·2	0·0
Syria												
All goods	292·7	0·1	281·9	0·4	0·0	0·1	14·5	10·7	1·2	1·7	98·5	0·0
Primary products	289·3	0·0	281·8	0·6	0·0	0·1	14·5	7·4	1·7	0·0	98·3	0·0
Manufactures	3·4	0·0	0·0	0·0	0·0	0·0	0·0	3·4	0·0	1·7	0·2	0·0
Taiwan												
All goods	725·6	15·0	720·9	9·1	15·0	0·0	0·0	0·0	0·0	229·3	113·1	0·0
Primary products	121·7	19·0	117·1	8·1	19·0	0·0	0·0	0·0	0·0	0·0	14·1	0·0
Manufactures	603·9	14·2	603·9	9·4	14·2	0·0	0·0	0·0	0·0	229·3	99·0	0·0

Thailand											
All goods	425.3	3.7	357.8	4.8	3.7	29.1	3.7	0.0	10.3	5.7	24.8
Primary products	362.0	3.6	317.4	3.3	3.4	9.1	11.5	0.0	0.0	0.2	21.9
Manufactures	63.3	3.9	40.3	7.3	5.7	20.1	0.2	0.0	10.3	5.5	2.9
Togo											
All goods	196.2	0.0	153.6	0.0	0.0	0.0	0.0	0.0	1.7	0.3	0.0
Primary products	192.5	0.0	153.4	0.0	0.0	0.0	0.0	0.0	0.0	0.0	0.0
Manufactures	3.7	0.0	0.2	0.0	0.0	0.0	0.0	0.0	1.7	0.3	0.0
United Arab Emirates											
All goods	2614.8	0.0	2613.8	3.0	0.0	1.1	1.0	0.0	0.2	1009.7	0.0
Primary products	2613.1	0.0	2612.8	1.3	0.0	0.3	3.7	0.0	0.0	1009.6	0.0
Manufactures	1.8	2.2	1.0	5.4	3.9	0.8	0.0	0.0	0.2	0.1	0.0
Tunisia											
All goods	495.7	0.4	244.6	3.1	0.3	0.4	8.8	0.6	40.3	78.9	114.0
Primary products	395.5	0.5	239.1	3.7	0.3	0.4	8.8	2.5	0.0	69.7	114.0
Manufactures	100.2	0.0	5.5	0.0	0.0	0.0	0.0	0.0	40.3	9.2	0.0
Uganda											
All goods	110.3	0.0	17.1	0.0	0.0	0.0	8.0	93.2	0.0	0.0	0.0
Primary products	110.0	0.0	17.1	0.0	0.0	0.0	8.0	92.8	0.0	0.0	0.0
Manufactures	0.4	0.0	0.0	0.0	0.0	0.0	0.0	0.3	0.0	0.0	0.0
Tanzania											
All goods	149.9	0.0	87.5	0.0	0.0	0.0	0.0	62.2	2.0	0.5	0.0
Primary products	137.0	0.0	78.4	0.0	0.0	0.0	0.0	58.6	0.0	0.1	0.0
Manufactures	12.8	0.0	9.2	0.0	0.0	0.0	0.0	3.7	2.0	0.4	0.0
Uruguay											
All goods	117.2	2.2	59.5	5.4	2.5	23.9	1.5	0.0	1.4	12.5	33.7
Primary products	92.2	2.9	56.2	5.2	2.4	2.2	15.9	0.0	0.0	2.4	33.7
Manufactures	25.0	0.6	3.3	5.9	4.9	21.7	0.0	0.0	1.4	10.0	0.0
Venezuela											
All goods	905.6	0.7	850.5	3.4	0.7	54.4	0.1	0.0	0.7	245.9	0.2
Primary products	893.3	0.7	843.5	2.5	0.7	49.0	0.1	0.0	0.0	245.4	0.2
Manufactures	12.3	0.2	6.9	5.7	0.4	5.4	0.0	0.0	0.7	0.4	0.0
Zaire											
All goods	1173.8	0.0	1010.7	0.0	0.0	0.0	0.0	163.1	0.0	2.2	0.0
Primary products	1155.5	0.0	1010.4	0.0	0.0	0.0	0.0	145.1	0.0	1.8	0.0
Manufactures	18.3	0.0	0.4	0.0	0.0	0.0	0.0	17.9	0.0	0.4	0.0
Zambia											
All goods	787.2	0.0	766.3	0.6	0.0	0.0	0.0	21.0	0.0	0.0	0.0
Primary products	786.2	0.0	765.7	0.8	0.0	0.0	0.0	20.5	0.0	0.0	0.0
Manufactures	1.0	0.0	0.5	0.0	0.0	0.0	0.0	0.5	0.0	0.0	0.0

APPENDIX TABLE 2. Trade Barriers Facing Individual Developing Countries in Japan

Source and kind of imports	Total imports Value ($m)	Weighted average rate	Imports subject to MFN Value ($m)	Average rate Unweighted	Weighted	Imports under GSP Value ($m)	Weighted rate	Other preferences Value ($m)	Weighted rate	Imports subject to NTBs ($m) Export restraints	Licensing plus quotas	Variable levies
Argentina												
All goods	229·0	4·7	199·7	8·4	5·0	29·3	3·2	0·0	0·0	0·0	28·3	0·0
Primary products	183·7	1·7	179·6	6·3	1·3	4·1	21·9	0·0	0·0	0·0	1·9	0·0
Manufactures	45·4	16·8	20·1	11·1	37·8	25·2	0·1	0·0	0·0	0·0	26·4	0·0
Bahrain												
All goods	375·1	5·0	375·0	4·7	5·0	0·0	0·0	0·0	0·0	0·0	306·8	0·0
Primary products	374·9	5·0	374·9	5·2	5·0	0·0	0·0	0·0	0·0	0·0	306·8	0·0
Manufactures	0·1	0·0	0·1	0·0	0·0	0·0	0·0	0·0	0·0	0·0	0·0	0·0
Brazil												
All goods	657·2	7·5	578·3	11·0	8·4	78·9	0·4	0·0	0·0	0·0	332·1	0·0
Primary products	555·7	8·0	533·8	11·1	8·3	22·0	0·8	0·0	0·0	0·0	284·0	0·0
Manufactures	101·5	4·5	44·6	11·0	9·8	56·9	0·3	0·0	0·0	0·0	48·1	0·0
Brunei												
All goods	884·8	6·6	884·8	3·8	6·6	0·0	0·0	0·0	0·0	0·0	0·0	0·0
Primary products	884·2	6·6	884·2	5·7	6·6	0·0	0·0	0·0	0·0	0·0	0·0	0·0
Manufactures	0·7	0·0	0·7	0·0	0·0	0·0	0·0	0·0	0·0	0·0	0·0	0·0
Chile												
All goods	404·3	0·8	315·7	3·3	1·0	88·7	0·0	0·0	0·0	0·0	246·3	0·0
Primary products	403·8	0·8	315·1	4·1	1·0	88·6	0·0	0·0	0·0	0·0	246·3	0·0
Manufactures	0·5	0·0	0·5	0·0	0·0	0·0	0·0	0·0	0·0	0·0	0·0	0·0
Cuba												
All goods	443·7	32·9	443·6	31·8	32·6	0·1	84·1	0·0	0·0	0·0	0·0	0·0
Primary products	438·7	32·9	438·6	52·4	32·9	0·1	15·1	0·0	0·0	0·0	0·0	0·0
Manufactures	5·0	0·0	5·0	1·0	0·0	0·0	0·0	0·0	0·0	0·0	0·0	0·0
Egypt												
All goods	168·7	0·2	165·7	21·6	0·2	3·0	0·9	0·0	0·0	0·0	0·6	0·0
Primary products	167·1	0·2	165·4	45·2	0·2	1·7	1·7	0·0	0·0	0·0	0·6	0·0
Manufactures	1·5	1·7	0·3	5·3	1·4	1·3	1·7	0·0	0·0	0·0	0·0	0·0

Hong Kong												
All goods	273·1	5·9	159·9	9·0	6·9	113·2	4·4	0·0	0·0	0·0	13·3	0·0
Primary products	59·1	3·2	55·8	7·1	3·0	3·3	6·6	0·0	0·0	0·0	7·1	0·0
Manufactures	213·9	6·7	104·1	10·0	9·1	109·8	4·3	0·0	0·0	0·0	6·2	0·0
India												
All goods	658·2	6·1	580·7	8·2	6·6	77·6	2·7	0·0	0·0	0·0	366·2	0·0
Primary products	562·0	6·2	537·8	6·0	6·5	24·2	0·3	0·0	0·0	0·0	361·2	0·0
Manufactures	96·2	5·9	42·9	10·5	8·4	53·4	3·8	0·0	0·0	0·0	5·0	0·0
Indonesia												
All goods	4571·5	2·4	4539·1	6·7	2·4	32·3	3·4	0·0	0·0	0·0	656·5	0·0
Primary products	4558·1	2·4	4532·3	6·4	2·4	25·8	3·7	0·0	0·0	0·0	656·3	0·0
Manufactures	13·4	3·5	6·8	7·3	4·7	6·5	2·3	0·0	0·0	0·0	0·2	0·0
Iran												
All goods	4766·2	2·7	4755·9	5·9	2·7	10·3	2·7	0·0	0·0	0·0	93·0	0·0
Primary products	4763·2	2·7	4753·2	5·1	2·7	10·0	2·7	0·0	0·0	0·0	93·0	0·0
Manufactures	3·0	1·5	2·7	7·2	1·5	0·3	1·2	0·0	0·0	0·0	0·0	0·0
Iraq												
All goods	201·6	2·7	201·6	2·6	2·7	0·0	0·0	0·0	0·0	0·0	11·4	0·0
Primary products	195·5	2·8	195·5	1·6	2·8	0·0	0·0	0·0	0·0	0·0	11·4	0·0
Manufactures	6·1	0·0	6·1	4·4	0·0	0·0	0·0	0·0	0·0	0·0	0·0	0·0
Republic of Korea												
All goods	1568·0	7·1	984·4	9·2	9·6	583·7	2·8	0·0	0·0	0·0	304·3	0·0
Primary products	534·2	7·3	475·2	8·9	7·4	59·0	6·7	0·0	0·0	0·0	260·4	0·0
Manufactures	1033·8	7·0	509·2	9·4	11·7	524·7	2·4	0·0	0·0	0·0	43·9	0·0
Kuwait												
All goods	2131·9	2·9	2131·9	3·7	2·9	0·0	0·0	0·0	0·0	0·0	366·5	0·0
Primary products	2131·6	2·9	2131·6	4·2	2·9	0·0	0·0	0·0	0·0	0·0	366·5	0·0
Manufactures	0·3	0·0	0·3	1·3	0·0	0·0	0·0	0·0	0·0	0·0	0·0	0·0
Libya												
All goods	364·0	2·7	364·0	1·3	2·7	0·0	0·0	0·0	0·0	0·0	0·0	0·0
Primary products	364·0	2·7	364·0	2·7	2·7	0·0	0·0	0·0	0·0	0·0	0·0	0·0
Manufacture	0·0	0·0	0·0	0·0	0·0	0·0	0·0	0·0	0·0	0·0	0·0	0·0
Malaysia												
All goods	979·0	1·0	917·9	5·9	0·8	61·1	3·1	0·0	0·0	0·0	31·1	0·0
Primary products	922·8	0·9	881·6	4·0	0·8	41·2	3·8	0·0	0·0	0·0	26·5	0·0
Manufactures	56·2	2·5	36·3	9·2	2·9	19·9	1·7	0·0	0·0	0·0	4·6	0·0

APPENDIX TABLE 2 continued

Source and kind of imports	Total imports Value ($m)	Total imports Weighted average rate	Imports subject to MFN Value ($m)	Imports subject to MFN Average rate Unweighted	Imports subject to MFN Average rate Weighted	Imports under GSP Value ($m)	Imports under GSP Weighted rate	Other preferences Value ($m)	Other preferences Weighted rate	Imports subject to NTBs ($m) Export restraints	Imports subject to NTBs ($m) Licensing plus quotas	Imports subject to NTBs ($m) Variable levies
Mexico												
All goods	308.4	8.7	281.5	11.6	9.4	26.8	1.1	0.0	0.0	0.0	52.1	0.0
Primary products	275.1	9.3	270.0	13.2	9.5	5.2	1.5	0.0	0.0	0.0	48.5	0.0
Manufactures	33.3	3.2	11.6	9.8	7.5	21.7	1.0	0.0	0.0	0.0	3.6	0.0
Nigeria												
All goods	448.9	2.7	445.7	1.7	2.7	3.2	1.0	0.0	0.0	0.0	2.8	0.0
Primary products	448.6	2.7	445.5	1.1	2.7	3.1	1.0	0.0	0.0	0.0	2.8	0.0
Manufactures	0.2	2.5	0.2	6.3	2.5	0.0	2.3	0.0	0.0	0.0	0.0	0.0
Peru												
All goods	297.0	1.6	290.0	7.7	1.6	7.0	0.4	0.0	0.0	0.0	205.8	0.0
Primary products	294.5	1.6	289.2	4.7	1.6	5.3	0.2	0.0	0.0	0.0	205.8	0.0
Manufactures	2.5	2.8	0.7	11.5	6.9	1.8	1.1	0.0	0.0	0.0	0.0	0.0
Philippines												
All goods	1104.8	11.0	995.1	12.3	8.3	109.7	36.3	0.0	0.0	0.0	487.9	0.0
Primary products	1067.7	11.3	978.7	14.6	8.3	89.1	44.2	0.0	0.0	0.0	487.8	0.0
Manufactures	37.1	4.8	16.4	9.3	8.0	20.7	2.2	0.0	0.0	0.0	0.1	0.0
Saudi Arabia												
All goods	5238.3	2.9	5237.9	2.5	2.9	0.4	0.0	0.0	0.0	0.0	1063.8	0.0
Primary products	5235.4	2.9	5235.4	3.0	2.9	0.0	0.0	0.0	0.0	0.0	1063.8	0.0
Manufactures	2.9	0.0	2.5	0.0	0.0	0.4	0.0	0.0	0.0	0.0	0.0	0.0
Singapore												
All goods	619.0	3.9	559.7	7.5	4.2	59.2	0.8	0.0	0.0	0.0	530.9	0.0
Primary products	547.8	4.0	542.7	6.3	4.0	5.1	6.0	0.0	0.0	0.0	522.5	0.0
Manufactures	71.2	2.5	17.0	8.8	9.6	54.1	0.3	0.0	0.0	0.0	8.4	0.0
Taiwan												
All goods	955.2	10.6	586.8	10.6	13.2	368.4	6.5	0.0	0.0	0.0	153.0	0.0
Primary products	438.1	15.8	372.2	11.7	14.7	65.8	21.8	0.0	0.0	0.0	117.1	0.0
Manufactures	517.1	6.1	214.6	9.3	10.4	302.5	3.1	0.0	0.0	0.0	35.9	0.0

Thailand												
All goods	685·8	13·1	643·5	9·3	13·7	42·3	2·8	0·0	0·0	0·0	50·0	0·0
Primary products	586·8	13·4	575·6	8·9	13·6	11·2	2·5	0·0	0·0	0·0	24·4	0·0
Manufactures	99·0	11·1	67·9	9·9	14·8	31·1	3·0	0·0	0·0	0·0	25·6	0·0
United Arab Emirates												
All goods	2116·0	2·7	2116·0	5·3	2·7	0·0	0·0	0·0	0·0	0·0	0·0	0·0
Primary products	2115·7	2·7	2115·7	1·5	2·7	0·0	0·0	0·0	0·0	0·0	0·0	0·0
Manufactures	0·3	0·4	0·3	11·7	0·3	0·0	0·0	0·0	0·0	0·0	0·0	0·0
Zaire												
All goods	108·9	0·0	74·8	0·2	0·0	34·2	0·0	0·0	0·0	0·0	46·5	0·0
Primary products	108·4	0·0	74·2	0·0	0·0	34·2	0·0	0·0	0·0	0·0	46·5	0·0
Manufactures	0·6	0·0	0·6	1·0	0·0	0·0	0·0	0·0	0·0	0·0	0·0	0·0
Zambia												
All goods	321·9	0·5	22·5	1·4	7·2	299·3	0·0	0·0	0·0	0·0	2·5	0·0
Primary products	321·2	0·5	21·9	2·8	7·5	299·3	0·0	0·0	0·0	0·0	2·5	0·0
Manufactures	0·7	0·0	0·7	0·0	0·0	0·0	0·0	0·0	0·0	0·0	0·0	0·0

APPENDIX TABLE 3. Trade Barriers Facing Individual Developing Countries in the United States

Source and kind of imports	Total imports		Imports subject to MFN			Imports under GSP		Other preferences		Imports subject to NTBs ($m)		
	Value ($m)	Weighted average rate	Value ($m)	Average rate Unweighted	Weighted	Value ($m)	Weighted rate	Value ($m)	Weighted rate	Export restraints	Licensing plus quotas	Variable levies
Algeria												
All goods	1088·7	0·9	1088·7	8·1	0·9	0·0	0·0	0·0	0·0	0·0	1021·7	0·0
Primary products	1084·5	0·9	1084·5	2·4	0·9	0·0	0·0	0·0	0·0	0·0	1021·7	0·0
Manufactures	4·2	2·6	4·2	10·7	2·6	0·0	0·0	0·0	0·0	0·0	0·0	0·0
Angola												
All goods	378·2	0·5	378·1	1·9	0·5	0·0	0·0	0·0	0·0	0·0	191·2	0·0
Primary products	376·3	0·5	376·3	2·7	0·5	0·0	0·0	0·0	0·0	0·0	191·2	0·0
Manufactures	1·8	0·0	1·8	0·0	0·0	0·0	0·0	0·0	0·0	0·0	0·0	0·0
Argentina												
All goods	372·0	3·7	238·3	9·8	5·7	133·6	0·0	0·0	0·0	2·0	72·0	0·0
Primary products	256·8	3·9	180·5	5·8	5·5	76·3	0·0	0·0	0·0	0·2	72·0	0·0
Manufactures	115·1	3·2	57·8	12·4	6·4	57·3	0·0	0·0	0·0	1·8	0·0	0·0
Bahamas												
All goods	936·3	0·8	920·6	5·9	0·8	15·6	0·0	0·0	0·0	0·0	704·8	0·0
Primary products	886·8	0·9	882·4	5·9	0·9	4·4	0·0	0·0	0·0	0·0	704·8	0·0
Manufactures	49·5	0·0	38·2	5·9	0·0	11·3	0·0	0·0	0·0	0·0	0·0	0·0
Brazil												
All goods	1671·4	2·8	1378·2	10·5	3·3	293·2	0·0	0·0	0·0	53·2	405·2	0·0
Primary products	1234·3	1·9	1096·8	4·9	2·2	137·5	0·0	0·0	0·0	4·0	405·2	0·0
Manufactures	437·1	5·1	281·4	13·6	7·9	155·7	0·0	0·0	0·0	49·2	0·0	0·0
Chile												
All goods	300·3	0·8	291·7	5·2	0·8	8·6	0·0	0·0	0·0	0·0	5·1	0·0
Primary products	293·0	0·8	285·3	2·9	0·8	7·7	0·0	0·0	0·0	0·0	5·1	0·0
Manufactures	7·3	0·1	6·4	10·4	0·1	0·9	0·0	0·0	0·0	0·0	0·0	0·0
Colombia												
All godds	511·5	3·1	488·2	13·7	3·2	23·3	0·0	0·0	0·0	32·8	63·6	0·0
Primary products	408·7	1·0	404·0	3·8	1·0	4·6	0·0	0·0	0·0	1·0	63·6	0·0
Manufactures	102·8	11·5	84·2	16·6	14·1	18·7	0·0	0·0	0·0	31·8	0·0	0·0
Costa Rica												
All goods	169·4	3·3	131·2	11·4	4·3	38·3	0·0	0·0	0·0	11·4	70·4	0·0
Primary products	154·2	1·2	118·1	3·3	1·6	36·1	0·0	0·0	0·0	0·2	70·4	0·0
Manufactures	15·2	24·4	13·1	19·0	28·5	2·2	0·0	0·0	0·0	11·2	0·0	0·0

Dominican Republic												
All goods	470·4	2·8	444·2	11·8	2·9	26·3	0·0	0·0	0·0	5·6	0·0	256·8
Primary products	451·4	2·5	430·6	7·9	2·7	20·8	0·0	0·0	0·0	0·0	0·0	256·8
Manufactures	19·0	8·8	13·6	18·2	12·3	5·5	0·0	0·0	0·0	5·6	0·0	0·0
Equador												
All goods	472·5	0·9	472·5	11·9	0·9	0·0	0·0	0·0	0·0	1·6	0·0	290·0
Primary products	466·5	0·9	466·5	6·6	0·9	0·0	0·0	0·0	0·0	1·2	0·0	290·0
Manufactures	6·0	6·8	6·0	15·1	6·8	0·0	0·0	0·0	0·0	0·4	0·0	0·0
El Salvador												
All goods	160·6	3·5	148·9	16·5	3·7	11·7	0·0	0·0	0·0	13·1	0·0	28·8
Primary products	132·0	0·8	129·9	5·2	0·8	2·1	0·0	0·0	0·0	0·5	0·0	28·8
Manufactures	28·6	15·8	19·0	19·8	23·7	9·6	0·0	0·0	0·0	12·6	0·0	0·0
Gabon												
All goods	162·3	1·2	162·3	6·4	1·2	0·0	0·0	0·0	0·0	0·0	0·0	141·4
Primary products	161·8	1·2	161·8	1·3	1·2	0·0	0·0	0·0	0·0	0·0	0·0	141·4
Manufactures	0·5	2·4	0·5	8·4	2·4	0·0	0·0	0·0	0·0	0·0	0·0	0·0
Ghana												
All goods	125·4	1·0	122·9	6·8	1·0	2·5	0·0	0·0	0·0	0·0	0·0	9·8
Primary products	124·2	1·0	121·8	2·1	1·0	2·4	0·0	0·0	0·0	0·0	0·0	9·8
Manufactures	1·2	3·4	1·1	10·2	3·8	0·1	0·0	0·0	0·0	0·0	0·0	0·0
Guatemala												
All goods	209·6	1·4	197·3	12·0	1·4	12·3	0·0	0·0	0·0	1·5	0·0	60·0
Primary products	198·4	1·2	189·1	3·9	1·2	9·3	0·0	0·0	0·0	0·0	0·0	60·0
Manufactures	11·2	4·3	8·2	16·0	5·9	3·0	0·0	0·0	0·0	1·5	0·0	0·0
Haiti												
All products	114·2	8·4	86·3	15·3	10·9	25·9	0·0	0·0	0·0	47·6	0·0	7·0
Primary products	28·8	0·2	18·9	3·5	0·4	7·9	0·0	0·0	0·0	0·4	0·0	7·0
Manufactures	85·4	10·9	67·4	18·4	13·8	18·0	0·0	0·0	0·0	47·2	0·0	0·0
Honduras												
All products	133·1	2·0	116·6	11·4	2·3	16·5	0·0	0·0	0·0	2·4	0·0	24·8
Primary products	125·8	1·5	109·9	7·7	1·7	15·9	0·0	0·0	0·0	0·1	0·0	24·8
Manufactures	7·3	10·2	6·7	14·9	11·1	0·6	0·0	0·0	0·0	2·3	0·0	0·0
Hong Kong												
All products	1611·3	11·0	1163·6	14·6	15·2	447·7	0·0	0·0	0·0	488·3	0·0	1·2
Primary products	27·0	1·9	15·4	6·4	3·4	11·6	0·0	0·0	0·0	10·2	0·0	1·2
Manufactures	1584·3	11·1	1148·2	16·6	15·4	436·1	0·0	0·0	0·0	478·1	0·0	0·0

APPENDIX TABLE 3 continued

Source and kind of imports	Total imports		Imports subject to MFN			Imports under GSP		Other preferences		Imports subject to NTBs ($m)		
	Value ($m)	Weighted average rate	Value ($m)	Average rate Unweighted	Weighted	Value ($m)	Weighted rate	Value ($m)	Weighted rate	Export restraints	Licensing plus quotas	Variable levies
India												
All products	553·0	3·9	490·1	12·2	4·4	62·9	0·0	0·0	0·0	70·6	33·9	0·0
Primary products	185·2	0·9	170·7	4·0	1·0	14·5	0·0	0·0	0·0	0·4	33·9	0·0
Manufactures	367·9	5·4	319·5	15·0	6·3	48·4	0·0	0·0	0·0	70·2	0·0	0·0
Indonesia												
All products	1686·3	0·7	1686·3	9·0	0·7	0·0	0·0	0·0	0·0	1·2	1154·3	0·0
Primary products	1661·5	0·7	1661·5	3·8	0·7	0·0	0·0	0·0	0·0	0·1	1154·3	0·0
Manufactures	24·8	2·7	24·8	11·6	2·7	0·0	0·0	0·0	0·0	1·1	0·0	0·0
Iran												
All products	2132·1	1·0	2132·1	4·6	1·0	0·0	0·0	0·0	0·0	20·7	1911·5	0·0
Primary products	2100·3	0·9	2100·3	4·6	0·9	0·0	0·0	0·0	0·0	0·0	1911·5	0·0
Manufactures	31·8	7·7	31·8	13·1	7·7	0·0	0·0	0·0	0·0	20·7	0·0	0·0
Israel												
All products	279·0	5·0	218·4	14·0	7·0	60·6	0·0	0·0	0·0	25·9	5·0	0·0
Primary products	27·7	3·5	23·2	8·5	4·2	4·5	0·0	0·0	0·0	1·0	5·0	0·0
Manufactures	251·3	5·7	195·2	15·9	7·3	56·1	0·0	0·0	0·0	24·9	0·0	0·0
Jamaica												
All products	232·5	2·2	225·8	12·5	2·2	6·7	0·0	0·0	0·0	8·4	38·6	0·0
Primary products	137·6	1·6	133·6	5·1	1·6	4·0	0·0	0·0	0·0	0·0	38·6	0·0
Manufactures	94·9	3·1	92·2	17·0	3·2	2·7	0·0	0·0	0·0	8·4	0·0	0·0
Republic of Korea												
All goods	1424·2	12·8	1188·6	12·8	15·3	235·6	0·0	0·0	0·0	289·3	2·3	0·0
Primary products	296·6	5·5	291·2	4·7	5·6	5·4	0·0	0·0	0·0	9·6	2·3	0·0
Manufactures	1127·6	14·7	897·4	15·6	18·5	230·2	0·0	0·0	0·0	279·7	0·0	0·0
Malaysia												
All goods	761·8	1·6	714·4	9·9	1·8	47·4	0·0	0·0	0·0	8·3	65·4	0·0
Primary products	548·5	0·3	541·6	2·1	0·4	6·9	0·0	0·0	0·0	0·0	65·4	0·0
Manufactures	213·2	5·0	172·8	15·1	6·2	40·5	0·0	0·0	0·0	8·3	0·0	0·0
Mexico												
All goods	3358·8	4·5	2464·0	10·9	6·2	894·8	0·0	0·0	0·0	199·5	287·7	0·0
Primary products	1390·5	3·6	991·9	6·3	5·0	398·5	0·0	0·0	0·0	12·0	287·7	0·0
Manufactures	1968·4	5·2	1472·1	14·0	7·0	496·3	0·0	0·0	0·0	187·5	0·0	0·0

Netherlands Antilles												
All goods	1995·5	0·9	1993·6	6·5	0·9	2·0	0·0	0·0	0·0	0·0	1355·1	0·0
Primary products	1978·9	0·9	1978·0	0·7	0·9	0·9	0·0	0·0	0·0	0·0	1355·1	0·0
Manufactures	16·6	3·0	15·6	11·0	3·2	1·0	0·0	0·0	0·0	0·0	0·0	0·0
Nigeria												
All goods	3287·5	0·9	3287·5	5·6	0·9	0·0	0·0	0·0	0·0	0·0	3042·1	0·0
Primary products	3285·4	0·9	3285·4	1·8	0·9	0·0	0·0	0·0	0·0	0·0	3042·1	0·0
Manufactures	2·1	3·3	2·1	8·6	3·3	0·0	0·0	0·0	0·0	0·0	0·0	0·0
Peru												
All goods	587·2	1·2	347·4	10·5	2·1	239·8	0·0	0·0	0·0	0·8	176·8	0·0
Primary products	576·2	1·2	338·8	3·0	2·1	237·4	0·0	0·0	0·0	0·3	176·8	0·0
Manufactures	11·0	2·2	8·6	16·0	2·8	2·4	0·0	0·0	0·0	0·5	0·0	0·0
Philippines												
All goods	1118·2	5·4	1015·8	13·9	5·9	102·4	0·0	0·0	0·0	73·5	503·7	0·0
Primary products	937·2	3·1	862·5	5·6	3·4	74·7	0·0	0·0	0·0	1·2	503·7	0·0
Manufactures	181·0	17·1	153·3	17·7	20·2	27·7	0·0	0·0	0·0	72·3	0·0	0·0
Saudi Arabia												
All goods	1672·6	0·9	1672·6	5·9	0·9	0·0	0·0	0·0	0·0	0·0	1515·6	0·0
Primary products	1665·0	0·9	1665·0	0·5	0·9	0·0	0·0	0·0	0·0	0·0	1515·6	0·0
Manufactures	7·6	0·0	7·6	8·7	0·0	0·0	0·0	0·0	0·0	0·0	0·0	0·0
Singapore												
All goods	541·2	6·5	394·8	11·3	9·0	146·4	0·0	0·0	0·0	68·5	32·5	0·0
Primary products	92·8	1·2	90·4	1·8	1·2	2·3	0·0	0·0	0·0	1·8	32·5	0·0
Manufactures	448·4	7·6	304·4	15·5	11·3	144·0	0·0	0·0	0·0	66·7	0·0	0·0
Taiwan												
All goods	2089·5	10·8	1446·0	13·4	15·5	643·5	0·0	0·0	0·0	436·3	32·4	0·0
Primary products	166·0	4·7	144·5	6·6	5·4	21·5	0·0	0·0	0·0	20·3	32·4	0·0
Manufactures	1923·5	11·3	1301·5	15·7	16·7	622·0	0·0	0·0	0·0	416·0	0·0	0·0
Thailand												
All goods	179·3	5·0	165·2	11·5	5·5	14·2	0·0	0·0	0·0	23·5	6·1	0·0
Primary products	123·7	0·9	121·8	5·0	1·0	1·9	0·0	0·0	0·0	0·5	6·1	0·0
Manufactures	55·6	14·1	43·4	15·1	18·1	12·3	0·0	0·0	0·0	23·0	0·0	0·0
Trinidad and Tobago												
All goods	1248·8	1·3	1230·8	7·3	1·3	18·1	0·0	0·0	0·0	1·9	1073·2	0·0
Primary products	1231·8	1·2	1217·0	4·7	1·2	14·9	0·0	0·0	0·0	0·5	1073·2	0·0
Manufactures	17·0	3·7	13·8	9·5	4·6	3·2	0·0	0·0	0·0	-1·9	0·0	0·0

APPENDIX TABLE 3 *continued*

Source and kind of imports	Total imports		Imports subject to MFN			Imports under GSP		Other preferences		Imports subject to NTBs ($m)		
	Value ($m)	Weighted average rate	Value ($m)	Average rate Unweighted	Weighted	Value ($m)	Weighted rate	Value ($m)	Weighted rate	Export restraints	Licensing plus quotas	Variable levies
United Arab Emirates												
All goods	365·0	0·9	365·0	9·0	0·9	0·0	0·0	0·0	0·0	0·0	344·1	0·0
Primary products	363·4	0·9	363·4	6·6	0·9	0·0	0·0	0·0	0·0	0·0	344·1	0·0
Manufactures	1·6	0·7	1·6	10·3	0·7	0·0	0·0	0·0	0·0	0·0	0·0	0·0
Venezuela												
All goods	4677·4	0·7	4677·4	9·2	0·7	0·0	0·0	0·0	0·0	0·7	3002·1	0·0
Primary products	4640·2	0·7	4640·2	5·9	0·7	0·0	0·0	0·0	0·0	0·0	3002·1	0·0
Manufactures	37·2	1·8	37·2	10·7	1·8	0·0	0·0	0·0	0·0	0·7	0·0	0·0

Notes

1. See Prebisch (1964). Specifically, Prebisch called for (1) international commodity agreements to give developing country producers of primary products the same sort of price-support and price-stabilisation assistance enjoyed by farmers in developed countries; (2) preferential access for exports of manufactures and semi-manufactures from developing countries to developed country markets; (3) preferential arrangements among developing countries to allow them to gain the advantages of specialisation in larger markets.
2. General Assembly Resolution 2626 adopted in 1970. For a discussion of the recent performance of LDCs in relation to the growth targets established in the Strategy see UNCTAD (March 1977a).
3. The International Development Strategy calls for each industrial nation to provide a minimum net flow of financial resources (gross disbursements of grants, loans and direct portfolio investment, less repayments of principle and disinvestment) amounting to 1 per cent of its GNP to developing countries. Of the total, more than two-thirds—0·7 per cent of GNP—should be in the form of official development assistance. Other important targets of the Strategy are a 6 per cent growth rate for real product, a growth rate of 3·6 per cent in gross product per head, an 8 per cent growth rate for manufacturing output. The important aid target has never been approached, with the 17 member states of the OECD Development Assistance Committee providing about 0·35 per cent of their collective GNP in the form of development assistance in 1970–1. See UNCTAD (1973d) for a discussion of the primary objectives of the Strategy.
4. General Assembly Resolutions 3201 (S VI) and 3202 (S VI). A principle difference between these resolutions and the International Development Strategy is that the Strategy attempted to resolve the development problem through a series of measures operating within the existing institutional framework. In contrast, the Declaration and Programme of Action call for a restructuring of the institutional framework of the international order itself.
5. Resolution 3281 (XXIV). Two of the more controversial of the Charter's propositions were (1) the affirmation of each state's 'full permanent sovereignty' over its natural resources and economic activities in addition to the 'right to nationalise, expropriate or transfer ownership' of foreign property with compensation decided upon by domestic tribunals, and (2) that 'all states have the *duty* [author's italics] to co-operate in achieving

221

adjustments in prices of exports of developing countries in relation to the prices of imports'. This latter provision has been interpreted to mean that developed countries were obligated to refrain from all efforts to break producer or similar developing country cartels.

6. The Manila Declaration (i.e., the position paper of the Group of 77 countries for the UNCTAD IV meetings in Nairobi) stresses the dual objective of stabilising and supporting commodity prices. Specifically, the Declaration calls for 'effective application of appropriate measures and procedures for indexing the price of commodities exported by developing countries to the prices of manufactures imported from developed countries' as well as 'reduction of excessive fluctuations in commodity prices and supplies in the interests of both producers and consumers'. See UNCTAD (May 1976a).

7. As an illustration, in 1972 copper constituted about 70 per cent of Chile's export earnings, 90 per cent for Zambia, and 60 per cent for Zaire. Sugar accounted for about 90 per cent of Mauritius' exports, and 80 per cent for Cuba and Reunion. Cotton is of prime importance to a number of developing countries, accounting for over 60 per cent of Sudan and Chad's export earnings, and about 45 per cent for Egypt. Tea was Sri Lanka's major export crop accounting for 60 per cent of export revenues, while 65 per cent of Ghana's originated from cocoa.

8. Provisions for establishing an International Trade Organisation (ITO) were negotiated in Cuba from November 1947 to March 1948, and were embodied in a document known as the Havana Charter. More than 50 countries participated in the negotiations and managed to reconcile divergent positions represented by 800 amendments to the draft charter sufficiently to agree upon a code of conduct for international trade. The ITO never formally came into operation since the United States and the United Kingdom refused to ratify the Charter. However, during the preparatory sessions a group of 23 countries agreed to negotiate tariff concessions which resulted in the formation of the General Agreement on Tariffs and Trade in January 1948.

9. Since 1950 there have been only five comprehensive international commodity agreements covering cocoa, coffee, wheat, sugar and tin. Of these, only the agreements for cocoa, tin, and coffee have been successfully renegotiated. UNCTAD attributes these failures to a reluctance of consuming countries to intervene in free markets, and the fact that the case by case approach, which has been employed for negotiations, tends to accent the commercial interests of industrial countries as buyers of a particular product.

10. Several studies have indicated that the figure of $3 billion suggested by UNCTAD is too low for the complete programme. For example, Kreinin and Finger (1976) estimate that buffer stocks worth about $9 billion would have been required to hold tin and copper prices to within 15 per cent of their trend value over the period 1956–73. Thus, the value of stocks required for these two commodities alone are three times UNCTAD's estimate for the complete programme. In a related study, Krause (1975) argues that establishing buffer stocks at too low a level may destabilise rather than partially stabilise commodity prices.

11. Improving conditions of LDC access to industrial country markets is a common theme that runs through much of the United Nations' thinking on current development problems. See in particular UNCTAD (December 1975) or UNCTAD (June 1973).

12. Several recent studies have challenged the view that the external environment has more of a retardation effect on the development effort than the internal policies pursued by many LDCs. Kreinin and Finger (1976) suggest that 'the harm that the LDCs inflict upon themselves exceeds what the developed nations do to them. For example, very steep and highly variable import duties designed to facilitate import substitution to the hilt cause gross misallocation of resources, discriminate against exports, and result in widespread production at negative value added. Having pursued such an import policy, LDC policy-makers proceed to wonder why the multinational companies attracted to invest in them have a strong preference toward producing for the heavily protected domestic market, as against the export market.' Similar arguments have been advanced in Grubel (1977).

CHAPTER 2

1. See Kindleberger (1958, pp. 238–59) for a more detailed analysis of these foreign trade models. Other studies which discuss the influence of trade on development include Helleiner (1972) and Meier (1968). An excellent synopsis of recent thinking on the role of trade in development is contained in Diaz-Alejandro (1975).

2. Suppose that one man-day of labour produces 60 bushels of wheat or 20 yards of textiles in the United States, and 20 bushels of wheat or 10 yards of textiles in the United Kingdom. Even though labour is more productive absolutely in the USA, there are different degrees of relative advantage. The United States has a 3 to 1 advantage in wheat and only 2 to 1 advantage in textiles. Since the USA is relatively more productive in wheat, while the UK is least disadvantaged in textiles, both nations will be better off if they specialise in these items and trade. For a proof see Kreinin (1975, pp. 218–55).

3. Trade was also thought to provide an important stimulus to capital accumulation and the availability of other domestic factors. The benefits associated with trade result in higher incomes, which increases the capacity to save. Increased funds are thus made available for new investment, while the incentive to invest is strengthened by increased returns and wider markets associated with international trade.

4. A variant of this argument emphasises the potential importance of economies of scale in production. Classical free trade based on comparative advantage may give less than an optimal allocation of resources because of increasing returns to scale which may not be achieved under free-trade prices and volumes. With protection and higher prices, an increase in scale may result which could *ultimately* lead to a lower price than that which would prevail under trade based on the *initial* conditions of comparative advantage.

5. See Keesing (1967). Haberler (1959) also accents four distinct ways in which developing countries can realise dynamic gains from trade: the provision of the material means of development in the form of capital goods, machinery, and raw and semi-finished materials; access to technological knowledge, skills, managerial talents and entrepreneurship; the receipt of capital through international investment; and the stimulating influence of competition.

6. A discussion and empirical analysis which identifies industries that experience scale economies is presented in Moroney (1967). Economists generally concur that scale economies result from such factors as cost savings associated with bulk purchase orders, opportunities to make fuller use of managerial skills, and the ability to effectively utilise research and development.

7. The difference between scale economies and specialisation should be noted. Specialisation implies the realisation of cost-savings due to the adoption of new production techniques in which capital and labour are used in narrower, more well defined activities, or in different proportions. Thus, the production function is being altered. Economies of scale refer to savings that accrue as production volumes are increased, but with the same factor proportions and techniques employed.

8. In a historical perspective, declining transportation costs associated with improvements and technological innovations in shipping played a key role in opening new markets to trade, which allowed producers to achieve many economies associated with scale effects and specialisation. Reduction in the cost of carriage also enabled specialisation and division of labour on a national and international basis to replace the relatively self-sufficient economies that previously predominated in the Western world. For a discussion of the interactions between declining transportation costs, expanding markets and development, see North (1958).

9. A criticism which has been directed at multinational corporations is that these organisations may not adopt production technologies which are optimal for the needs of the developing country. Capital intensive techniques have been selected, or skilled workers imported from abroad, while the local labour force is employed in positions requiring menial skills with no educational benefit. In these cases, the manufacturing or production activities are conducted in a form of 'enclaves' with few important benefits extending to most of the local population. Two situations which reflect some of these problems are discussed in Gadiel (1966) and Lim (1968).

10. In assessing the contribution of international trade to development, Meier (1968, p. 220) stresses the potential importance of these educational effects in noting 'perhaps of even more value than the direct importation of material goods is the fundamental educative effect of trade. A deficiency of knowledge is a more pervasive handicap to development than is the scarcity of any other factor. Contact with more advanced economies provides an expeditious way of overcoming this deficiency. The implementation of technical know-how and skills is an indispensable source of technological progress, and the importation of ideas in general is a potential stimulus to development. Not only is this vital for economic change in itself, but also for

political and socio-cultural advances which may be the necessary preconditions of economic progress. By providing the opportunity to learn from
the achievements and failures of the more advanced countries, and by
facilitating selective borrowing and adaptation, foreign trade can help
considerably in speeding up a poor country's development.'

11. The central figure in Schumpeter's analysis of the development process is
the entrepreneur, the individual who undertakes new combinations of the
factors of production. These innovations may take any one of the following
forms: (1) the introduction of a new good, (2) the development of a new
method of production, (3) the development of a new source of raw material
supply, (4) the opening of a new market, or (5) the reorganisation of an
industry. Often these innovational activities will provide an important long-
term stimulus to economic growth and development. See Schumpeter
(1934).

12. The potential advantages and disadvantages of import-substitution as a
development strategy are discussed by Little, Scitovsky, and Scott (1970,
pp. 59–79) and in Diaz-Alejandro (1975).

13. Studies which have been undertaken indicate that the levels of protection in
some LDCs are often very high with nominal rates reaching 100 or 200 per
cent. Protection at these levels can cause serious distortions in factor
markets or between industries. Serious discriminatory effects against
agriculture often result from the high levels of industrial protection. For
analyses and information on protection policies in some developing
countries see Balassa and Associates (1971).

14. This shift in the composition of import demand can have important
consequences in periods of low foreign exchange reserves. As long as
finished goods are imported, an occasional inability to pay for these items
lowers living standards by making the products unavailable. When these
goods are produced domestically with the aid of imported components, an
inability to purchase these materials can cause work stoppages, unemployment, and a reduction of incomes generated by domestic manufacturing.

15. Situations in which import-substitution policies have produced some
favourable results are discussed in Baer (1972) and Hirschman (1968).

16. Risk aversion will lead investors to participate less in activities subject to
unstable prices and earnings than their private or social profitability
demands. Instability may also lead to excessive investment in boom
periods, and excessive retrenchment in times of slack demand. Fluctuations
in investment can result in shortages or excess capacity, which has a further
disequilibrating effect on prices. Capital wastage may occur if construction
begun during an expansion is abandoned and left to deteriorate during
contractions. Other possible consequences of instability include the reduction of savings rates and the creation of inflationary pressures.

17. This classification scheme is suggested by Morton and Tulloch (1977, p. 99).

18. The problem of price instability for several commodities falling in groups
one and two is aggravated by a price-quantity cobweb cycle in which
current quantity changes are associated with price fluctuations which
occurred several years in the past.

19. While adverse *consequences* of export instability are discussed in a
forthcoming section, the basic *cost* is that of carrying, or borrowing,

sufficient foreign exchange reserves to enable the economy to operate over the fluctuations. The relative size of exports in total gross national product will be a major factor determining the magnitude of this cost (see Table 2.1).

20. Obviously, the commodities in which a country specialises have an important influence on stability of export prices and earnings. For example, one recent empirical study found that revenues from food exports were considerably more stable than proceeds from most other commodities. Short-term prices for items in which producers have some degree of countervailing power (such as bauxite, manganese, and petroleum) are also likely to be more stable than in markets where producers do not have some degree of market control.

21. For simplicity, the country is assumed to export equal shares of the two products, since a modification of equation 2–1 would be required if the shares differ. A related analysis of a firm's incentive to diversify is presented in Scherer (1970, pp. 101–2).

22. Empirical investigations which have found a positive association between export concentration and instability include Massel (1970) and Michaely (1962). However, different conclusions are reached in MacBean (1966). To some extent the conflicting results may be due to deficiencies in the measures used in these studies. This point is discussed by Tuong and Yeats (1976).

23. The United Nations has identified 13 problem commodities which combine low growth with unstable prices. These commodities are further classified as: those in actual or potential long-term surplus due to excess supply, and commodities facing serious competition from synthetics. The first group includes coffee, sugar, tea and rice, while cotton, rubber, lauric oils, jute, wool, hides and skins, sisal, essential oils and vanilla are included in the second category.

24. Some economists have argued that the terms of trade (i.e., the relative purchasing power) of commodities have declined against manufactures over the long run. This is used as another argument for LDCs' diversifying out of traditional exports into manufactures. The empirical evidence concerning declining terms of trade is mixed, but many studies have supported the proposition.

25. Relationships between product bulk, fragility, and freight costs can have an important influence on the location of processing activity. For example, *supply oriented* industries are those where processing tends to be located near raw material sources due to the fabricated goods having markedly lower shipping costs. For the most part these commodities are weight-losing in processing, or increase substantially in value. *Market oriented* commodities add weight or bulk, or become more fragile with processing (furniture, plywood and veneers, beverage bottling, etc.), and tend to be processed near major markets. Transport costs for *footloose industries* are generally unimportant, and changes in weight or volume are small. For a discussion of the influence of transport costs on industry location see Kindleberger (1968, pp. 93–101).

26. A number of subsequent studies elaborated on, or disputed, some of Kravis' conclusions. See among others Crafts (1973), Adams (1973), and Hanson (1977).

27. Crafts (1973) has challenged these first two conclusions arguing that Kravis did not account for the secondary and induced effects (i.e., dynamic productivity gains of the classical analysis) of trade on growth. Crafts also finds fault with the use of the rate of growth of the share of exports in domestic product (E/Y) as a measure of the importance of trade since the two variables are correlated. If the marginal propensities to save and import fall in an appropriate range, the expansion in exports would cause domestic product to grow even faster. Thus, the ratio (E/Y) would decline and fail to reveal the true contribution of exports to growth.

28. Using gross national product as a measure of market size, Kravis finds that the relative GNPs of the centre to the periphery countries was about 2 to 1 one hundred years ago, while today the ratio stands at about 4 or 5 to 1. Thus, the current markets for developing countries are potentially more important than in the past. It is also observed (p. 851) that the protectionist policies of industrial countries reduce the effective size of markets and lower the development potential of trade for LDCs.

29. If $D_{o,j}$ and $D_{t,j}$ represent world demand for product j at time o and t respectively, while $s_{o,j}$ is the developing country's share of the world market in the initial time period, the world market factor $(E_{w,i})$ for country i is defined by,

$$E_{w,i} = \sum^{j} (s_{o,j})(D_{t,j} - D_{o,j}) \qquad (2\text{--}2)$$

while the competitive factor index $(E_{c,i})$ is estimated from,

$$E_{c,i} = \sum^{j} (s_{t,j} - s_{o,j})(D_{o,j}) \qquad (2\text{--}3)$$

The third index, the diversification factor, is set equal to the actual change in exports minus each of the above elements.

30. A separate test for the period 1860–1900 arrives at similar conclusions regarding the relative importance of the demand and competitive factors. See Hanson (1977).

31. A separate body of literature, commonly referred to as 'two-gap' analysis, has developed around the premise that developing countries are relatively powerless to influence the level of their export earnings. For an exposition of this theory see Chenery and Strout (1966).

32. See Meier (1968, pp. 239–48). The role of these 'preconditions' is emphasised (p. 248) as an explanation of why trade may fail to stimulate growth. 'No matter how strong the stimulus from trade, it is essential that the prior development of the society and its economy should result in a positive and self-reinforcing response to it. If this necessary foundation exists, international trade can then release latent indigenous forces which can exploit, in turn, the stimulus from the export sector and produce further transformative effects throughout the economy. Unlike this favourable situation, however, the domestic economy of some poor countries remains fragmented and compartmentalised, the transfer of resources from less productive to more productive employment has been restricted, and the linkage of markets and their subsequent extension have been handicapped.

The secondary round of activities induced by an increase in exports has thereby been cut short, and the dynamic gains from trade have not been fully realized.'

33. Internal policies LDCs might pursue which could promote exports and more favourable growth prospects are discussed in Little, Scitovski and Scott (1970, pp. 231–69). It should also be noted that these internal constraints are not independent of external factors. If trade barriers in industrial countries were liberalised, this would heighten the attractiveness of export markets. In response, forces might be set in motion within the LDCs to enable producers to take better advantage of these profitable opportunities. In other words, internal changes can result from external stimuli.

CHAPTER 3

1. For example, the average yearly variation in prices of 50 primary commodities studied by the United Nations Secretariat was 14 per cent per annum over the period from 1900 to 1950. The report notes that, as the value of exports fluctuates widely, a specialised country lacks control over national income, money supply, fiscal policy, etc., and hence over its rate of development. See United Nations (1952). In a more recent study, Massell (1970) shows that LDCs have experienced fluctuations in export earnings which are 50 per cent greater than those of developed countries over the period 1950–66.

2. In retrospect, the decade of the 1960s was a remarkably prosperous period for the LDCs. One set of estimates suggests that the exports of developing countries whose foreign exchange earnings were not primarily from petroleum rose by 6 per cent per year in the 1960s as compared with a corresponding rate of 0·8 per cent in the previous decade. See Cohen and Sisler (1971). This period of relative prosperity largely ended with the OPEC price rises in the early 1970s which had profound effects on world employment, demand and trade.

3. For example, over the period 1950–73 exports of developing countries in Asia rose approximately 535 per cent from $7·7 billion to $49·2 billion. In contrast, exports from Saudi Arabia rose almost 20 times their 1950 level of $340 million, while Korea's exports were more than 15 times their earlier value of $23 million. Exports from Hong Kong also registered an increase of about 670 per cent which was well above the Asian average. In Africa, the overall increase of about 550 per cent is inflated by Nigeria's increase in petroleum exports of close to 1400 per cent, while Libya exported over $3 billion in 1973 from a base of only $11 million in 1950.

4. The LINK project is a large-scale econometric effort which ties together individual econometric models that have been estimated for the world's industrial economies. As such, the model permits analysis of the effects of various policy measures on world trade, employment, capital flows, and other international economic variables. The system was broadened considerably with the recent inclusion of models for developing countries. For a description see Klein, Moriguchi, and Van Peeterssen (1975).

5. The decline in developing country market shares for primary products is a long-run phenomenon that has serious economic implications. For example, Cohen (1968) notes that if developing countries had maintained their 1952–4 market position for 23 primary commodities exported to North America and Europe, their 1962–4 foreign exchange earnings would have been almost $900 million higher. This loss may have been as much as 20 per cent of the foreign aid flow to LDCs in 1962. Chapter 5 in this book argues that the protectionist policies of industrial countries, and the growing tendency for these governments to subsidise agricultural exports, have been a major factor accounting for the displacement of the LDC producers in world markets.

6. Other factors have led to a lower share of primary commodities in developing country exports. Competition from synthetics has been keen in some areas, particularly the substitution of manmade fibres for various natural textiles. Maizels (1965) suggests that inroads by synthetics may have resulted in an LDC trade loss of $1·5 billion a year by the early 1960s. In addition, some developing country policy actions appear to have excessively pushed industrialisation projects to the extent that production advantage in primary commodities was sacrificed. Finally, the unstable political and social conditions existing in many developing countries have caused some industrial nations, particularly Japan, to shift to Australia, Canada, South Africa or the United States for stable supplies of raw materials.

7. An alternative diversification index is defined by,

$$H_j = \left[\sum \left(\frac{x_i}{X} \right)^2 \right]^{\frac{1}{2}} \qquad (3\text{--}2)$$

where x_i is the value of commodity i exports, and X is the total of country j's exports. This measure also ranges between zero and one, with the latter indicating complete concentration of exports. This index has some statistical problems, however, in that it cannot distinguish between a country broadly diversified in a common group of products, like agriculture, as opposed to another which exports a wider range of commodities. See Tuong and Yeats (1976).

8. This index value was computed with data from the period 1960–70 and is defined by,

$$F_j = \frac{100}{n} \sum \frac{|x_t - \hat{x}_t|}{\hat{x}_t} \qquad (3\text{--}3)$$

where x_i is the value of aggregate export earnings of country j at time t, $\hat{x}_t$ is the corresponding exponential trend value, and n is the number of years covered.

9. See Yeats (in press). For a description of the United States off-shore assembly provisions and an analysis of their influence on the level and composition of imports see Finger (September 1976).

10. For a theoretical and technical discussion of problems in the measurement of terms of trade see Kindleberger (1956).

11. Maizels (1965, p. 13) states that 'there is no doubt that over the past decade

(i.e., the late 1950s and early 1960s) the underdeveloped areas have suffered a sharp deterioration in their terms of trade, equivalent to a loss of some $4 billion, or about one-eighth of their total current export earnings'. Alternative views tend to regard these changes in primary commodity terms of trade as long-term cyclical phenomena. Declining terms of trade in one period lower real investment, which results in reduced output and higher real prices in future intervals.

12. One set of estimates suggests the income elasticity of demand for developing country primary products during the 1960s ranged between 0·65 and 0·75 in the United States and European Economic Community, but was actually negative in the United Kingdom. See Cohen and Sisler (1971).

13. See United Nations (1950) or United Nations (1963).

14. A divergent view is presented in Haberler (1961). Meier (1968, pp. 41–65) also suggests that long-term movements in the terms of trade for developing countries may have improved due to quality changes in their imports, access to a wider range of imports, and a relative decline in *ad valorem* transportation costs.

15. See UNCTAD (1968). This source provides the exact SITC code designation for each processing stage. As an indication of their overall importance, the products comprising these processing chains accounted for about 50 per cent of developing country non-petroleum exports to OECD nations in 1974.

16. See United Nations (various issues a). Information on the USSR's imports from developing countries was taken from UNCTAD (April 1977). Similar information on the USSR's imports was not available for 1964.

17. These totals include imports by Denmark, France, Germany, Japan, Sweden, the United Kingdom and the United States. Altogether, these seven countries accounted for over 70 per cent of total OECD imports from developing countries in 1974. They therefore constitute the major markets for LDC products.

18. Massive shifts in Japan's sources of supply resulted in sizeable foreign exchange losses for some developing countries. For example, in 1964 Japan received about 82 per cent of her iron ore requirements from LDCs, but by 1974 their share declined to about 44 per cent. This reduction in market share, caused by greatly expanded imports from Australia, resulted in a $800 million trade loss for developing countries. Though not as dramatic, Canada and South Africa also made important inroads into LDC metal ore markets over the decade.

19. As indicated earlier, many economists have called for diversification of LDC exports away from traditional goods into semifinished items and manufactures. Yet the analysis of market share information shows this policy may have caused sizeable annual losses in foreign exchange if it resulted in insufficient investments for modernisation and expansion of primary good capacity. While this analysis does not contest the need for LDCs to diversify exports, the estimated trade loss of $1·4 billion indicates the necessity of striking a proper balance between new investment in primary and processed good production capacity.

20. The change in the primary product ratio overstates somewhat the deconcentration which has occurred due to the declining LDC market

shares. For example, if developing countries had maintained their overall market position (46 per cent) for these items, these exports would have accounted for 55 per cent of the 1974 total. Thus, a decline of 3 percentage points in the primary product ratio is *not* due to actual deconcentration, but a market loss for primary goods.

21. There is no single satisfactory measure of market size. However, the population adjusted figures probably indicate an upper limit to the potential developing country trade. For example, if Soviet imports were to match the average of the Western countries deflated by GNP, this would imply an LDC trade expansion of about $3·5 billion. A related study, which employs international price comparisons, also concludes that the trade barriers erected by Soviet block states are often many times higher than in the market economy countries. See Pryor (1966).

22. A key question centres on the extent to which this shift has spread through the developing countries as a group, as opposed to several fast growing exporters of manufactures. Table 3.3 suggests that changes in overall composition of exports are due to a relatively few countries as most concentration indices remained relatively stable.

23. Kreinin (1977) suggests that the primary economic effects of the OPEC price increases were: a severe blow, both direct and indirect, through the shrinkage of Western markets, to the external and internal position of developing countries; a marked contribution to the world-wide inflation; a strong contractionary impact on the economies of the industrial OECD countries (superimposed upon other recessionary trends occurring at that time); and an unfavourable effect on the balances of payments and currency markets of the industrial nations.

24. Prior to the OPEC price rise, UNCTAD estimated that developing countries could attain a 6 per cent target growth rate for gross product if the economically advanced countries provided 1 per cent of their GNP in net financial resource transfers. In a subsequent study UNCTAD (April 1976b) revised its estimate upward by 50 per cent if LDCs are to attain the International Development Strategy target growth rate by 1980.

CHAPTER 4

1. The advantage of specific tariffs is that they remove an incentive to falsify customs invoices in order to reduce import taxes. Since these fixed-charge-per-unit tariffs are imposed irrespective of product value, under-reporting import values will not reduce the tariff liability as it will for *ad valorem* duties. The disadvantage of specific tariffs is that their protective effect can be eroded by inflation, while they may also have a differential impact on various grades of similar goods.

2. Some indication of the importance of a c.i.f. versus an f.o.b. rate base can be derived from recent United States import statistics which now show the transportation and insurance cost components of imports. Using India as an illustration, shifting to a c.i.f. base would effectively raise US import tariffs on textile fabrics (SITC 653) and travel goods (SITC 831) by 15 to 25 per cent, on crude materials (SITC 276) by about 35 to 40 per cent, while

import duties on nonferrous base metal ores, which have an *ad valorem* transport rate of over 50 per cent of the f.o.b. price, would rise by over 40 per cent. For data and an analysis of India's transportation costs on exports to the USA see Yeats (October 1977).

3. For example, the tariff schedules may list an *ad valorem* duty of 20 per cent on a chemical product which sells for $100 per ton on the foreign market. However, if the equivalent ASP price for this item is set at $175 this figure will be used for valuation purposes and the actual tariff will be 35 per cent of the foreign f.o.b. price. Grubel and Johnson (1967) estimate that the ASP system generally raised benzenoid chemical tariffs by about 70 to 100 per cent above the median rate of 26 per cent published in the US tariff schedules.

4. A further complexity is that, under many GSP schemes, imports from a specific country may lose their preferential status after certain ceilings or quotas are surpassed. Thus, if preferential exports from (say) Korea to the EEC, were to exceed a predetermined annual level, further shipments of these goods would lose their preferential status and have to be imported under normal MFN rates. It has been suggested that these ceilings often seriously retard the operation of some GSP programmes due to the uncertainty as to whether a given export shipment will qualify for preferential tariff treatment when it actually arrives in the foreign market.

5. This comparison excluded duty free imports, or items imported under very low tariffs (i.e., *ad valorem* equivalent rates of less than 0.5 per cent). Tariff lines in which either the developed or developing country group had less than $5000 in exports were also excluded from the analysis. Thus, the empirical tests were performed on the common set of products which were exported jointly to Switzerland by developed and developing countries.

6. It is interesting to note that the equivalent *ad valorem* rate on developing country products fell below that for industrial countries by 4·5 per cent or more in close to 6 per cent (73) of the tariff lines. An examination of the basic data indicates that there are two types of goods in which this unusual 'reverse' incidence occurs. First, there is the case where the developing countries are producing specialty products, such as Near-Eastern tobacco, which have higher unit values due to quality or related differentials. Second, with Swiss agricultural tariffs being levied on a weight basis, there is evidence that the LDC-industrial country product-weight ratio is even lower than the corresponding value ratio in a number of tariff lines.

7. For example, the average *ad valorem* incidence of the specific tariffs on manufactures in SITC 6 is 5·7 per cent for industrial countries and 12·1 per cent for LDCs; in SITC 8 (Miscellaneous Manufactured Articles) the tariff rate is 4·6 per cent as opposed to 10·1 per cent for developing countries. Employing a sample of about 200 tariff line items Yeats (March 1976) found similar evidence that United States specific tariffs impose *ad valorem* equivalents on LDC manufactures which are roughly double (19·2 as opposed to 10·4 per cent) those on industrial country products.

8. On the positive side, the protective effect of specific tariffs can be seriously eroded by inflation. Yeats (March 1976) estimates that over the period 1966–72 import price increases reduced the overall *ad valorem* equivalents

of United States specific tariffs by about 20 per cent.

9. The four-digit Brussels Tariff Nomenclature (BTN) level generally represents the lowest level of aggregation at which tariff comparisons can be made, i.e., at which imports into individual countries can be summed up to obtain combined trade weights. In other words, world trade weights could not be used for averaging tariffs *within* each four-digit BTN heading due to the number of divergent sub-classifications used by various countries. For derivation of a four-digit BTN tariff average only two methods are available, computation of a simple average of tariff line data, or a weighting by each country's own imports can be used. After this is done, the estimated four-digit rates can be combined via one of the weighting systems (*a* through *e*) to make international comparisons of tariffs at higher levels of aggregation.

10. For a detailed analysis of the results of the Kennedy Round negotiations see Preeg (1970) or Evans (1971). An analysis of the Kennedy Round results from the viewpoint of the developing countries is presented in UNCTAD (1968).

11. See GATT (June 1966). UNCTAD has added some items to this list whose low capital and high unskilled labour input requirements would seem to make them likely candidates for future production in LDCs.

12. However, subsequent analysis will show that import tariffs do not constitute the most important trade restraints for either agricultural products or textiles in the EEC. Here a system of variable import levies is applied to agricultural products whose *ad valorem* equivalents will be shown to frequently dwarf tariff rates which are also applied to these items. Agricultural imports are strictly controlled by Japan through a system of licensing requirements which insulate domestic producers from low cost foreign competition. Finally, textile and clothing exports from a number of LDCs are strictly limited in all industrial markets by a variety of export restraints which are part of the current Multifibre Arrangements.

13. For an excellent non-technical discussion of the implications of these assumptions, as well as other points concerning the effective protection model see Grubel (1971), while a more complete technical discussion can be found in Michaely (1977).

14. Assume a 20 per cent tariff is applied to a product which sells for $10 on the world market, while its raw material inputs, which account for 60 per cent of the free trade production value, are not subject to an import duty. Since the tariff raises the domestic price of the product, protection permits the producer to operate with a value added of $6 as opposed to a value added of $4 under free trade. The effective tariff would be 50 per cent ($6−$4)/$4, as opposed to a nominal tariff of 20 per cent.

15. Continuing with the previous example, if a duty of 10 per cent is levied on material inputs for product *j*, production costs could rise by 60 cents. However, as indicated by equation 4–6, the effective tariff rate accounts for the combined effects of duties on inputs and the final product. While the tariff on the final good adds $2 to free trade value added, the input tariff lowers this coefficient by 60 cents. Thus, the joint effect of the two tariffs results in a value added of $5.40, which is 35 per cent (the effective tariff

rate) above the free trade level. It should be noted that the effective tariff can be negative. This situation may occur when the weighted tariffs on inputs exceed that on the final product.

16. Alternatively, some effective rate studies have employed actual input shares from Belgium and the Netherlands as approximations to free trade coefficients under the assumption that these countries have low protection profiles. However, this procedure has come under attack since it has been demonstrated that Benelux tariffs can cause serious bias if undeflated input shares are used for the derivation of effective protection estimates. Also, Benelux seems to have substituted nontariff barriers for tariffs in a number of important industries, with the result that the former cause important distortions in production shares from free trade values.

17. For example, the 35 per cent effective tariff indicated in the previous example means that foreign producers must operate with a value added of about $1·04 which is 26 per cent lower than their counterparts in the protected market. Since returns to factors of production are artificially raised in the industrial nation, market forces lead to a larger allocation of labour and capital in the import competing sector than would occur in the absence of protection. Conversely, the relatively lower return reduces capital availability in the export sector of the LDC. Thus, the effective rate of protection serves as an index which shows the extent to which returns to productive factors must be curtailed if developing countries are to export to the protected industrial markets.

18. Noting that the denominator in equation 4–6 is an alternative expression for the free trade value added coefficient, this formulation can be recast as,

$$E_j = (t_j - \bar{t}_i + \bar{t}_i V_j)/V \qquad (4\text{–}8)$$

where $\bar{t}_i$ is the weighted average tariff on inputs. Division by t_j gives the effective rate of protection as a multiple of the nominal rate for the end product,

$$E_j/t_j = (1 - \alpha)/V_j + \alpha \qquad (4\text{–}9)$$

where α is the ratio of the nominal protection for inputs over that for the final product. Equation 4–9 has been used to derive the functional relations shown in Figure 4.2

19. Tumlir and Till (1971) estimated effective protection for a common group of industries using four different averaging procedures to derive *ad valorem* tariffs, and showed that different systems of weights for tariff averaging produce sizeable changes in ERP estimates as well as different rankings of industries by effective protection levels.

20. Recent studies have shown that effective rate estimates must also be regarded with caution due to problems associated with inaccurate input coefficients. For example, Yeats (February 1976) demonstrated that effective protection estimates may be considerably in error when production data pertaining to a previous period are used for derivation of current ERP estimates. Also, Sampson (1974) has shown that the error in input coefficients associated with substitution among factors of production may be significant.

21. Effective protection from both tariffs and transport charges can be derived from the following equation for a country which levies import duties on a free-on-board basis,

$$E_j = \frac{(t_j + r_j) - \sum a_{ij}(t_i + r_i)}{1 - \sum a_{ij}} \tag{4-11}$$

where r_j and r_i are *ad valorem* transport rates for the final product and its material inputs.

22. As shown by equation 4–10.1, the effective rate equals the nominal rate on the end product (t_j) when this duty equals the (weighted) average input tariff. Since this condition held rather closely for a number of the primary goods, the stage 1 nominal tariffs have been reproduced in Table 4.6 as approximations to the effective protection rates.

23. These overall results are subject to the biases involved in any form of tariff averaging. For example, if OECD trade-weighted averages had been used, the average effective rates shown for the stage 3 and 4 products would have been higher due to the overall importance of textile products. Somewhat stronger evidence of escalation can be observed in pre-Kennedy Round effective rates. However, the deeper cuts in tariffs for manufactures than semi-finished goods seems to have acted as an equalising factor for items falling in stages 2 to 4.

24. For a complete derivation see MacPhee (1974, pp. 44–6). The European import demand elasticities employed in the present analysis were estimated by several individuals for the UNCTAD Secretariat. Since estimates of import supply elasticities were scarce and were considered less reliable than the other data, the trade expansion simulations were run under the assumption of unitary supply. Also, for the European countries, estimates of *ad valorem* equivalents for variable levies were added to existing tariffs when simulating the effect of removal of a trade barrier.

25. There is some justification for believing that removal of the EEC barriers may result in the LDCs, increasing exports above these predicted levels. Since the import figures recorded in Table 4.8 exclude intra-trade among EEC member states, the expansion estimates are downward biased to the extent that non-EEC sources can displace these trade flows. In the absence of the artificial protective barriers, it appears that some of this intra-trade would become unprofitable and be directed to foreign sources of supply.

26. Other empirical studies have reached similar conclusions concerning the magnitudes of LDC trade expansion associated with a removal of tariff barriers on their exports. In an empirical analysis of the effects of the Kennedy Round, Finger (March 1976) estimated LDC tariff elasticities which ranged from 5·4 for the EEC to 9·5 for the USA. While such estimates are subject to margins of error, they suggest that the LDC trade response to tariff cuts is on the order of 5 to 9 times the percentage reduction in import duties.

CHAPTER 5

1. It appears that a further qualification should be added for some of UNCTAD's group B measures; they must be applied in a differential manner which raises relative prices or production costs of foreign firms. In other words, to be classified as a nontariff barrier the measure must discriminate in favour of domestic producers. Failure to make this important distinction may have led to the classification of some measures as NTBs without the required evidence concerning discrimination. For example, health and sanitary regulations are considered to be nontariff restraints since they raise production costs of foreign producers, yet these same measures are applied to firms operating in the domestic market. Unless the regulations are differentially enforced with the specific intent of raising foreign production costs relative to domestic producers, they should not be considered NTBs.

2. Global quotas fix the total amount of a particular product that can be imported from any source during a given time period, while selective or discriminatory quotas perform the same function with regard to specific foreign suppliers. Several other types of quotas exist. Seasonal quotas are used in the agricultural sector to limit imports to periods when there is no domestic harvest, or when supply conditions are tight. With a tariff quota, a predetermined volume of imports is admitted under a base tariff rate with additional imports incurring higher duties. Voluntary restraints are bilateral agreements under which individual countries agree to reduce exports to a particular market where they are viewed as disruptive. These measures have steadily grown in importance, as the GATT estimates they now cover between 3 to 5 per cent of world trade.

3. Domestic procurement and content regulations may be considered forms of quantitative restraints since they can effectively limit imports. For example, discriminatory government procurement promotes public purchases of goods and services from domestic sources even when competitive import supplies are less costly. Domestic content regulations also require fixed percentage purchases from domestic units although foreign goods may be more attractively priced. Tied aid is a corollary to this type of NTB. Under tied aid programmes, recipient countries are required to purchase goods in the donor nation even though more competitive terms may be offered by other suppliers.

4. For example, certificates of origin may be required either as standard practice or sporadically at the discretion of customs officials. Different customs invoicing procedures are employed by importing nations demanding thorough familiarity on the part of exporters with valuation regulations. In some cases, incidental fees or taxes may be required on importation, or customs stamps may have to be purchased. There may also be provisions which prevent the refund of duties paid on defective items which are re-exported. Apart from these explicit customs matters, inadequate port and warehousing facilities, or high transfer charges, may be a source of additional costs, delays, or other uncertainty which constitute negative influences on trade.

5. Under the GATT regulations, Article XI prohibits application of quanti-

tative restraints to imports from other contracting members. However, the list of exceptions includes provisions to alleviate critical shortages of foodstuffs; enforcement of domestic restraints on particular products; removal of temporary agricultural surpluses (Article XI); balance of payments adjustments (Article XII); enforcement of domestic health and sanitary measures (Article XX), and measures dictated by national security (Article XXI). A concession is made to developing countries in that Article XVIII permits their use of quantitative restraints to protect infant industries.

6. Since exporters are interested in maximising total export earnings, a quota could cause a change in the composition of exports from low to high price items within the quantitative restriction. The reduced availability of the low priced good will disproportionately effect consumers of such items, i.e., the quota could effectively constitute a regressive tax on low income groups. In addition, if exporters were able to shift from low to higher priced items this would reduce the initial favourable change in the balance of payments for the country applying the quantitative restriction.

7. For analyses of similarities and differences in trade effects of tariffs and quotas see Bhagwati (1965), Kreinin (1970), Shibata (1968) and Walter (March 1971).

8. When considered from the viewpoint of the limit pricing model, further differences between the consequences of tariffs and quotas become apparent. Limit pricing suggests that firms may purposely hold prices at competitive levels to discourage entry by outsiders. Under tariffs, domestic firms are still faced with the threat of foreign competition if their prices become excessive. Thus, the uncertainty as to the potential reaction of foreign firms, and the amount of the tariff they may be willing to absorb, can have a moderating influence on price and production policies of domestic producers. In other words, the *threat of entry* causes them to follow more competitive pricing practices. However, with a quota this competitive stimulus is missing since the measure sets an upper limit to the market share and extent of potential entry by foreign firms.

9. The adverse effects of quantitative restraints may be far more serious for LDCs who are only in the process of developing their export sectors than for more mature economies such as Korea, Brazil, Hong Kong or Taiwan. For the countries just starting the industrialisation process, the quantitative restraints may lock them into minor market shares and not permit achievement of favourable scale effects associated with larger production volumes and rapid export growth.

10. Appendix Tables 1 to 3 provide tabulations of individual developing countries' exports which are covered by nontariff restrictions in the European Economic Community, Japan and the United States.

11. While the UNCTAD inventory has been established primarily to serve the needs of the developing countries, the United States have developed a similar data source for their own negotiators. For a description of the procedures used in the construction of the inventory see United States Tariff Commission (1974).

12. The measure suffers from the problems of any 'own trade-weighted' index in that products facing very restrictive NTBs will enter the calculation with

zero or low weights. The index is therefore downward biased since it fails to account for the most trade restrictive NTBs. An alternative to weighting the coverage of national nontariff measures by a country's own imports would be to employ OECD trade weights. This measure is defined as

$$O_j = \frac{M_{r,\,w}}{M_{j,\,w}} \tag{5–3}$$

where $M_{r,\,w}$ represents the sum of OECD imports to which the country applies its NTBs, while $M_{j,\,w}$ indicates the total OECD imports of commodity group j.

13. The comparisons illustrate one of the serious problems associated with the use of NTB inventories; there is no way to differentiate between the trade restrictive effect of the various restraints. Thus, the United States health standards are counted equal to the EEC variable levies even though the latter have a far greater impact on price margins. The case for classifying health standards as NTBs is so marginal the forthcoming analysis argues that, in many instances, they should not be considered as such.

14. Disruption was defined in Article X and in Annex C to the arrangement as a situation containing the following elements,
    (1) a sharp and substantial increase or potential increase of imports of particular products from particular sources;
    (2) these products are offered at prices which are substantially below those prevailing for similar goods of comparable quality in the market of the importing country;
    (3) there is serious damage to domestic producers or threat thereof;
    (4) the price differentials referred to in item (2) do not arise from governmental intervention in the fixing or formation of prices, or from dumping practices.

15. See Roningen and Yeats (1977). When the NTB *ad valorem* equivalents derived in this study are tested in a partial equilibrium trade model of the sort developed in Chapter 4, it is estimated that removal of these restraints would increase textile imports by the United States and France by about 35 to 45 per cent.

16. See UNCTAD (1973a, p. 149). This document also analysed the economic effects of Japan's restrictions on leather footwear and concluded that imports would have been close to 60 per cent higher in the absence of these measures. The implied trade loss for developing countries is put at $6 million.

17. It should be stressed that a potential weakness of such a tabulation is that it merely shows the *actual* trade values covered by the nontariff restraints, but gives no indication as to the *potential* trade which would occur in the NTBs' absence.

18. The product groups on which this study was based are; prepared and preserved meats, prepared and preserved vegetables, household and ceramic articles, prepared and preserved fruits and juices, starch derivatives and products, sugar confectionery and chocolate. In a related study, Ingo Walter (May 1971) ranked indices of LDC comparative advantage for 60 three-digit SITC products with coverage ratios for nontariff barrier

application. The positive significant correlation coefficient was interpreted as further evidence that the NTBs are used to discriminate against developing country products.

19. This point was clearly recognised by the US Tariff Commission (1974, p. 40) which noted; 'When specific trade barriers are to be identified and dealt with, it becomes necessary to add limitations or qualifications to very broad definitions (of NTBs). A frequently used qualification has been to limit the definition to government laws, regulations, policies, or practices that are intended to protect domestic producers from foreign competition. A key aspect of this qualification has been put in terms of equal market access for foreign and domestic products; and *if discrimination is absent* [author's italics] a trade barrier is not recognised to exist.'

20. This problem seems to be an integral part of any tabulation of nontariff trade restraints, i.e., reporting units are frequently not able to differentiate between real and imagined barriers. For example, in its study the US Tariff Commission (1974, p. 43) noted: 'It is clear from the public submissions in the Commission's investigations that businessmen and traders generally regard as "barriers" to their trade virtually any policy, action or arrangement—whether governmental or non-governmental and regardless of purpose—which increases cost of delivering their product in a market. In these submissions, numerous complaints did not involve any element of actual discrimination or even implied discrimination against the imported product.'

21. A further problem with the inventory approach is that if any one country reports a restriction, it must normally be assumed that the measure applies equally to all exporters of that product. For example, health standards which restrain imports from a relatively few countries (say those in North Africa) are assumed to apply to all nations. The problem is that an inventory can merely indicate whether or not a trade restraint exists. It cannot tell how important the restraint is, nor how many individual nations are influenced by the measure.

22. The GATT has established a two-fold test for non-discriminatory operation of state trading agencies, namely, the use of objective conditions of purchase or sale as the basis for trading decisions, and the provision of adequate opportunities for all contracting parties to compete for the trade involved. To date, only three fully documented cases have been brought before the GATT involving complaints that state agencies were not acting in accord with the established standards. In contrast, UNCTAD has recorded virtually all reported cases of state trading in its inventory with little analysis to determine if the GATT standards were being violated. For a discussion of how state trading should function within the GATT framework see Baban (1977).

23. For example, 72 per cent of agricultural production is covered by price support schemes plus external protection, while 25 per cent of total output has exclusively external protection. In general, price support programmes have been applied to products in which the EEC wishes to maintain self-sufficiency. Finally, supplementary production aid covers 2·5 per cent of production, and aid at a fixed rate per hectare accounts for 0·6 per cent.

24. Specifically, production subsidies permitted the EEC domestic price of olive

oil to fall to 64 per cent of the producer price over 1967–72. In this situation, external protection was lower than would have been required in the absence of this support. High production subsidies for olive oil result in reduced demand for other substitute products such as peanut oil, coconut oil, and corn oil.

25. While the value of the variable levy may be changed frequently, published estimates indicate that figures shown in Table 5.4 are generally representative of their longer-term levels. For some products, however, they may be low. For example, during 1968–9 and 1969–70, the *ad valorem* incidence of the levies was over 500 per cent on butter while those for sugar ranged from 110 per cent to 330 per cent. See UNCTAD (1972).

26. See Sampson and Yeats (1976). This study indicates that Sweden has taken the lead in extending the variable levy system outside the agricultural sector and now uses these special charges to control imports of some plastics and chemicals falling in SITC 5.

27. A further point worth noting is that a clear tendency exists for both the level and coverage of EEC protection to expand in recent years. For example, over the interval 1968–73, the Community extended the Common Agricultural Policy to include additional commodities—notably wine, tobacco and fishery products. Governmental expenditures in support of agricultural markets in the Community have also increased markedly from about $500 million in 1960, to $1500 in 1967, and reached $2400 million in 1969.

28. Similar conclusions emerge from a comparison of Swedish tariffs and import levies on a common group of agricultural products, although the divergence may in fact be somewhat larger. See Sampson and Yeats (1976, pp. 886–7).

29. A related study has attempted to evaluate empirically levels of agricultural price support in industrial countries. Norway and Switzerland emerge as the most highly protected economies with average levels of agricultural prices more than 100 per cent above world levels in 1968–9. Estimates for other countries are; Sweden—80 per cent, Austria— 39 per cent, Benelux—74, France—66, West Germany—69, Italy—78, and Great Britain—31 per cent. See Gulbrandsen and Lindbeck (1973, p. 38). A study of United States agricultural protection also revealed some very high effective rates; 143 per cent for food grains, 100 per cent for cotton, 204 per cent for peanuts, and 590 per cent for sugar. See Wipf (1971).

30. These results are based on a large-scale world food agricultural econometric model which has been developed at UNCTAD and the FAO. For purposes of this exercise, the world has been subdivided into 28 basic countries or producer regions, and supply and demand equations have been estimated for all major food products. The levels of agricultural protection tested in these simulations were those in effect during 1970. For a description see UNCTAD (March 1972).

31. However, many developing countries are large net importers of certain agricultural products. For example, India and the Philippines import wheat, rice, and cotton, while Brazil and Pakistan import wheat. Taiwan imports soybeans, cotton, and wheat—all in substantial quantities. Removal of agricultural protection in the industrial markets would raise both world demand and prices for these commodities, with the result being a loss

to the developing countries who are net importers.

32. General Agreement on Tariffs and Trade (1958). For a critique which points out some of the problems in trying to use price differentials for measuring NTBs see Holzman (1969).

33. See Dardis (1967) and Pryor (1966). As measured by price differentials for goods exported by LDCs, the Pryor study finds trade barriers erected by socialist countries are more than four times higher than in Western market economy countries.

34. The formula employed for estimating the *ad valorem* incidence of the nontariff restraints (B_j) was,

$$B_j = (P_{dj}/P_{wj}) - (N_j + T_j) - 1 \cdot 0 \tag{5-9}$$

where P_{dj} and P_{wj} are domestic and world prices for commodity j, N_j is the nominal tariff rate, and T_j is the estimated *ad valorem* incidence of various taxes. Products covered by subsidies should be excluded from the domestic-world price comparison since these payments will mask the incidence of NTBs. It should be noted that equation 5–9 still incorporates the effect of international transport charges which work to maintain price differentials between consumer nations.

35. Estimates of United States transport costs were taken from Finger and Yeats (1976), while German rates were estimated by Moneta (1959). While no similar comprehensive study exists on Japan's transport costs, comparison of c.i.f. and f.o.b. import-export values suggested an average *ad valorem* freight rate of slightly over 15 per cent.

CHAPTER 6

1. At the start of the Kennedy Round negotiations, the American delegation suggested that tariffis, with a minimum of exceptions, be reduced by 50 per cent with the cuts phased over five annual instalments. However, the EEC had reservations about this approach since its tariffs were concentrated in the 10 to 20 per cent range while the US duties were more widely dispersed with some even exceeding 100 per cent. Unless something was done about these peaks, the EEC tariffs would be uniformly low while the US would still be left with substantial protection for some items. As an alternative, the EEC offered a proposal which incorporated larger percentage cuts in high tariffs, thus *harmonising* or equalising tariffs between countries. What finally emerged was a compromise between these and other proposals.

2. For example, the price of imports in the consuming market can be assumed equal to,

$$p_d = p_f (1 + t_0) \tag{6-1}$$

where p_f is the delivered foreign price of the commodity (an adjustment is required if tariffs are levied on the f.o.b. base) and t_0 is the *ad valorem* tariff. If the import duty is reduced to t_1, the domestic price can change by,

$$p_d = (t_0 - t_1)/(1 + t_1) \tag{6-2}$$

Multiplication of this expected price change, or some variant incorporating supply elasticities, by the elasticity of import demand yields the projected change in imports. A study which employed this approach is Balassa and Kreinin (1967).

3. A compendium of results and survey of studies which estimate international trade elasticities is published in Stern (1976).

4. Equations 4–12 to 4–15 develop a partial equilibrium model incorporating supply and demand elasticities which can be employed for this approach. If estimates for supply elasticities are not available, one may be forced to employ the simpler model outlined in equations 6–1 and 6–2, or to assume a relevant range for this parameter and determine the sensitivity of results to changes in these values.

5. Proper evaluation of the trade effects of alternative tariff formulas requires a model such as that indicated by equations 6–1 and 6–2 be used in connection with appropriate supply and demand elasticities for individual products. Depth of tariff cut is employed here as a very rough approximation to the results from a partial equilibrium trade model.

6. Algebraically, the value of trade creation (TC_i) for good i can be measured from

$$TC_i = M_i n_i [\Delta t_i / (1 + t_i)] \qquad (6\text{-}5)$$

where M is the initial level of donor country imports from beneficiaries, n_i is the import demand elasticity, while Δt_i and t_i are the change and initial tariff values. Trade diversion (TD_i) can be approximated by,

$$TD_i = TC_i(Mn_i / V_i) \qquad (6\text{-}6)$$

where n represents donor country imports from non-beneficiaries and V is domestic production. For a proof see Baldwin and Murray (1977).

7. The EEC scheme actually consists of three distinct types of quotas. First, *overall* tariff quotas are established for each product on the basis of 1974 imports plus a supplement of 5 per cent of imports from all other sources in the most recent year. Second, the EEC allocates these total ceilings among member states so that eight separate donor ceilings are created for each product group. Finally, quotas limit the share of each product which may be filled by any one beneficiary to no more than 50 per cent, with limits as low as 15 per cent for some sensitive goods.

8. The United States employs a competitive need criteria which has negative effects similar to the EEC limitations. The US ceilings stipulate no beneficiary shall continue to receive preferential tariff treatment on products where its US exports exceed $25 million (subject to a growth factor), or where it has over 50 per cent of the United States import market for that item.

9. Baldwin and Murray (1977) cite a case where Portland Cement exported by East Africa will not qualify for US tariff preferences even if wholly produced there since indirect costs of this item account for 68 per cent of ex-facory cost.

10. Since the United States did not initiate their Generalised System of Preference plan until 1976, the US figures are estimates which apply indicated preferences to the 1974 trade values. Also, the EEC figures

include imports under the GSP as well as special preferences extended to associate developing countries. For a breakdown of trade under these two preference systems see Appendix Tables 1 to 3.

11. A tabulation shows that 56 per cent of United States OAP imports from developing countries were composed of electronics products while 13 per cent were machinery. Miscellaneous metal products and other manufactures each accounted for 10 to 11 per cent of the total while textiles had about 8 per cent. See Finger (1975).

12. Recent estimates of the trade creation effect of the EEC's Generalised System of Preferences are in the range of $100 to 110 million, while the US off-shore assembly provisions are reported to increase LDC exports by $96 to 130 million. No estimates of OAP trade creation were made for the European Market, nor for GSP trade creation in the United States. See Finger (1975).

13. These conclusions are based on annual trade flows and assume that the GSP will continue in perpetuity. However, if this programme is limited to a 10 or 20 year period, the policy implications are even more strongly tilted in favour of MFN tariff cuts.

14. See UNCTAD (June 1976). Evidence suggests that LDCs should strongly resist any exceptions to the general formula eventually agreed upon. In the Kennedy Round, exceptions were made on tariffs for many products of export interest to developing countries with the result that cuts in these duties were well below average. In cases, effective protection may have actually increased where reductions in input tariffs were larger than those for the final good.

15. Problems associated with negotiating the removal of NTBs are discussed in Gerard and Victoria Curzon (1971) and Lloyd (1974).

16. The official attitude of the Common Market during the Kennedy Round was that agriculture is a matter 'replete with social, political, and economic considerations and that agricultural systems do not constitute an appropriate topic for multilateral trade negotiations'. As such, the EEC tabled all efforts to draw agricultural NTBs into the negotiations.

17. For agricultural or other homogeneous products, UNCTAD proposes the computation of tariff equivalents for quotas through the average unit differential between domestic price and landed cost (c.i.f. plus fixed duties and charges). Quota enlargement might then proceed according to some fixed time schedule giving a constant yearly reduction in the price difference. This approach would also yield much useful information on the magnitudes of protection afforded by NTBs and should be extended to as many products as feasible.

18. Extension of the GSP concept to nontariff restraints would not call for changes in the machinery or philosophy of the programmes, merely a broadening of their scope. Indeed, qualifications such as special rules of origin could be applied to NTBs with little or no administrative changes. It has been argued that the GSP is one of the most promising approaches for relaxing quantitative restraints that limit developing countries' exports. This could also be a way of compensating developing countries for any loss of preferential tariff margins due to MFN duty cuts. See Murray and Walter (1977).

19. A growing variant of the quantitative restriction is the voluntary export restraint. These trade controls are accepted by exporters for fear that quantitative restrictions, or other more detrimental barriers, might be imposed. While the proposals for liberalising quantitative restraints apply, UNCTAD has made specific suggestions for this restriction:
    (1) Departures from the standstill through application of voluntary restraints should be subject to internationally agreed criteria, consultation, and review procedures. Such departures should be temporary and for short duration.
    (2) Existing restraints should not be renewed nor their coverage extended.
    (3) Existing restraints should be subject to multilateral consultations, review and surveillance with a view toward liberalisation as soon as possible.
    (4) Countries should provide for a reasonable growth of imports pending elimination of the voluntary restraints.

20. Japan's internal price support for rice is set at such high levels that this nation has changed from a major importer to a rice exporter. This has resulted in sizeable revenue losses for some rice-exporting countries of Southeast Asia. Compensation should be arranged for these and related trade losses.

21. Products whose import is frequently controlled by discretionary licensing include processed food and beverages, motor fuels, aluminium products, construction equipment, textile fabrics, precious metals, electronic components, motorcycles, certain chemicals and pharmaceuticals, glassware and rubber manufactures.

22. According to Article XVII paragraph 1, state trading is deemed to exist when a government agency exports or imports for resale. However, the term also covers cases in which an autonomous, or quasi-autonomous, enterprise receives exclusive power from the government to import or export a product. State trading organisations typically prevail in the following product groups: cereals, alcoholic beverages, antibiotics, vaccines and medicaments, yarns and cordage, fertilisers, vegetable alcaloids, smokers' supplies, ethyl alcohol, and tobacco products.

23. At the request of a contracting party, governments sponsoring state trading organisations are obligated to supply information about these concerns' operations, as well as data on import mark-ups during a representative period. The aim of these and related provisions is to prevent the monopolies from setting domestic retail prices which impair tariff concessions bound in national schedules.

24. UNCTAD (June 1973, pp. 18–20) has suggested modifications in state trading regulations to promote LDC trade. In particular, the extension of preferences to developing countries through lower resale mark-ups on their products is worthy of attention. Since the requirements of individual state trading organisations are very diverse, they create special problems for developing countries who may not be familiar with all variations. Efforts are needed to harmonise these regulations where possible. Finally, UNCTAD has stressed the need for the wine monopolies of developed countries to broaden purchases from LDCs in order to create opportunities in this profitable market.

25. State trading organisations in centrally planned economies may charge retail prices for LDC food products which are more than three or four times those in Western countries. These higher prices have a severe limiting effect on developing country exports. See Pryor (1966).
26. See Baldwin (1970, pp. 78–80). It is important to note the distinction between state trading and government procurement. In the former, goods are purchased for resale, while in government procurement goods are bought for the states' consumption.
27. As an illustration, Baldwin (1970, p. 144) cites a case where the maximum permissible speed for tractors is 17 miles per hour in France, 13 miles per hour in Germany, and only 10 miles per hour in the Netherlands. This means that French producers must modify their tractors for export to Germany or the Netherlands, and that tractors produced in these countries are not as competitive in the French market as those produced by local firms.
28. According to section (2a) of the Code, 'Adherents shall ensure that mandatory standards are not prepared, adopted or applied with a view toward creating obstacles to international trade. They shall likewise ensure that neither mandatory standards themselves nor their application have the effect of creating an unjustifiable obstacle to international trade.'

CHAPTER 7

1. See Finger and Yeats (1976). For a theoretical analysis which examines the influence of transportation costs on the volume and composition of international trade see Kindleberger (1968).
2. While the developed market economy countries only accounted for 31·4 per cent of total loadings in 1974, their share of unloadings was 78·3 per cent. In contrast, LDCs had 63·1 per cent of loadings and 18·4 per cent of unloadings. These differences reflect the composition of trade; bulk unprocessed material and petroleum transported from developing to developed countries, while trade in the opposite direction is largely composed of machinery and fabricated goods.
3. Since many shipping lines headquartered in developed countries have found that registration of vessels under flags of convenience conveys substantial tax benefits, or is a means of evading strict safety and labour regulations, the figures shown in Table 7.2 understate the actual control of industrial nations on world shipping. While accurate figures are difficult to obtain, it is generally conceded that the United States is the primary owner of vessels in the open registry category, while Japan is a close second.
4. An unambiguous distinction between various types of shipping does not exist. However, a differentiation is generally made between liner, tramp, bulk carrier or tanker operations. The primary difference between cargo liners and tramps is that the former are intended to satisfy demand for regular transit over a fixed route. Thus, liners are vessels with given itineraries calling at predetermined ports at fixed intervals. Tramps, in comparison, are cargo vessels which do not have fixed routes, but which carry dry cargo in bulk over long distances. Some construction differences

exist in that liners are usually able to generate higher speeds, and their holds are often compartmentalised for carrying finished or semi-finished manufactures, or even such 'sensitive' goods as butter, sugar, coffee, cocoa, etc. However, liners and tramps are similar enough that the latter may be pressed into service on liner routes from time to time. *Bulk carriers* differ significantly from these two in that these specialised containers are designed primarily for the transport of ores, coal, grains, etc., while *tankers* carry primarily liquid cargoes. For a discussion of these different types of markets and operations see Metaxes (1971).

5. UNCTAD (1975d) gives a listing of the conferences and an indication of the principal routes covered. As an indication of the importance of the conferences, Richards (1967) puts their share of the world general cargo trade at about 95 per cent.

6. However, a comparison between the actual *level* of tramp and liner rates, whether in the long term or short run, is not valid because each refers to a different type of service. The liner rate normally includes cargo handling charges and the tramp rate usually does not. The tramp rate is a whole ship rate whereas the liner rate is a parcel rate. The liner provides regular service ready for use when a shipper wants it and need not be used when the exporter has nothing to ship, whereas a tramp ship provides a service only when an exporter who can fill a ship wants it. For the same reasons, a comparison of tramp and liner rates in relation to the value of the product carried is not valid.

7. While not specifically directed at the developing country complaints, most empirical studies have concluded that the *overall* level of conference profits is quite low. For example, in an analysis of conference pricing and practices the Rochdale Committee observed: 'It is doubtful whether, in the aggregate, for any considerable period since World War II profits have been at a level which would be considered adequate by any normal commerical standard.'

8. See Fashbender and Wagner (1973, pp. 24–42). Evidence of discrimination also exists for United States steel products. For example, one investigation noted that it cost $38·25 per long ton to ship steel tubing from New York to the German Federal Republic, while a German exporter pays a freight cost of $20·75 for shipping a slightly lighter metric ton in the opposite direction. The inquiry demonstrated that freight charges for American steel exports to Japan, France and the German Federal Republic averaged about 60 per cent above corresponding import rates.

9. Cited in R. T. Brown (1968, p. 145). Resolution XXI of the Organisation of American States.

10. This conclusion was reached by a number of investigators including Koch (1968). Other related studies have also demonstrated that commodity value may be a key determinant of ocean freight rates. See Lipsey and Weiss (1974) or Bryan (1974).

11. The potential success of these organisations can be judged through reference to the recent activities of the Australian Meat Board, a government sponsored agency, which, by direct intervention, caused a rollback of a 13·5 per cent increase in liner freight rates. For details of the operation of shippers' organisations see UNCTAD (November 1976).

12. See Yeats (October 1976). In a related study Fashbender and Wagner (1973) examined seemingly high rate differentials for homogeneous goods shipped from different ports and concluded that they could be accounted for by operating factors such as volume of traffic, duration of voyage, time in harbour, quality of vessels employed, differences in loading or unloading equipment. As such the evidence concerning port discrimination is largely mixed and can vary from case to case.

13. If demand is also perfectly inelastic the outcome is indeterminant. The key point emerging from Figure 7.1a is that demand conditions fail to influence who bears freight costs if supply is inelastic: the entire burden falls on the exporter. While the discussion is framed in terms of absolute levels, the analysis is equally valid for analysing *changes* in transport costs.

14. Introduction of transport costs in Figure 7.1a does not shift the supply schedule since exporters offer the same quantity at all price levels. In other words, the export price is completely demand determined. However, in Figure 7.1b freight costs mean that supply price in the importing market must be higher (by the amount of freight) at any given level of quantity. Exporters would only be willing to *continue* offering ON if they receive price OP. The increase in delivered price (CP), borne by domestic consumers, goes to pay freight costs.

15. After a survey of the literature, Balassa and Kreinin (1967) use import demand elasticities of -0.39 and -0.29 for simulations of the effects of tariff cuts on imports of primary products in the United States and Common Market, while elasticities of -4.12 and -3.09 were employed for manufactured goods.

16. Currency adjustment factors, to account for the unsettled monetary conditions, also had a strong influence on liner rates. For a tabulation of the bunker and currency surcharges which occurred see UNCTAD (1975d). In a related study, Finger and Yeats (1976, p. 174) compared changes in tramp and liner freight rate indices with United States unit value indices for imports. Their analysis led to the conclusion that the average *ad valorem* freight rate rose by about 4 percentage points over the 1970s. An increase of this magnitude would be sufficient to offset tariff reductions negotiated during the Kennedy Round.

17. Economists have noted that importers may have an incentive to under-invoice imports in order to blunt the impact of high tariffs. If there are large purposeful inaccuracies in the United States customs data this would bias estimates of transportation factors. For several reasons it is felt that this is not the case. Firstly, Chapter 4 showed that the US employs *specific* duties on about 35 per cent of its tariff line items. These fixed import charges remove the incentive to under-invoice, since they are applied independent of product value. Secondly, many of the United States nominal tariffs are now quite low, averaging about 7 per cent. As such, minimal gains would accrue from falsification of customs data, while the penalties could be quite severe if noted by the authorities.

18. For examples of studies which have employed this technique for estimation of transport costs incurred by individual exporting countries see Yeats (October 1976) or (October 1977).

19. Correlations between LDC transport costs for the United States with those

published by Moneta (1959) for the Federal Republic of Germany are positive and significant. This suggests that freight rates shown in the forthcoming analysis are generally an accurate guide to LDC penetration costs for both European and American markets. However, there are exceptions. Some Latin American freight costs appear lower for the United States market, while developing countries in North Africa have lower transport costs for Germany.

20. Guinea's major export product (noncalcined bauxite ore) accounted for $20·7 million of this country's total $22·9 million in c.i.f. exports. The transport factor for this item was about 60 per cent.

21. The United Kingdom and Japan are among India's chief competitors for the United States textile market. Examination of the United States import statistics indicates these nations face *ad valorem* transport charges of from 4 to 6 per cent, or approximately 15 percentage points below India.

22. This exceptional figure is due primarily to shipments of ilmenite sand which has a transport factor of over 200 per cent on shipments (c.i.f.) of approximately $800000. India may not be making optimal use of bulk shipping methods for this product, as a comparison with Australian figures shows the latter to have a transport factor for United States shipments which is more than 100 percentage points lower.

23. The actual magnitude of an f.o.b. export increase associated with reduced freight costs is dependent upon the supply and demand elasticities for the products involved. Any investment in port or transport improvements may normally be considered economically feasible if the export revenue increase, plus domestic linkage effects from increased output in the foreign trade sector, exceeds the innovation's cost. In a related discussion, Laing (1977) notes that the total export revenue increase from port cost reduction measures may be double the value of the transport savings on the *original* volume of manufactured goods.

24. There are variations of the containerised shipping approach; all of which require that packaging be done outside the vessel so berth time is reduced. For example, 'roll-on/roll-off' ships for cars, trains, and mobile containers are one popular variant. LASH (lighters-along-ship) are 'lift-on/lift-off' type vessels designed primarily to carry barges which can be lifted on and off the container ship by specially built cranes. For a discussion of the unitised cargo approach see UNCTAD (1975c)

25. See International Bank for Reconstruction and Development (1973). Shipping economists are generally agreed that considerable economies of scale can be achieved in the transport of items like grains, iron ore, coal, bauxite and phosphate. Some studies also suggest that economies can result from adapting bulk methods for commodities currently exported by liner services, i.e., timber, sugar, rubber, and jute.

26. Tramp or bulk carrier markets are much more susceptible to competitive pressures, so the element of monopoly pricing inherent in liner rate policy is missing. Also tramp and charter rates normally exclude handling charges so any improvement in port facilities should be directly realised by exporters. See UNCTAD (1969, p. 11–16).

References

N. A. Adams, 'A Note on Trade as a Handmaiden of Growth', *Economic Journal*, 81 (March 1973), 210–12.

R. L. Allen and Ingo Walter, 'An Analysis of the Impact of Nontariff Measures Imposed by Developed Market Economy Countries on Representative Products of Export Interest to Developing Countries', *UNCTAD Secretariat Working Paper* (Geneva: United Nations, mimeo 1970).

Roy Baban, 'State Trading and the GATT', *Journal of World Trade Law*, 11 (August 1977), 334–53.

W. Baer, 'Import Substitution Industrialization in Latin America: Experiences and Interpretations', *Latin American Research Review*, 7 (Spring 1972), 95–122.

Bela Balassa and Mordechai Kreinin, 'Trade Liberalization under the Kennedy Round: the Static Effects', *Review of Economics and Statistics*, 49 (May 1967), 125–37.

Bela Balassa and Associates, *The Structure of Protection in Developing Countries* (Baltimore: Johns Hopkins Press, 1971).

Robert Baldwin, *Nontariff Distortions of International Trade* (Washington: The Brookings Institution, 1970).

Robert Baldwin and Tracy Murray, 'MFN Tariff Reductions and Developing Country Trade Benefits under the GSP', *Economic Journal*, 87 (March 1977), 30–46.

Jagdish Bhagwati, 'On the Equivalence of Tariffs and Quotas', in R. E. Baldwin (ed.), *Trade, Tariffs and Growth* (Chicago: Rand McNally, 1965).

T. R. Brown, *Transportation and Development* (Los Angeles: University of California, mimeo 1968).

Ingrid Bryan, 'Ocean Liner Freight Rates', *Journal of Transport Economics and Policy*, 8 (May 1974), 161–73.

Hollis B. Chenery and Alan M. Strout, 'Foreign Assistance and Economic Development', *American Economic Review*, 56 (September 1966), 679–733.

C. Clague, 'The Trade Effects of Tariff Preferences', *Southern Economic Journal*, 38 (January 1972), 449–55.

Benjamin Cohen, 'Relative Effects of Foreign Capital and Larger Exports on Economic Development', *Review of Economics and Statistics*, 50 (May 1968), 281–4.

Benjamin Cohen, 'The Less Developed Countries' Exports of Primary Commodities', *Economic Journal*, 78 (June 1968), 334–43.

Benjamin Cohen and Daniel Sisler, 'Exports of Developing Countries in the 1960s', *Review of Economics and Statistics*, 53 (November 1971), 354–61.

Committee of Inquiry into Shipping, *Report Presented to Parliament by the President of the Board of Trade* (London: HMSO, 1966).

N. F. Crafts, 'Trade as a Handmaiden of Growth: an Interchange', *Economic Journal*, 81 (September 1973), 875–89.

Gerard and Victoria Curzon, *Global Assault on Nontariff Barriers* (London: Trade Policy Research Centre, 1971).

Richard Dardis, 'Intermediate Goods and the Gains from Trade', *Review of Economics and Statistics*, 49 (November 1967), 502–9.

Carlos F. Diaz-Alejandro, 'Trade Policies and Economic Development', in Peter B. Kenan (ed.), *International Trade and Finance: Frontiers for Research* (Cambridge: Cambridge University Press, 1975).

Robert F. Emery, 'The Relation of Exports and Economic Growth', *Kyklos*, 20 (Fasc. 2, 1967).

European Economic Community, *Marchés Agricoles* (Brussels: European Economic Community, various issues).

John W. Evans, *The Kennedy Round in American Trade Policy* (Cambridge, Mass: Harvard University Press, 1971).

Karl Fashbender and Wolfgang Wagner, *Shipping Conferences, Rate Policy and Developing Countries* (Hamburg: Verlag Weltarchiv, 1973).

J. M. Finger, 'Tariff Provisions for Offshore Assembly and the Exports of Developing Countries', *Economic Journal*, 85 (June 1975), 365–71.

J. M. Finger, 'Effects of Kennedy Round Tariff Concessions', *Economic Journal*, 86 (March 1976), 87–95.

J. M. Finger, 'Trade and Domestic Effects of the Offshore Assembly Provisions in the U.S. Tariff', *American Economic Review*, 66 (September 1976), 598–611.

J. M. Finger and A. J. Yeats, 'Effective Protection by Transportation Costs and Tariffs: a Comparison of Magnitudes', *Quarterly Journal of Economics*, 90 (February 1976), 169–76.

D. L. Gadiel, 'International Trade and Economic Development in Papua-New Guinea', *Economic Record*, 42 (June 1966), 274–91.

General Agreement on Tariffs and Trade, *Trends in International Trade*, (Geneva: GATT, 1958).

General Agreement on Tariffs and Trade, *Products Notified as Being of Export Interest to Less Developed Countries* (Geneva: GATT, June 1966).

General Agreement on Tariffs and Trade, *Basic Documentation for Tariff Study* (Geneva: GATT, June 1966).

General Agreement on Tariffs and Trade, *Import Measures, Variable Levies and Other Special Charges* (Geneva: GATT, 1971).

Hans Glismann and Axel Neu, 'Towards New Agreements on International Trade Liberalization—Methods and Examples of Measuring Nontariff Trade Barriers', *Weltwirtschaftliches Archiv*, 107 (April 1971), 235–71.

Harry G. Grubel and Harry G. Johnson, 'Nominal Tariff Rates and United States Valuation Practices: Two Case Studies', *Review of Economics and Statistics*, 44 (May 1967), 138–42.

Herbert G. Grubel, 'Effective Tariff Protection: a Non-Specialist Introduction to the Theory, Policy Implications and Controversies', in Herbert G. Grubel and Harry G. Johnson (eds.), *Effective Tariff Protection* (Geneva: GATT, 1971).

Herbert G. Grubel, 'The Case Against the New International Economic Order', *Weltwirtschaftliches Archiv*, 113 (April 1977), 284–307.

Odd Gulbrandsen and Assar Lindbeck, *The Economics of the Agricultural Sector* (Stockholm: Almqvist and Wiksell, 1973).

Gottfried Haberler, *International Trade and Economic Development* (Cairo: National Bank of Egypt, 1959).

Gottfried Haberler, 'Terms of Trade and Economic Development', in Howard S. Ellis (ed.), *Economic Development for Latin America* (New York: St Martins Press, 1961).

John R. Hanson, 'More on Trade as a Handmaiden of Growth', *Economic Journal*, 87 (September 1977), 554–8.

P. Harff, *The Contribution of National Shipping Fleets to the Economic Development of Latin-American Countries* (Gottingen: Assen Press, 1970).

Trevor D. Heaver, 'A Theory of Shipping Conference Pricing and Policies', *Maritime Studies and Management*, 1 (July 1973), 17–30.

G. K. Helleiner, *International Trade and Economic Development* (Middlesex: Penguin Books, 1972).

B. Hindley, 'The UNCTAD Agreement on Preferences', *Journal of World Trade Law*, 5 (November: December 1971), 694–702.

A. O. Hirschman, 'The Political Economy of Import Substituting

Industrialization in Latin America', *Quarterly Journal of Economics*, 87 (February 1968), 1–32.

Franklyn D. Holzman, 'Comparison of Different Forms of Trade Barriers', *Review of Economics and Statistics*, 51 (May 1969), 159–65.

International Bank for Reconstruction and Development, 'The International Market for Iron Ore: Review and Outlook', *Bank Staff Working Paper No. 160* (Washington: I.B.R.D., 1973).

D. Gale Johnson, 'Sugar Program: Costs and Benefits', in D. Gale Johnson *et al*, *Foreign Trade and Agricultural Policy* (Washington: Government Printing Office, 1967).

Joint Economic Committee, Congress of the United States, Hearings Before the Subcommittee on Federal Procurement and Regulation, *Discriminatory Ocean Freight Rates and the Balance of Payments* (Washington: Government Printing Office, April 1965).

Donald Keesing, 'Outward-Looking Policies and Economic Development', *Economic Journal*, 77 (June 1967), 303–20.

Charles Kindleberger, *The Terms of Trade: A European Case Study* (Cambridge, Mass: M.I.T. Press, 1956).

Charles Kindleberger, *Economic Development* (New York: McGraw Hill, 1958).

Charles Kindleberger, *International Economics* (Homewood: Richard Irwin, 1968).

L. R. Klein, C. Moriguchi and A. Van Peeterssen, 'The Link Model of World Trade', in Peter B. Kenan (ed.), *International Trade and Finance: Frontiers for Research* (Cambridge: Cambridge University Press, 1975).

A. G. M. Koch, *Current Pricing Behavior in Liner Shipping* (Bergen: Institute for Shipping Research, 1968).

Lawrence Krause, 'The Theory of Exhaustible Resources and International Commodity Agreements', paper presented at the *Southern Economics Association Meetings*, New Orleans, November 1975.

Irving Kravis, 'Trade as a Handmaiden of Growth: Similarities Between the Nineteenth and Twentieth Centuries', *Economic Journal*, 80 December 1970), 850–72.

M. E. Kreinin, 'The Equivalence of Tariffs and Quotas Once Again', *Kyklos*, 23 (March 1970), 165–9.

M. E. Kreinin, *International Economics: A Policy Approach* (New York: Harcourt, 1975).

M. E. Kreinin, 'OPEC Oil Prices and the International Transfer

Problem', *Journal of World Trade Law*, 11 (January: February 1977), 75–8.

M. E. Kreinin and J. M. Finger, 'A Critical Survey of the New International Economic Order', *Journal of World Trade Law*, 10 (December 1976), 493–512.

E. T. Laing, 'The Distribution of Benefits from Port Investment', *Maritime Policy and Management*, 4 (January 1977), 141–54.

Youngil Lim, 'Trade and Growth: The Case of Ceylon', *Economic Development and Cultural Change*, 16 (January 1968), 245–61.

R. E. Lipsey and M. Y. Weiss, 'The Structure of Ocean Transport Charges', in D. E. Farr (ed.), *Explorations in Economic Research*, 1 (New York: National Bureau of Economic Research, 1974).

Ian Little, Tibor Scitivsky and Maurice Scott, *Industry and Trade in Some Developing Countries* (London: Oxford University Press, 1970).

Peter Lloyd, 'Strategies for Modifying Nontariff Distortions', in Hugh Corbet and Robert Jackson (eds.), *In Search of a New World Economic Order* (London: Trade Policy Research Centre, 1974).

A. I. MacBean, *Export Instability and Economic Development* (Cambridge: Harvard University Press, 1966).

Craig MacPhee, *Restrictions on International Trade in Steel* (Lexington: Lexington Books, 1974).

Alfred Maizels, *World Trends and Problems in the 1960s* (London: Woolwich Polytechnic, 1965).

B. F. Massel, 'Export Instability and Economic Structure', *American Economic Review*, 60 (September 1970), 618–30.

Gerald Meier, *The International Economics of Development* (New York: Harper and Row, 1968).

B. N. Metaxes, *The Economics of Tramp Shipping* (London: Athlone Press, 1971).

Michael Michaely, *Concentration in International Trade* (Amsterdam: North Holland, 1962).

Michael Michaely, 'Exports and Growth: An Empirical Investigation', *Journal of Development Economics*, 4 (March 1977), 49–53.

Michael Michaely, *Theory of Commercial Policy* (Oxford: Philip Allan, 1977).

J. S. Mill, *Principles of Political Economy* (London: Longmans, 1848).

Carmellah Moneta, 'The Estimation of Transport Costs in International Trade', *Journal of Political Economy*, 67 (February 1959), 41–58.

John R. Morony, 'Cobb-Douglas Production Functions and Returns to

Scale in U.S. Manufacturing Industry', *Western Economic Journal*, 5 (December 1967), 39–51.

Kathryn Morton and Peter Tulloch, *Trade and Developing Countries* (London: Croom Helm, 1977).

Tracy Murray, 'Preferential Tariffs for LDCs', *Southern Economic Journal*, 40 (July 1973), 35–46.

Tracy Murray and Ingo Walter, 'Quantitative Restrictions, Developing Countries and GATT', *Journal of World Trade Law*, 11 (September: October 1977), 391–421.

Douglas North, 'Ocean Freight Rates and Economic Development', *Journal of Economic History*, 18 (December 1958), 537–55.

Raul Prebisch, *Towards a New Trade Policy for Development* (New York: United Nations, 1964).

Ernest Preeg, *Traders and Diplomats* (Washington: The Brookings Institution, 1970).

W. Prewo and J. Geraci, 'Bilateral Trade Flows and Transportation Costs', *Review of Economics and Statistics*, 59 (March 1977), 67–76.

Frederic Pryor, 'Trade Barriers of Capitalist and Communist Nations Against Foodstuffs Exported by Tropical Underdeveloped Nations', *Review of Economics and Statistics*, 57 (November 1966), 406–11.

P. J. Richards, 'Shipping Problems of Underdeveloped Countries', *Oxford Bulletin of Economics and Statistics*, 29 (August 1967), 177–93.

Vernon Roningen and Alexander Yeats, 'Nontariff Distortions of International Trade: Some Preliminary Empirical Evidence', *Weltwirtschaftliches Archiv*, 113 (January 1977), 613–25.

Gary Sampson, 'On Factor Substitution and Effective Tariff Rates', *Review of Economic Studies*, 41 (April 1974), 293–6.

Gary Sampson and Alexander Yeats, 'Do Import Levies Matter? The Case of Sweden', *Journal of Political Economy*, 84 (August 1976), 881–91.

Gary Sampson and Alexander Yeats, 'Tariffs and Transport Barriers Facing Australian Exports', *Journal of Transport Economics and Policy*, 4 (May 1977), 112–38.

F. M. Scherer, *Industrial Market Structure and Economic Performance* (Chicago: Rand McNally, 1970).

J. A. Schumpeter, *The Theory of Economic Development* (Cambridge: Harvard University Press, 1934).

A. Shibata, 'On the Equivalence of Tariffs and Quotas', *American Economic Review*, 58 (March 1968), 137–41.

Adam Smith, *An Inquiry into the Nature and Causes of the Wealth of*

Nations, Edwin Cannan (ed.) (New York: Random House, 1937).

Robert M. Stern, 'Evaluating Alternative Formula for Reducing Industrial Tariffs', *Journal of World Trade Law*, 10 (January: February 1976), 50–64.

Robert M. Stern, *Price Elasticities in International Trade: An Annotated Bibliography* (Toronto: Macmillan, 1976).

Jan Tumlir and Ladislav Till, 'Tariff Averaging in International Comparisons', in Harry G. Grubel and Harry G. Johnson (eds.), *Effective Tariff Protection* (Geneva: GATT, 1971).

Ho Dac Tuong and Alexander Yeats, 'A Note on the Measurement of Trade Concentration', *Oxford Bulletin of Economics and Statistics*, 38 (November 1976), 299–310.

United Kingdom Political and Economic Planning Organisation, *Atlantic Tariffs and Trade* (London: UKPEP, 1962).

United Nations, *The Economic Development of Latin America* (New York: United Nations, 1950).

United Nations, *Instability in Export Markets of Developing Countries* (New York: United Nations, 1952).

United Nations, *Towards a Dynamic Development Policy for Latin America* (New York: United Nations, 1963).

United Nations, *Commodity Trade Statistics* (New York: United Nations, various issues a).

United Nations, *World Trade Annual* (New York: Walker and Company, various issues b).

United Nations Commission for Asia and the Far East, *Intraregional Trade Projections: Effective Protection and Income Distribution*, 2 (Bangkok: United Nations, 1972).

UNCTAD, *Shipping and the World Economy* (New York: United Nations, 1966).

UNCTAD, *The Kennedy Round Estimated Effects on Tariff Barriers* (New York: United Nations, 1968).

UNCTAD, *Liberalization of Tariffs and Nontariff Barriers* (Geneva: United Nations, December 1969).

UNCTAD, *Level and Structure of Freight Rates, Conference Practices and Adequacy of Shipping Services* (New York: United Nations, 1969).

UNCTAD, 'Agricultural Protection and the Food Economy', *Research Memo. Number 46* (Geneva: United Nations, March 1972).

UNCTAD, *Commodity Problems and Policies* (Geneva: United Nations, 1972).

UNCTAD, *Liberalization of Nontariff Barriers* (Geneva: United Nations, June 1973).

UNCTAD, 'Access to Markets', in *Proceedings of the United Nations Conference on Trade and Development* (New York: United Nations, 1973a).

UNCTAD, *Berth Throughput* (New York: United Nations, 1973b).

UNCTAD, *Relationship Between Changes in Freight Rates and Changes in Costs of Maritime Transport and the Effect on the Export Trade of Developing Countries* (Geneva: United Nations, 1973c).

UNCTAD, *Trade and Development Policies in the 1970s* (New York: United Nations, 1973d).

UNCTAD, 'Proceedings of the United Nations Conference on Trade and Development', vol. 2, *Merchandise Trade* (New York: United Nations, 1973e).

UNCTAD, *Measures to Expand Processing of Primary Commodities in Developing Countries* (Geneva: United Nations, December 1975).

UNCTAD, *Country Studies on Export Diversification: A Suggested Outline* (Geneva: United Nations, 1975b).

UNCTAD, *Review of Maritime Transport, 1972–73* (New York: United Nations, 1975c).

UNCTAD, *Review of Maritime Transport, 1974* (New York: United Nations, 1975d).

UNCTAD, *Background Study on the Impact on Employment of International Policy Measures in the Field of Trade and Development* (Geneva: United Nations, April 1976a).

UNCTAD, *Trade Prospects and Capital Needs of Developing Countries, 1976–80* (Geneva: United Nations, April 1976b).

UNCTAD, *Manila Declaration and Programme of Action* (Nairobi: United Nations, May 1976a).

UNCTAD, 'Summary of Trade Barriers and Preferences Facing Individual Developing Countries in Major Developed Markets', *Research Memo. Number 57* (Geneva: United Nations, May 1976b).

UNCTAD, *New Directions and New Structures for Trade and Development* (Nairobi: United Nations, May 1976c).

UNCTAD, *An Overview of Tariff Reduction Formula for the Group of 77* (Geneva: United Nations, June 1976).

UNCTAD, *The Effectiveness of Shippers' Organizations* (Geneva: United Nations, November 1976).

UNCTAD, *Handbook of International Trade and Development Statistics* (New York: United Nations, 1976).

UNCTAD, *The Evolution of a Viable International Development*

Strategy (Geneva: United Nations, March 1977a).

UNCTAD, *Review of Maritime Transport, 1976* (Geneva: United Nations, March 1977b).

UNCTAD, 'Imports of the Union of Soviet Socialist Republics from Developing Countries', *Research Memo. Number 51* (Geneva: United Nations, April 1977).

United States Department of Commerce, *Highlights of U.S. Export and Import Trade* (Washington: Bureau of the Census, 1975).

United States International Trade Commission, *Protection in Major Trading Countries* (Washington: USITC, 1975).

United States Tariff Commission, *Trade Barriers: An Overview* (Washington: U.S. Tariff Commission, 1974).

Ingo Walter, 'Nontariff Barriers and the Free-Trade Area Option', *Banca Nazionale del Lavoro Quarterly Review*, 22 (March 1969), 16–45.

Ingo Walter, 'On the Equivalence of Tariffs and Quotas: Comment', *Kyklos*, 24 (March 1971), 46–50.

Ingo Walter, 'Nontariff Barriers and the Export Performance of Developing Countries', *American Economic Association Papers and Proceedings*, 61 (May 1971), 195–205.

Ingo Walter and Jae Chung, 'The Pattern of Nontariff Obstacles to International Market Access', *Weltwirtschaftliches Archiv*, 108 (March 1972), 122–35.

Ingo Walter, 'Nontariff Protection Among Industrial Countries: Some Preliminary Empirical Evidence', *Economia Internazionale*, 25 (May 1972), 335–54.

Lary Wipf, 'Tariffs, Nontariff Distortions and Effective Protection in U.S. Agriculture', *American Journal of Agricultural Economics*, 53 (August 1971), 423–30.

Alexander Yeats, 'Effective Tariff Protection in the United States, the European Economic Community and Japan', *Quarterly Review of Economics and Business*, 14 (Summer 1974), 41–50.

Alexander Yeats, 'An Analysis of the Effect of Production Process Changes on Effective Protection Estimates', *Review of Economics and Statistics*, 58 (February 1976), 81–5.

Alexander Yeats, 'An Analysis of the Incidence of Specific Tariffs on Developing Country Exports', *Economic Inquiry*, 14 (March 1976), 71–80.

Alexander Yeats, 'An Analysis of the Incidence of Tariffs and Transport Costs on Indonesian Exports', *Bulletin of Indonesian Economic Studies*, 12 (October 1976), 326–42.

Alexander Yeats and Gary Sampson, 'An Evaluation of the Common Agricultural Policy as a Barrier Facing Agricultural Exports to the European Economic Community', *American Journal of Agricultural Economics*, 59 (February 1977), 99–106.

Alexander Yeats, 'Effective Protection for Processed Agricultural Commodities: a Comparison of Industrial Countries', *Journal of Economics and Business*, 29 (Fall 1977), 31–9.

Alexander Yeats, 'A Comparative Analysis of Tariffs and Transportation Costs on India's Exports', *Journal of Development Studies*, 14 (October 1977), 97–107.

Alexander Yeats, 'Do International Transportation Costs Increase with Fabrication? Some Empirical Evidence', *Oxford Economic Papers*, 29 November 1977), 458–71.

Alexander Yeats, 'On the Accuracy of Partner Country Trade Statistics', *Oxford Bulletin of Economics and Statistics* (in press).

Index